THE ARCHITECTURE OF ENGINEERS

EDITED BY

MARISTELLA CASCIATO

PIPPO CIORRA

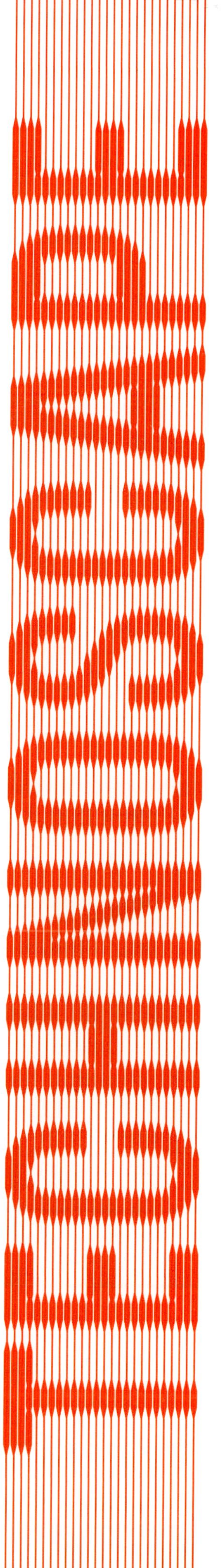

INDEX

EXHIBITION PLAN

01		TEATRO REGIO
02		SYDNEY OPERA HOUSE
03		EPFL – ROLEX LEARNING CENTER
04		MEISO NO MORI MUNICIPAL FUNERAL HALL
05		SICLI COMPANY BUILDING
06		OPEN CHAPEL IN PALMIRA
07		MARKET (SOKO) LA KARIAKOO
08		GARE TGV RAILWAY STATION
09		KIMBELL ART MUSEUM
10		KIMBELL ART MUSEUM EXPANSION
11		MENIL COLLECTION
12		CENTRE POMPIDOU
13		BROADGATE EXCHANGE HOUSE
14		BURGO PAPER MILL
15		MASP – MUSEU DE ARTE DE SÃO PAULO
16		MAM – MUSEU DE ARTE MODERNA DO RIO DE JANEIRO
17		SCHOOL IN LEUTSCHENBACH
18		HSBC MAIN BUILDING
19		JOHNSON WAX RESEARCH TOWER
20		BURJ KHALIFA TOWER
21		875 NORTH MICHIGAN AVENUE SKYSCRAPER
22		BANK OF CHINA TOWER
23		CCTV HEADQUARTERS
24		HALL OF NATIONS AND HALLS OF INDUSTRIES
25		GC PROSTHO MUSEUM RESEARCH CENTER
26		HÖHENRAUSCH.2 – BRÜCKEN IM HIMMEL (BRIDGES IN THE SKY)
27		GRAND ROOF, FESTIVAL PLAZA, EXPO '70
28		AMERICAN PAVILION, EXPO '67
29		IRIS DOME
30		PALAZZETTO DELLO SPORT
31		EDEN PROJECT
32		FUJI PAVILION, EXPO '70
33		BRUGES PAVILION
34		STEVE JOBS THEATER
35		CHURCH OF CHRIST THE WORKER AND OUR LADY OF LOURDES
36		NORDPARK RAILWAY STATIONS
37		MULTIHALLE
38		OLYMPIASTADION, OLYMPIAHALLE AND SCHWIMMHALLE
39		SNOWDON AVIARY, ZSL LONDON ZOO
40		PHILIPS PAVILION, EXPO '58
41		YOYOGI NATIONAL GYMNASIUM

SECTIONS

THIN SHELLS
MODULAR SPANS
FLOATING VOLUMES
TALL BUILDINGS
SPACE FRAMES
DOMES
ALTERNATIVE MATERIALS
LIGHT MEMBRANES
DIE ANGEWANDTE WIEN
UNIVERSITÄT STUTTGART
MIT CAMBRIDGE
IUSS EUCENTRE PAVIA
TU BERLIN
ETH ZÜRICH
TUDELFT

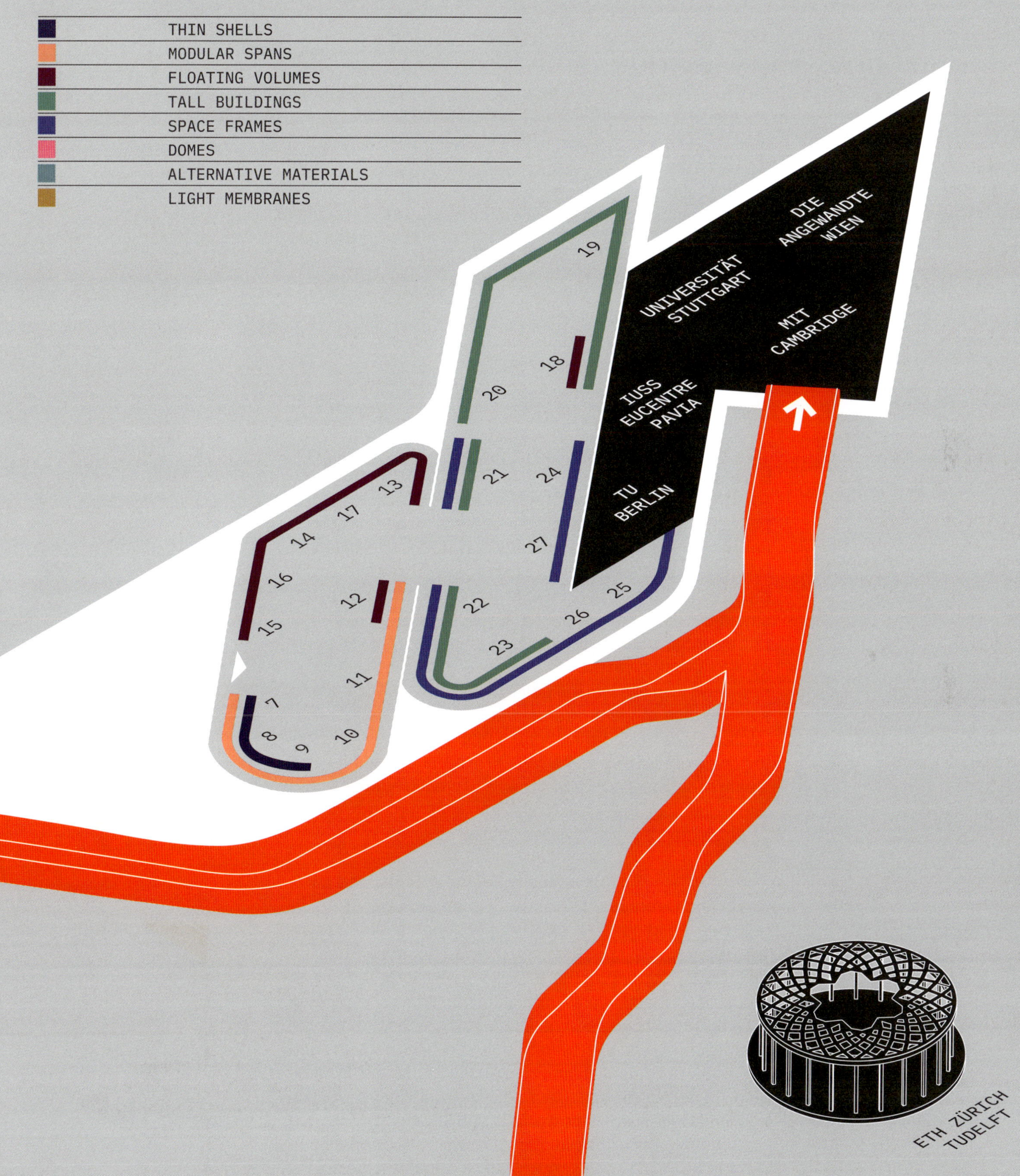

PREFACE

Giovanna Melandri

PRESIDENT
FONDAZIONE MAXXI

Technoscape. The Architecture of Engineers is a manifesto exhibition for the MAXXI, for a few sound reasons. Because this space, from the outset, was intended and has come to be confirmed as the national museum of modern and contemporary architecture that Italy was missing, an international, interdisciplinary reference point and a place for discussion and debate. Because in our mission, and I might say, in our identity, the study of the most innovative trends and the most original designers is essential to rekindle interest—long-stifled—in the dilemmas and solutions that arise in new ways in urban life, the politics of sustainability, and the safeguarding of the environment and local territories. And because as a museum-laboratory that never tires of exploring and experimenting, the MAXXI is committed to forging a path of dialogue between aspects of creativity, knowledge and technology that have often been kept separate, and to driving experimentation without barriers.

These are the elements that inspired curators Pippo Ciorra and Maristella Casciato to offer us *Technoscape*, an immersive, documented journey into the parallel universes of structural engineering and technological innovation. Looking at the period from 1945 to today and focusing on masterworks created in the most wide-ranging contexts, that have become icons of our cities, the exhibition describes and intertwines languages, connections and influences from architecture, construction sciences, the evolution of materials, digital technologies, and finally, artificial intelligence applied to the design, fabrication, maintenance and management of buildings and cities. A boundary line —today no longer seen as such, but pioneering at the time— was crossed, but there is little understanding and even less awareness of it.

Traditional exposition instruments (drawings, images, models) and interactive exhibition itineraries (created in collaboration with universities and research centers) reveal approaches to space, construction methods and cultural outlooks, laying out a critical analysis of recent periods in architecture and urban design, up to the surging acceleration of the last few decades. *Technoscape* has the courage to grapple "in real time" with the transformations that digital technology proposes—beyond our little everyday concerns—designing places that offer more authentic forms of social interaction, and that we can "inhabit" with the sense of a community.

These sorts of projects make use of unexpected contributions, convergences between new technical knowledge and various environmental sciences, between low-tech and robotics, to grasp and concretize a revolutionary idea: the smart city. Think of bio-composite and "intelligent" materials, transparent woods, green alternatives to cement that have lower energy costs. Think of nanotechnologies applied to lighter, more durable claddings. The future is already here, pervading our world. Not without reason, *Technoscape* is complemented by the spotlight exhibition *inGenio. Visionary ideas by Sergio Musmeci*, a small but illuminating selection of designs curated by Tullia Iori. The exhibition collects materials belonging to our gold mine of an archive, pioneering works which have never been brought to fruition and have been so far ahead of the times, and today seem more relevant and stimulating than ever.

TECHNOSCAPE.
THE ARCHITECTURE OF ENGINEERS

We live in a time when the alliance between science and the arts that is characteristic of the relationship between engineering and architecture seems to be one of the many urgently necessary conditions for the survival of the planet, at least in an inhabitable version. To respond to questions that go along with this scenario, the MAXXI has dedicated a major exposition to the past, present and possible future of technical, structural and digital intelligence applied to the architectural and environmental design of object and materials. In line with a series of large post-war exhibitions (MoMA 1964, Centre Pompidou 1997) and in keeping with the great importance within the MAXXI's collection of the design heritage of great Italian engineers (Nervi and Musmeci first and foremost), the project aims to document a number of masterpieces of structural engineering, from 1945 to today, that have embodied both the autonomous energy of increasingly advanced scientific and "inventive" research and experimentation, and the products of a series of extraordinary collaborations between architects and structural designers.

To delineate the boundaries of such a broad theme, and one so relevant to the role that architecture can play in the near future, the MAXXI made a few very specific choices. Firstly, to limit the scope, with very few exceptions, to the architecture of buildings, where the collaboration between the structural designer and the architect must be most intense. Then, to reserve a space for milestones that preceded the Second World War: seminal works, from Shukhov to Torroja, from Freyssinet to Wachsmann, from Arup to Nervi, without which we cannot understand successive developments. Finally, to organize the exhibition not chronologically or by type of use, but offering visitors a series of possible paths to follow, along which works are grouped according to eight structural themes, identified in a non-defined and non-definitive way. The *Thin Shells* section gathers projects based on the statics of thin reinforced concrete surfaces, often in shapes that are far from elementary; *Modular Spans* are structures that are "put together," made up of the repetition of elements assembled at the work site; the *Floating Volumes* section comprises buildings with structures that correspond to complex frames made to support architectures with overhangs or cantilevers, or that are raised above ground; *Tall Buildings* obviously aim for maximum height; *Space Frames* are assemblages of three-dimensional modular elements; the *Domes* section includes various approaches to the self-supporting roof with arch section; *Alternative Materials* highlights cases where designers seek to enhance the characteristics of one of more construction materials; *Light Membranes* refer to tensile structure and the production of free forms generated through the plastic use of various types of materials.

While until the end of the last century, or rather, until the advent of computers and digital technology, the development of engineering had been fairly vertical, tied to mathematical and technological progress immediately reflected in materials and construction methods, today engineering tends to also, and above all, expand horizontally, increasingly bringing spheres of scientific research applied to space into dialogue with architecture and design. To explore this sector of engineering, *Technoscape. The Architecture of Engineers* has involved seven research centers linked to academic institutions with a committed focus on the field of relations between technologies and design disciplines: the MAXXI asked each center to show the results of their research through self-produced installations, which are displayed inside and outside the exhibition route.

TOTAL ENGINEERING OR THE ART OF CONSTRUCTING

Maristella Casciato

I would distinguish the difference
between the engineer and the
architect by saying the architect's
response is primarily creative,
whereas the engineer's
is essentially inventive.[1]

PETER RICE,
IN MEMORIAM

The exhibition *Technoscape. The Architecture of Engineers* is a window onto one of the most heated debates of the past century and a half, the historical-critical lines of which have been defined by torrents of words and numerous expositions. The theme brings with it a question: is there an architecture of engineering, or, to put it more directly, how do the engineer's craft and technique relate with the architect's production, and vice-versa? Do creativity and inventiveness merge, or clash? Obviously, the question is much more complex than this, given that it involves strictly constructive themes like those concerning materials and their invention and use, along with subjects related to the socio-political effects of certain structural choices, in terms of their economic and ecological significance as well as their impact on users and the community.

Finally, as will be taken into consideration below, technical choices are never neutral, as the eight decades that separate us from the Second World War have not failed to demonstrate. In the opening essay of the

---

1   Peter Rice, "The Role of the Engineer," in *An Engineer Imagines* (London: Artemis, 1994), 72.

↑   Alexander Graham Bell kissing his wife Mabel Hubbard Gardiner
     Bell, who is standing in a tetrahedral kite, Baddeck, 1903. Courtesy
     Prints and Photographs Division, Library of Congress, Washington

↑   Walther Bauersfeld, Zeiss Planetarium, Jena, 1922. ZEISS Archive

encyclopedic volume that accompanied the exposition *L'Art de l'ingénieur. Constructeur, entrepreneur, inventeur*, Antoine Picon pondered (and he was not the only one) how structural invention and "imaginaire social" (collective imagery) had been connected, with very different results, since the years of the French Revolution and the successive Second Industrial Revolution.

But, without too much hesitation, Picon also acknowledged the limits of this relationship: "[...] the qualifier of 'democratic' attached to the art of structural engineering is not entirely self-evident." And he continued, emphasizing the technocratic and authoritarian current that the social mission of engineering had grappled with in numerous situations of political conflict, and concluded by asserting that "the project of a use of technologies which, after having contributed to dividing humankind by bringing forth social classes [...] would gather them again around a common ideal of prosperity and exchange, has not lost its seductiveness. [...] technology may well lead to a kind of redemption in the form of a return in force of the collective, the community. This, in any case, is the secret dream of many engineers."[2]

In line with this reflection, another of the authors contributing to this publication takes the example of the Madrilenian engineer Félix Candela, who during the civil war years had seen the shattering of his idealistic aspirations for an imminent technical revolution. It was only after emigrating to Mexico that Candela was able to reconcile his personal and intellectual freedom with a genuine interest in lightweight structures. The freedom/lightness binomial, more than a metaphor, had become the emblematic signature of his masterpieces.[3]

Before moving on to consider how, when and why, during the decades after the Second World War, the art of structural engineering became the raw material that profoundly altered architects' thinking and the architectural forms to which that art was applied, a few thoughts on the harbingers of that sea change highlight some unresolved aporias.

Particularly in more economically advanced countries, it was the processes of modernization accompanying industrial growth that generated the greatest challenges with regard to the development of the truly *modern*—simultaneously dynamic, complex and contradictory—thinking that came to bear on the art of building.

2   Antoine Picon, *L'Art de l'ingénieur. Constructeur, entrepreneur, inventeur*, catalog of an exhibition of the same title (Paris: Éditions du Centre Pompidou, 1997), 37–40.

3   Guy Nordenson, "Constellations. Ideas and Things," in *Seven Structural Engineers: The Felix Candela Lectures*, eds. Guy Nordenson and Terence Riley (New York: The Museum of Modern Art, 2008), 9–15.

↑   Vladimir Grigoryevich Shukhov, Shukhov Tower, Moscow, 1922.
© Shukhov Tower Foundation

↑   Eugène Freyssinet, Hangar Airship, Orly, 1923. Photo Studio
Chevojon. RIBA Collections

↑ Tecton Group, Ove Arup, Penguin Pool at London's Regent's Park Zoo, London, 1934. Photo Tony Taylor. Courtesy Arup

↑ Hans Leuzinger, Robert Maillart, GUNIT-Zementhalle for the Swiss National Exhibition, Zurich, 1939. Photo H. Wolf-Benders Erben. RIBA Collections

↑ Pier Luigi Nervi, Hangar, Orvieto, 1939. Courtesy Collezione MAXXI Architettura, Pier Luigi Nervi Archive

In that context, the primacy of engineering was becoming consolidated, establishing itself as the symbol of the creativity of the new man, whose values and visionary and progressive inclinations it interpreted. The heroic example of this primacy and of the dreams and collective imagination that converged around it was, and still remains, the Crystal Palace (1851), "mechanically conceived and realized" and "all ready-made and computed with mathematical exactitude."[4] The adventure of Joseph Paxto's structure, which at the time of its construction sparked volatile disputes as heated as the fire that eventually destroyed it (an earlier version of what would happen to Richard Buckminster Fuller's pavilion), sums up the two faces of modernization in the twentieth century: the "adventurous" one and the "routine" one, a very convincing description, too, of the aspirations and the contradictions of "total engineering,"[5] from which this exhibition takes its cues.

One factor that helps to explain the tension that inevitably developed between the pioneers of engineering—first those in England who experimented with structures in iron and steel, and later the French forerunners of reinforced concrete construction—and architects who, from the 1920s on, held a place of honor in the pantheon of modernity's heroes lies in how the histories of architecture were written.

The interpretative paradigm constructed by Sigfried Giedion in his book *Space, Time and Architecture* (1941) is the most convincing example, and its author was one of the first to deal with this contentious subject. In one chapter, Giedion tackled the theme of the structural innovations that came out of the Second Industrial Revolution and their potentiality over the course of the nineteenth century, during which architecture had become so banal that it was hardly worth talking about, while "[t]he seeds of a new architecture were planted at the moment when handwork gave place to industrialized production [...]. But as long as scientific and technological advances were used in architecture without being absorbed by it, the engineer remained subordinated and detached from the architect."[6]

While on one hand this observation neither preannounced nor served to alter Giedion's position, as he remained a fervent apostle of early-twentieth-century mo-

4   Marshall Berman, "Afterword: The Crystal Palace, Facts and Symbol," in *All that is Solid Melts into Air* (London: Verso, 2010), 235–48.

5   A paraphrase that takes cues from the ideal of a "total architecture" expressed by Walter Gropius beginning in the Bauhaus period and reconsidered in 1956 in the text *Scope of Total Architecture* (London: George Allen & Unwin, 1956).

6   Sigfried Giedion, "The evolution of new potentialities," in *Space, Time and Architecture. The Growth of a New Tradition* (Cambridge: Harvard University Press, 1941), 182–83.

dernity, his insistence on seeking out the roots of a new tradition laid the foundation for a continuity between the realm of architecture and the methods of engineering, of which Walter Gropius first, and later Charles-Édouard Jeanneret (better known as Le Corbusier) were early interpreters.

The former, in his essay *Die Entwicklung Moderner Industriebaukunst* used images of industrial buildings—grain silos and factory buildings—to express his ideal of "total architecture," the heroic form of which confirms the authority of the engineer, even though the latter was on the verge of legitimizing the architect's sphere of competence. Of those perfect organisms, Gropius wrote: "Specific form, with no random elements, clear outlines, order of elements, sequences of similar parts and unity of form and color will become the aesthetic instrument of modern architecture, in concert with the energy and economy of our everyday lives."[7]

Le Corbusier closely followed the path laid down by his German colleague, recognizing in it the roots of a way of thinking that identified a direct connection between the spirit of modern times and the spirit of construction. In the magazine *L'Esprit Nouveau*, a still-young Le Corbusier had already included a section dedicated to the "Esthétique de l'ingénieur," in which he made himself the spokesman for the idea that the modern engineer was the only person capable of showing architects the way towards a rational conception of design.[8] He revisited the theme in *Vers une architecture*, in the celebrated *Trois rappels à MM. les architectes*, extolling the engineer's authority and radicalizing his oppositional nature with regard to the architect. In the first of his *rappels* (calls), dedicated to the "volume," Le Corbusier used some of the photographs of grain silos that had appeared in Gropius' text, lending those "beautiful forms," completely free from any sort of ambiguity, a timeless character. He had already expressed his appreciation for the "useful," "strong," "salubrious designs" that engineers had produced up to that point, and had set forth a panegyric that certainly left his contemporaries no possible rejoinder: "Our Romans, our Gothics, our Louis XIV, those are now the engineers."[9]

<hr>

7   "Exakt geprägte Form, jeder Zufälligkeit, klare Kontraste, Ordnen der Glieder, Reihung gleicher Teile und Einheit von Form und Farbe werden entsprechend der Energie und Ökonomie unseres öffentlichen Lebens das ästhetische Rüstzeug des modernen Baukünstlers werden." Walter Gropius, "Die Entwicklung Moderner Industriebaukunst," in *Jahrbuch des Deutschen Werkbundes* (Jena: E. Diederichs, 1913), 19–20.

8   Thomas P. Hughes, "Appel aux industriels," in *L'Esprit nouveau: Le Corbusier et l'industrie 1920-1925*, ed. Stanislaus von Moos (Berlin: Ernst & Sohn, 1987), 26–31.

9   See S.R. [Simone Rümmele], "Silos," in Ibid., 167 and Jean-Louis Cohen, "Introduction," in Le Corbusier, *Toward an Architecture* (Los Angeles: Getty Publications, 2007), 4–10.

In the successive decades, the sectors in which engineers and architects continued to develop their experimentation ended up ever more frequently overlapping. Commonalities in methods were created, redefining approaches in both fields and producing fruitful interactions. Structural engineering, the focus of this exhibition, arose from obvious connections with mathematical sciences, calculation and the use of digital programs, but at the same time has regained its distinction as "art," which has driven architecture to go beyond its bounds, to find common ground in which rationality and aesthetic principles interact, and to give voice to an unconventional interdisciplinarity.[10]

10 See Hanif Kara and Andreas Georgoulias, eds., *Interdisciplinary Design. New Lessons from Architecture and Engineering* (Barcelona: Actar and Harvard Graduate School of Design, 2012).

THE SUBCONSCIOUS OF ARCHITECTURE

Pippo Ciorra

In the typical depiction of Italian post-war planning and design, relations between architecture and engineering were always rather difficult, conditioned by the idea that they supposedly pertained to different, clearly-defined fields of action. Architecture was public, political, more interested in the imaginativeness of design than in the reality of materials, and focused on language and on relations with history and urban values; engineering, on the other hand, was viewed with suspicion, because it was intrinsically more linked to production processes and thus to the market, to private enterprise, to the built object, to concreteness as opposed to utopia. As Italy was becoming modernized, every parent hoped his daughter would marry an engineer, and every romantic young girl appreciated the engineer, but eloped with the architect. The antagonism was further aggravated by the social roles of the two professions, as the stereotypically political-theoretical nature of architecture meant that many commissioners (or perhaps "clients" is a better term) often preferred, and in many cases still prefer, the concreteness of engineers to the challenging creativity of architects.

---

1   The MAXXI, with the fundamental presence in its collections of the archives of brilliant structural engineers like Pier Luigi Nervi and Sergio Musmeci, and of architects who lent great importance to structural planning, like Maurizio Sacripanti, is proof that the situation we have outlined contained various important "exception" zones in which the two disciplines intersected and overlapped in the work of figures who cannot be circumscribed within just one of the two professional spheres. In particular, the experience of the exhibition *Zevi's architects: History and counter-history of Italian architecture 1944-2000* (MAXXI, 25 April–23 September 2018, curators Pippo Ciorra and Jean-Louis Cohen) brought to light the work of a constellation of architects and engineers who tended to blur the lines between the professions described here.

↑   Eduardo Torroja Miret, Hipódromo de la Zarzuela, Madrid, 1941.
Archivo Torroja, CEHOPU-CEDEX

↑   Hassan Fathy, New Gourna Village, Luxor, 1948. © Roger-Viollet /
Roger-Viollet

With all the due and well-documented exceptions,[1] this situation of forced collaboration and "armed peace"[2] lasted at least until the 1970s, when the conventional wisdom[3] that saw Italian architecture as one of the strong points of the country's political and social evolution and a fine example for every other western context began to dissipate. Up to then, despite the enthusiastic propaganda and the rather biased view of the figure of the engineer[4] promulgated in the previous decades by Le Corbusier, for many, engineering really was what Antoine Picon called "the subconscious of architecture,"[5] a necessary component, but always considered a sort of secret infrastructure in the service of architectural inventiveness. Perhaps the first person to establish himself thanks to an explicit decision to challenge this dichotomy was Renzo Piano, artisan, architect and engineer. Or at least, he was the first one capable of establishing a completely different dialogue between peers with engineers. Piano obviously did not spring up from nothing: he falls into an important line of architects that comprises figures like Franco Albini and Jean Prouvé, who were extremely mindful of the capabilities of technologies and materials. But Piano's communicative stroke of genius lay in giving constructive processes the same civic dignity as inventive processes, and in completely overriding the idea of political action as pertaining to ideologies, groups or parties that intermediated between designers and "users." Piano was a trailblazer, but the simultaneous petering out of

---

2   The two professional profiles combine not only in the work of flamboyant and eclectic figures like Nervi or Luigi Pellegrin, but also in long-standing "couples" whose collaboration always managed to bring out the best in the two cultures. Ludovico Quaroni suffered when he could not have Musmeci as his engineer, Renzo Piano adored working with Peter Rice, Foster with Arup in various versions, Steven Holl with Guy Nordenson and so forth. All situations in which the architectural result would not have been the same if one of the two figures had not been present.

---

3   Jean-Louis Cohen's text *La coupure entre architectes et intellectuels, ou les enseignements de l'italophilie* (Brussels: Margada, 2015), despite the relatively remote date of its initial publication (1984), is still the most interesting reading on the Italian architectural-political hegemony in the 1960s and 1970s.

---

4   Antoine Picon defines the quality that modernist theoreticians attributed to engineering as "paradoxical"; i.e., engineers were allowed to generate beauty only if it was involuntary ("postuler que les réalisations des ingégneurs ne sont jamais abouties artistiquement que lorsqu'elles ne chercent pas á faire de l'art")! Antoine Picon, "Introduction," in *L'Art de l'ingénieur. Constructeur, entrepreneur, inventeur*, ed. Antoine Picon (Paris: Moniteur, 1997), 22. Catalog of an exhibition of the same title, presented at the Centre Pompidou, Paris, June 25–September 29, 1997.

---

5   Again in the introduction to the 1997 catalog, Picon asks: "L'art de l'ingégneur constituerait-il alors une sorte de subsconscient de la pratique artistique?," in Picon, *L'Art de l'ingénieur*, 23.

↑ Konrad Wachsmann, U.S. Air Force Aircraft Hangar, model, 1951.
Photo Harry Callahan. Konrad-Wachsmann-Archiv, Akademie der
Künste, Berlin. Courtesy Pace Gallery. © The Estate of Harry Callahan

↑ Fred Nicholas Severud, Matthew Nowicki, Dorton Arena, Raleigh,
North Carolina, 1953. State Archives of North Carolina

↑ Niels Gutschow, Ulrich Finsterwalder, Cement Industry Pavilion, Constructa Bauausstellung, Hannover, 1951. Photo Ramón Vázquez Molezún. Courtesy Servicio Histórico De La Fundación Arquitectura COAM

the Tendenza movement and Florentine Radicalism left the field virtually empty, and that space was occupied by new or rediscovered architects—Botta, Natalini post-Superstudio, Ungers, Scarpa and Kahn—who seemed to demonstrate a new and far more fervent sensitivity to matters of construction and materials.

At this point, a strange period began, in which frequent references to Vitruvius and other primary sources seemed to authorize some to assert that a bijective correspondence between architecture and construction was possible, as if for every building there was an ideal structural type, and every structure corresponded to an appropriate architectural language. Paolo Portoghesi spoke of a hypothetical "constructive probity"[6] in almost metaphysical terms; Kenneth Frampton undertook his studies of tectonics and initially seemed to fall in line with a hierarchy that favored architects (Sverre Fehn, Giorgio Grassi, the various exponents of his "regionalism") who tended to identify their work with a type of material, a corresponding structure and, ultimately, a congruent architectural language—an architecture of a tectonic nature, in short. But then the focus shifted to another pair of luminaries present in this exhibition, Jørn Utzon and Ove Arup, whose extraordinary collaboration on the Sydney Opera House served to clarify that constructive probity as the postmodernists articulated it does not exist, that the dialogue between engineer and architect is one that entails the empirical pursuit of an equilibrium and an infinite quantity of different choices and options, and that sometimes the success of a project may require the use of a very different structural solution than the ideal one.[7] The question was resolved once and for all by two of the authors of this volume, Guy Nordenson and Barry Bergdoll, united by a 2016 publication that collected thirty-nine of the American engineer's projects.[8] For Nordenson, according to Bergdoll, the idea of a building having a single, unique formal and structural identity makes no sense; the reality is a much more complex condition of continuous negotiation between form and calculation.[9] It is true, however, that at a certain point in

---

6   Paolo Portoghesi, *After modern architecture* (New York: Rizzoli, 1982). Translated by Theresa Davis from the Italian edition.

7   Kenneth Frampton reports a very clear declaration made by Ove Arup, who explained that the Sydney Opera House "is one of those not-infrequent cases where the best architectural form and the best structural form do not coincide" and where one must thus move forward based on an arbitrary decision that makes one discipline bow to the needs of the other. See Kenneth Frampton, *Studies in Tectonic Culture. The Poetics of Construction in Nineteenth and Twentieth Century Architecture* (Cambridge: The MIT Press, 1995). Translated by Theresa Davis from the Italian edition.

8   Guy Nordenson, *Reading Structures: 39 Projects and Built Works* (Zurich: Lars Müller Publishers, 2016).

9   Barry Bergdoll, "Engineering between Research and Expression," in Guy Nordenson, *Reading Structures*, 9.

↑ James Hardress de Warenne Waller, Ctesiphon concrete shell, 1953. Waller Album, Irish Architectural Archive (93/67)

↑ Jean Prouvé, Pavilion for the Centenary of Aluminum under construction, Paris, 1953. Photo Lucien Hervé. Institut pour l'histoire de l'aluminium

the late twentieth century, the *rapprochement*[10] Picon spoke of became more evident. It was evident in the implications of architectural languages that lent growing importance to the tectonic nature of the design projects that generated them, albeit with a still vaguely ancillary role for structural engineering. And it was even more evident with the emergence of a line of high-tech architectonic experimentation and production that relies considerably on the other side of engineering, the realm of geometry and frames, and aims to bring the dialogue between architectural form and structural solution to the forefront. Piano's contributions, among the most effective of the exponents of the English *nouvelle vague* of the 1960s (Cedric Price and Richard Rogers above all), and those of the engineering studios Arup, Frei Otto and SOM, along with the rediscovery of the heritage of Italian heroes of engineering (Nervi, Musmeci and many others) laid the groundwork for a line of experimentation on lightweight structures that still today has an enormous quantitative and qualitative impact on the excellence of the construction industry.

As we said, the amity between architects and engineers is necessary, but also unstable and fickle: in the decade following the explosion of high-tech, architects once again veered towards particularly sculptural and abstract form-generating processes that were inevitably destined to shunt the hard task of making buildings with daring and unrealistic geometries "stay upright" to structural engineering.

We need only consider Arup's herculean efforts to allow Peter Eisenman[11] to create columns that ended in mid-air before touching the ground, or the willingness of Frank O. Gehry and Daniel Libeskind's engineers to conceive more complex and counterintuitive structures than Utzon had designed for the Opera House. The overall impression, if we look back as far as the eighteenth- and nineteenth-century archeology of modern engineering, is that of a discipline becoming increasingly aware of its own expressive autonomy and of the role it can play in a dialogue with architecture. A sort of subconscious aspect of the built work that progressively emerges to establish a more attentive dialogue with form, function and the desire to create art. The dialogue becomes more productive in phases when the two disciplines' lines of progress run close together, resonating with one another. Which is what may be happening in the current historical period.[12]

In fact, the hypothesis of this exhibition is that we are now in one of those phases of maximum rapprochement of the two disciplines. Not unlike a century ago, at the

---

10   Picon wrote: "Le rapprochement de l'art e de l'ingénierie peut paraître évident au premier abord," in Antoine Picon, *L'Art de l'ingénieur*, 16.

---

11   The reference is obviously to the Wexner Center in Columbus Ohio, inaugurated in 1988, which underwent significant restoration by Arup before the end of the millennium.

dawn of modernism,[13] the impression is that architecture is being asked, a bit indiscriminately, to concretize the functional and political need for modernization of the inhabited world (and today, the uninhabited one as well). In the 1920s, this occurred by means of an interesting convergence of and mutual need for technological advancement—cement, steel, glass—and a radical figurative innovativeness, as in the case of Le Corbusier's five points, or the Bauhaus aesthetic. Today we have a very clear understanding of the enormous impact of technological innovations and functional demands, for example with regard to climate change and digital culture, but we do not have such a clear idea about the possible aesthetic response of architecture to these same questions—one that would be neither too ephemeral nor purely self-destructive. In short, the situation is reversed: a century ago, the discipline of architecture included structural innovations and was a direct interlocutor with society; today, the relationship between technology and society tends to be direct and apparently efficient, while architecture struggles to find a role that will allow it to survive, reinvent itself and contribute its own answers to social and environmental challenges. One of the objectives of the exhibition is thus to foster dialogue between the disciplines and stimulate architects to bring their ideas into a discussion with society at large.

The exhibition and the accompanying essays in this catalog show the full scope of the impressive results of experimentation in the field of structural engineering and its interaction with the expressive and functional aims of architects. But it is even more clear today than in the past, as Picon told us, that "structural engineering is no longer a humanistic discipline in itself, but rather a small part of the science of engineering."[14] With the advent of computer-assisted design and calculation, innovations in science and technology, and

---

12   The idea of a "rapprochement" between the two disciplines evoked by Picon at the beginning of his introduction to the 1997 exhibition catalog is still the same one which, under different conditions, now compels us to produce *Technoscape. The Architecture of Engineers*, a new context for penetrating dialogue, no longer between architecture and structural engineering, but between architecture and the many types of engineering that support it, fuel it, and in some cases outdo it.

---

13   While at the time of *Vers une Architecture* (1923) and Le Corbusier's mythography of engineering, technology appeared to be a device for improving the social value of architecture (construction in series, accessibility etc.), today many types of engineering can be essential tools to connect aesthetic experimentation with the many demands of the environment, the resource system, and the technologies we live in the midst of. As a perhaps less solid counterpoint to the milestones of a century ago—Le Corbusier and Bauhaus—one may want to juxtapose the New European Bauhaus project, a new platform for dialogue between creative professionals, society and science. (https://europa.eu/new-european-bauhaus/index_en.)

---

14   Picon, *L'Art de l'ingénieur*, 32.

the urgent need to involve planning and design in striving to tackle environmental issues, those who deal with the creation of inhabited spaces must dialogue with many more branches of engineering: environmental engineering, robotics, materials engineering, aerospace engineering, digital fabrication and others. For this reason, the exhibition brings together documentation of masterpieces of the architecture of engineering from the post-war period to today, and a series of explorations of the future world of engineering carried out in collaboration with some of the most important research centers from universities in Europe and abroad. We expect them to offer answers in terms of direct ecological actions accomplished via "natural" agents; the production of new materials, whether organic or synthetic; disaster mitigation; the smart management of data and urban spaces; and the use of robotics in various phases of design and planning, from fabrication to the dynamic autonomy of domestic and urban accoutrements.

TEATRO REGIO

	TURIN, ITALY
	1965–1973
ARCHITECTS	CARLO MOLLINO CARLO GRAFFI
ENGINEERS	SERGIO MUSMECI FELICE BERTONE ADOLFO ZAVELANI ROSSI MARCELLO ZAVELANI ROSSI

Turin's Teatro Regio, inaugurated in 1740, was destroyed by a fire in 1936; a competition for its reconstruction was launched, but the complex designed by the architect Carlo Mollino and the engineers Marcello and Adolfo Zavelani Rossi, who participated at an early stage, was not completed until 1973.

Mollino's structure interrelates with the Baroque spirit of the original theater via a distinctive and skillful use of sinuous curves for the side walls, balconies created in continuity with the ceiling, and the foyer. The concrete manifestation of Mollino's expressive ideas was made possible by the contribution of the engineer and entrepreneur Felice Bertone, who designed the hyperbolic paraboloid roof, and the engineer Sergio Musmeci who, thanks to his experience designing complex concrete structures, did the necessary calculations for the structural elements. Hence a system of ramps and catwalks took shape, characterized by "folding" exposed concrete surfaces and constructed using hollow beams with V-shaped sections.

↓ Teatro Regio, reinforced
concrete structure, view
from the foyer, Turin,
1973. Courtesy Collezione
MAXXI Architettura, Sergio
Musmeci Archive

SYDNEY
OPERA HOUSE

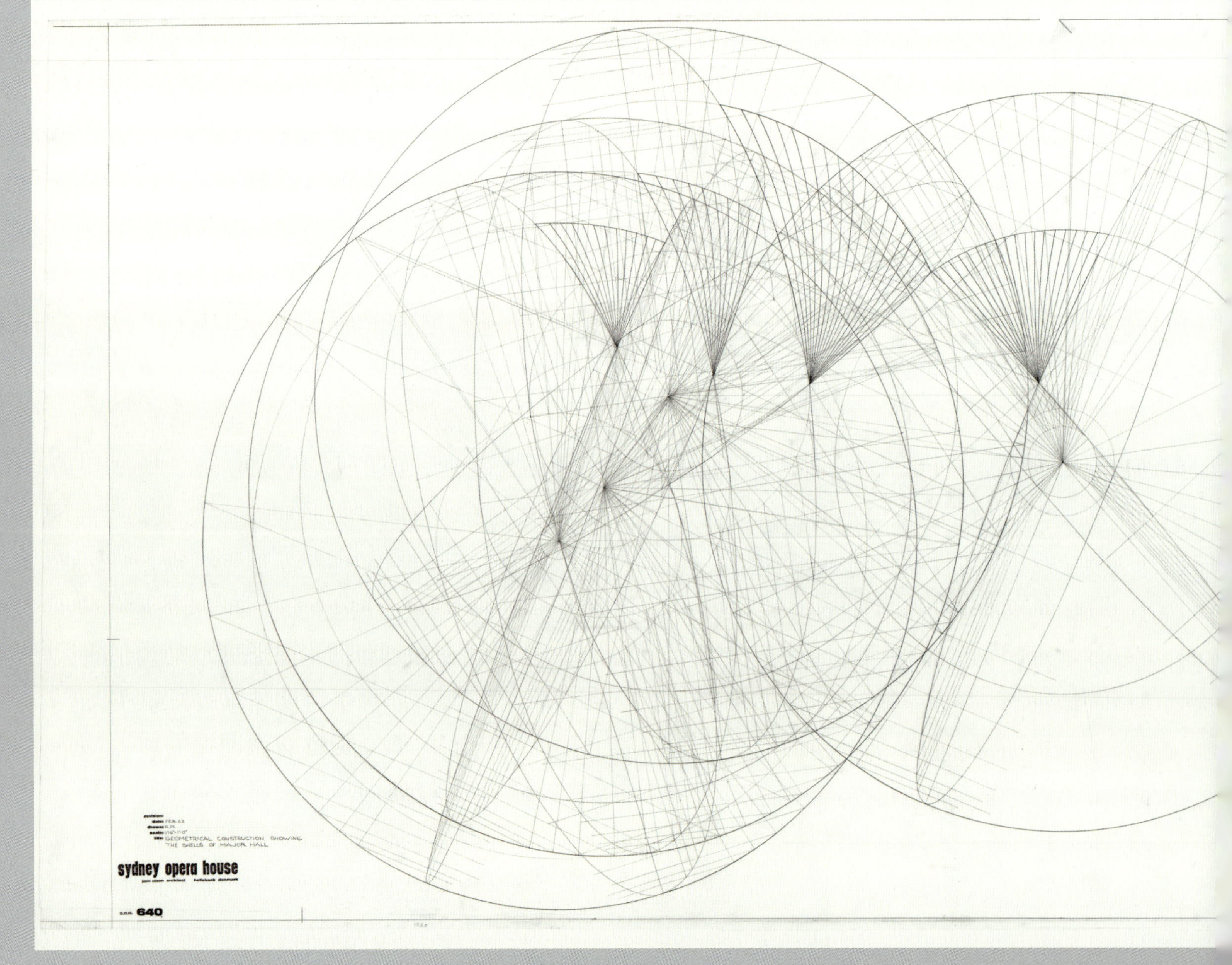

1957–1973

ARCHITECTS JØRN UTZON
HALL TODD & LITTLEMORE

ENGINEER OVE ARUP & PARTNERS
OVE NYQUIST ARUP
GERHARD JACOB "JACK" ZUNZ

A UNESCO World Heritage site since 2007, the Sydney Opera House is considered a paradigmatic example of the relationship between architect Jørn Utzon, and engineer Ove Arup. The provocative design's roots date back to 1957, when the not-yet-forty-year-old Utzon won the international competition with a visionary idea: a series of overlapping shells that would rise unencumbered over the bay. The sixteen-year gestation period between the competition and the 1973 inauguration entailed a complicated process of metamorphosis in which poetic concepts were adapted to economically and structurally pragmatic forms, thanks in part to innovative digital structural analysis models. The famous final plan, so immediate and simple in its compositional clarity, is the result of twelve phases of evolution that took the geometry of the structure from free curve to parabola, ellipse and circle. In the end, the key idea—a collective vision that came out of a climate of collaboration between Utzon's team and Arup's led by Jack Zunz—lay in inscribing the shells within a single spherical surface. This allowed both the prefabrication of the reinforced concrete ribs created by the firm Hornibrook Ltd, and the rationalization of the design for the tile facing. In 1966, Utzon abandoned the project, leaving the question of the glass façades unresolved, but they were masterfully designed by Peter Hall in 1968.

← Sydney Opera House, project, Sydney, 1973. Utzon Archives © The Utzon Center

EXHIBITING STRUCTURE AT MOMA 1932–1994

Barry Bergdoll

Beginning in the 1920s, architecture historians crafted, in real time, a narrative for emerging architectural modernism that equally established a canon of nineteenth and early twentieth-century engineering landmarks. As a genealogy for the audaciously new was forged, it was based on an insistence that modernity had come of age despite an ever-widening chasm over the course of the nineteenth century between architects, burdened by nostalgia, and engineers, by nature pragmatic and future-oriented. Le Corbusier, Mies van der Rohe, and Walter Gropius, in this telling, owed more to heroic engineers than to earlier architectural designers. This supposed "schism between architecture and technology"[1] was famously and influentially diagnosed by Sigfried Giedion in his lectures at Harvard in 1938–39 (later published as *Space, Time and Architecture*) as one of the main causes for alarm in surveying the "present state of our culture." Giedion professed a mission to help,

"anxious to find a way out of the apparent chaos of its contradictory tendencies."[2] There was much to be anxious about in 1939, but the Swiss historian and secretary of CIAM skirted the political. His zeal was to separate the progressive engineering wheat from the nostalgic architectural chaff in order to see the vectors of architectural progressivism more clearly. While the instrumentality of Giedion's historical argument, in texts from *Bauen in Frankreich. Bauen in Eisen. Bauen in Eisenbeton* of 1928 to *Mechanization Takes Command* of 1948, has been analyzed frequently in recent years,[3] the role of exhibitions aimed at reaching an even larger public in the task of bridging the chasm—in garnering aesthetic admiration as much for bridges as for opera houses—has received little attention. And this even for the exhibitions with which Giedion was himself involved. Museums, and the newly minted Museum of Modern Art in New York in particular, played a role in celebrating engineering as an integral part of the larger culture of building modernity and modernism, and making the case for a broad public.

From its inaugural exhibition, for which the museum's first director Alfred Barr coined the term "The International Style," MoMA set out to support an architecture in which engineering and aesthetics were intrinsically interwoven. "The aesthetic principles of the International Style are based primarily upon the nature of modern materials and structure and upon modern requirements in planning. Slender steel posts and beams, and concrete reinforced by steel have made possible structures of skeleton-like strength and lightness," co-curators Philip Johnson and Henry-Russell Hitchcock noted. The work of the museum was both to bridge professional splits and to rectify historical oversights: "engineering [...] remained until after the Great War outside the field of architecture. Buildings like the Crystal Palace in London were seldom considered as having architectural significance [...]. Since the War an international style has grown up throughout Europe [...]. Engineering was at last not only joined closely with architecture but made its basis."[4]

Attention paid by an *art* museum to engineering was a radical gesture, since large public museum collections in the nineteenth century had separated architecture and engineering firmly between institutions devoted to history and art and those devoted to science and technology. This mirrored earlier teaching collections, since from the late eighteenth century engineering and architectural models were held and deployed separately in their respective professional schools, and perhaps nowhere more dramatically than in France. By the 1880s the public could enjoy, in Paris, displays of engineering models in the galleries of the Conservatoire national des arts et métiers, while architecture could be seen, after 1889, in the Musée de Sculpture Comparée in the Palais du Trocadéro. After 1939, sectional models of Gothic cathedrals were prime features of the Musée des Monuments Français (as the Musée de Sculpture Comparée was rebaptized), and a few hundred meters away in Auguste Perret's majestic Musée des Travaux Publics, models of bridges, dams, and other engineering works were to be admired.

The novelty of the Museum of Modern Art was from the outset to display not only works of the traditional fine arts, including architecture, but also works produced by technical and machine production: photography, film, and even works of engineering as aesthetic buildings. A marriage between architecture and engineering was announced with the foundation of the Department of Architecture in 1932. Inevitably this would favor engineering as a factor in the production of aesthetic modern form, and display would be posited as much on appearance as any underlying technical inventiveness or advance. In 1933, Philip Johnson presented a small display of the underlying principles of the steel frame building as the condition for the development of the most American of building inventions, the skyscraper. The exhibition demonstrated that displaying engineering principles would often require supplemental didactic materials rather than the supposition that a built structure could be admired as art through a direct encounter with its representation in a model or photographs (drawings only became a frequent part of MoMA architecture exhibitions in the 1960s). *Early Modern Architecture: Chicago 1870-1910* included specially produced didactic diagrams of the steel frame construction that had revolutionized urban building.

In the prelude to the United States' entry into World War II, during which museums across the country felt an urgency to orient exhibitions, programs, and their public demeanor toward the war effort, a major exhibition celebrated the Tennessee

1   Sigfried Giedion, *Space, Time and Architecture: The Growth of a New Tradition* (Cambridge, MA: Harvard University Press, 1944), 146.

2   Giedion, *Space, Time and Architecture*, V.

3   See most recently Reto Geiser, *Giedion and America: Repositioning the History of Modern Architecture* (Zurich: gta Verlag, 2018) and Anthony Vidler, *Histories of the Immediate Present: Inventing Architectural Modernism* (Boston: MIT Press, 2008).

4   Henry-Russell Hitchcock and Philip Johnson, *Modern Architecture* (New York: The Museum of Modern Art, 1932), 19. On this seminal and influential exhibition see Terence Riley, *The International Style: Exhibition 15 and the Museum of Modern Art* (New York: Rizzoli, 1992) and Barry Bergdoll, "Modern Architecture: International Exhibition," in *Partners in Design: Alfred H. Barr Jr. and Philip Johnson*, ed. David A. Hanks (New York: The Monacelli Press, 2015), 136–47.

Valley Authority (TVA), a vast regional electrification project launched in 1933 by Franklin D. Roosevelt. The exhibition, like the TVA itself, embraced a synthesis of architecture and engineering, of landscape and infrastructure, of science and art that was at the heart of a national project that understood infrastructure and engineering as intertwined. From the very beginning, the TVA took public relations as an integral part of its massive undertaking.[5] With visitors' centers located at its most dramatic dams, and with cutting-edge graphic designers on staff, the TVA might be said to have put itself on display from the start. If it brought tourists to a region better known for rural poverty than a new synthesis of natural beauty and the engineering sublime, it also sought to broadcast its message and circulate its imagery. The show at MoMA was more a creation of the authority than of the museum's Department of Architecture. "Photographs and models included in the exhibition have been chosen to emphasize the basically modern design which has resulted from the harmonious collaboration of architect and engineer in this vast government project. Graphic diagrams will show the engineering control over the 700-mile Tennessee River and its effect upon the valley through which it flows, an area larger than England,"[6] explained the press release for a display which opened in late April 1941 first to an invited group of government officials, architects, engineers, and defense program officials, before being thrown open to the general public, already alerted by radio broadcasts. Yet the show also advanced the museum's agenda of effecting new alliances between architecture and engineering, as the press release underscored: "Distinguished by sober yet imaginative design, the architecture of the TVA [...] represents a close cooperation of architect and engineer with an understanding of each other's skills on a scale unmatched since the great utilitarian building campaigns of Imperial Rome."[7] Governmental and museum rhetorical stances were blending in ways that made clear that not only was the American public to be won over to the vast expense of the project, but also to imbibe a rhetoric of the engineering of a democratic country soon to be in conflict with totalitarian regimes with their own machines for celebrating engineering and infrastructural projects in publications, exhibitions and films. A film on the

TVA played daily in the museum's film theater and then accompanied the display on a national tour. David E. Lilienthal, director of the TVA, explained to the press: "Millions of Americans, we told ourselves, will see these structures. They will see in them a kind of token of the virility and vigor of democracy, of its concerns for living men and generations yet to come. We wanted these dams to have the honest beauty of a fine tool; for TVA was a tool to do a job for men in a democracy." And he went on "The dams must be the finest achievements of modern engineering skill. But what of their aesthetic quality, their form? These monuments would reflect for centuries the standard of American culture and the purpose of American life of our time. Should we follow the quite general practice of building the structures, and then add some decorations to make them 'pretty'? Should we raise up monoliths to see their giant shoulders against the floods of a thousand years, and then embellish their strength with the doo-dads and columns of a civilization now gone for a thousand years? [...] We had to search for architects who were not in a constant delirium of nostalgia for the past, men who could interpret the functional strength the engineers would build into these structures; and we had to find engineers willing to collaborate with architects with open and eager minds. The exhibit you have seen tells how well that union succeeded."[8] Wall-sized

---

5   See Tim Culvahouse, ed., *The Tennessee Valley Authority: Design and Persuasion* (New York: Princeton Architectural Press, 2007).

6   MoMA Press Release, April 21, 1941, "Museum of Modern Art will hold exhibition of TVA Architecture and Design," MoMA Archives, viewable online: https://assets.moma.org/documents/moma_press-release_325221.pdf?_ga=2.178816932.1887772004.1633972257-338071719.1611330555. Accessed October 11, 2021.

7   MoMA Press Release, April 28, 1941, "David E. Lilienthal, Director of the TVA, Opens Exhibition of TVA Architecture and Design at MoMA," 2, MoMA Archives, viewable online: https://assets.moma.org/documents/moma_press-release_325220.pdf?_ga=2.192119466.1887772004.1633972257-338071719.1611330555. Accessed October 11, 2021.

8   MoMA Press Release, "David E. Lilienthal," 1.

9   See Juliet Kinchin, "Machine Art: Elements of a New Beauty," in *Partners in Design: Alfred H. Barr Jr. and Philip Johnson*, 148–73.

10   MoMA Press Release, October 9, 1941, "Museum of Modern Art Exhibits Portable Defense Housing Unit and Bomb Shelter Made from Steel Grain Bin," 1–2, MoMA Archives, viewable online: https://assets.moma.org/documents/moma_press-release_325265.pdf?_ga=2.221440792.1887772004.1633972257-338071719.1611330555. Accessed October 11, 2021.

11   *Ibid.*

photo murals in the tradition of Bauhaus designer Herbert Bayer's exhibition designs transported visitors in midtown Manhattan to the valleys of the Tennessee River and to commanding positions hovering above towering dams.

Architecturally the museum would return again and again to putting the work of a quartet of architects before the public: Frank Lloyd Wright, Le Corbusier, Alvar Aalto, and particularly Mies van der Rohe, who was of course Philp Johnsons' idol. But for two decades from the inclusion of his Dymaxion House in the tenth anniversary show (which also inaugurated MoMA's first purpose-built home) in 1939 to the dramatic occupation of the sculpture garden by three large-scale experimental structures in 1959, Richard Buckminster Fuller would also be lionized over and over by the museum as an avant-garde inventor, a breaker of norms every bit as worthy of admiration as Picasso. Johnson, even before he arrived at MoMA to craft *Modern Architecture: International Exhibition*, had exhibited Fuller's Dymaxion House at the Harvard Society for Contemporary Art in 1930. In 1941, with America's entry into World War II all but inevitable, the idea of using MoMA's new sculpture garden for the occasional display of cutting-edge residential architecture—part of the museum's determination to shape middle-class

taste—was launched. Not however as originally planned with Frank Lloyd Wright's vision of the "Usonian house," in which future residents might act partly in a build-it-yourself fashion to create an architecture of timber and brick on organic principles. That prototype had run afoul of New York City Building Department permits in 1941. Rather prefabricated corrugated steel cylinders of the type used to store grain in the American heartland were given a place of honor in the sculpture garden, twinned and outfitted by Fuller as prototype ready-mades to fulfill the Federal government's call for wartime "defense housing." Fuller's "Dymaxion Deployment Unit" (repeating his trademark brand of Dynamic, Maximum, and Tension) created tension as much by its structural innovations in assembly as by juxtaposing fairly traditional internal furnishings supplied by Bloomingdale's Department Store with a below-grade bomb shelter. Fuller defined the vision of the modernist designer, one able to see the beauty in the new realities of life, a position first staked out when Johnson included airplane propellers and industrial springs displayed for aesthetic appreciation in his 1934 *Machine Art* show.[9] "Buckminster Fuller has for many years been known as a shatterer of traditions in the fields of engineering and housing [...]. His Dymaxion House caused furious discussion and controversy among architects because it broke all precedent and principles in conventional house building."[10] The spectacle of construction in the garden—the performance as much as the outcome—was as much a part of the display as the finished product since the house was built "from the top down, i.e., the steel segments of the roof were assembled and bolted together on the ground and raised by means of a collapsible mast extending through the ventilator opening at the top center of the roof. The roof was raised a little at a time to allow the circular segments composing the walls to be bolted on from the top down. When the wall was completed the foundation was laid: a circle of bricks flat from on the ground. The bricks were not mortared but sand was used to fill the interstices. With the wall resting on the tops of the bricks the collapsible mast was removed and taken out of the house. A sectional steel floor was then bolted to the lower rim of the walls and steel anchors attached by steel guy ropes were then sunk outside the house to a depth of two feet."[11] Fuller went on to explain that engineering thinking was not only about rapid assembly, but cost efficiency providing a "more comfortable dwelling unit of but a fraction of the weight of other dwellings of equal cubical content," as well as efficiency for air conditioning and radiant heating, retaining more easily a comfortable interior temperature. More topical, he alerted an ever more nervous public that "[t]he round house is easiest to camouflage from the air as it coincides with nature-forms such as trees and hillocks."[12] An interior display of Fuller's work constituted the first monographic display devoted to an "engineer" inventor who bridged architecture and engineering, although—or perhaps because—he had formal training in neither.

Fuller would remain the darling of MoMA curators after the war, but he was not alone as the museum celebrated the idea of systems of construction, rather than final compositions, as one possible answer to the question posed in the 1949 symposium "What is Happening to Modern Architecture," meant to counter growing regionalism. Already in 1946 a press release announcing the display of a "revolutionary new type of steel construction," sought to garner excitement for a large (1/2 inch scale) model of an airplane hangar designed by emigre architect Konrad Wachsmann. Wachsmann's experiments in lattice-type interlocking space frames were a visual and conceptual cousin of the way Fuller's work would later evolve with the geodesic dome series. "What may at first appear to be a giant plaything put together from a child's toy building set, the visitor to the MoMA will find on drawing nearer to a remarkable half-inch scale model of an airplane hangar of revolutionary construction. The great truss roof, which would actually measure 140×200 feet, is boldly cantilevered out from four supports of incredible lightness. The floor area is almost entirely unobstructed, and removable external walls allow maximum freedom of circulation."[13] Wachsmann's "mobilar" tube joint system that could be easily assembled on site, was juxtaposed in *Architecture in Steel: An Experiment in Standardization*, with a prototype of a mobile wall unit whose doors could be opened or removed without recourse to hinges or tracks. "Banks of these wall units are self-supporting and can be rolled away from the building in which they function, since they in no way affect the building's structural load."[14] The collaborative nature of the project was acknowledged in the press release: "Paul Weidlinger, civil engineer, worked out all the difficult calculations on stresses and functions which made this whole type of construction possible."[15]

MoMA's efforts to lionize engineers as well as architects reached a high point in 1947. Full-scale retrospectives—both featuring walk-in scale photographic enlargements to create environments—were devoted to the engineer Robert Maillart and to the architect Mies van der Rohe.[16] For a short while in the autumn, the two exhibitions could be seen nearly side by side. While Johnson worked hand-in-hand with Mies on the installation of his architecture which included elements of the vocabulary he had created for the expression of American steel, Giedion as guest curator

12 *Ibid.*

13 MoMA Press Release, February 4, 1946, "Museum of Modern Art Shows Revolutionary New Type of Steel Construction," 1, MoMA Archives, viewable online: https://assets.moma.org/documents/moma_press-release_325504.pdf?_ga=2.144892980.1887772004.1633972257-338071719.1611330555. Accessed October 11, 2021.

14 *Ibid.*

15 *Ibid.* On Weidlinger and Breuer see Guy Nordenson, "Marcel Breuer: *Structure* and Shadow," in *Marcel Breuer: Building Global Institutions*, eds. Barry Bergdoll and Jonathan Massey (Zurich: Lars Müller, 2018), 116–39.

16 On Mies see Barry Bergdoll, "Walk in Collage: Mies van der Rohe's 1947 Exhibition at MoMA," in *Mies van der Rohe: Montage/Collage*, eds. Andreas Beitin, Wolf Eiermann, and Brigitte Franzen (London: Koenig Books, 2017), 172–87.

17 MoMA Press Release, June 20, 1947, "Museum of Modern Art Exhibits Swiss Bridges Remarkable for Beauty and Engineering," 1, MoMA Archives, viewable online: https://assets.moma.org/documents/moma_press-release_325568.pdf?_ga=2.225160218.1887772004.1633972257-338071719.1611330555. Accessed October 11, 2021.

18 *Ibid.* This juxtaposition was recreated literally in a 2005 exhibition on Santiago Calatrava at The Metropolitan Museum of Art, New York.

19 Arthur Drexler, *8 Automobiles. An exhibition concerned with the esthetics of motorcar design*, at the Museum of Modern Art, New York, autumn 1951 (New York: The Museum of Modern Art, 1951), preface. Two years later a follow-up exhibition *Ten Automobiles* was staged.

20 MoMA Press Release, August 25, 1952, "Two Houses of the Future to be Exhibited," 1, MoMA Archives, viewable online: https://assets.moma.org/documents/moma_press-release_325859.pdf?_ga=2.251363462.1887772004.1633972257-338071719.1611330555. Accessed October 11, 2021.

21 *Ibid.*

was able to further his mission of bridging the chasm by celebrating his countryman Maillart in the "first exhibition of his work ever to be held."[17] Given all the laurels of an avant-garde artist, Maillart, who had died in 1940, was touted for his "constant struggle against official opposition and public apathy." Relegated to rural valleys far from official taste, the museum brought these radical inventions of Maillart's conviction in "structure as monolithic" into full public view, all the while celebrating their presence in an art museum: "One has only to compare Brâncuși's *Bird in Space* with the lines of Maillart's three-hinged arch bridges to observe his amazing combination of engineering with pure sculpture."[18] Engineering as sculpture would be declared over and over as the Department of Architecture and Design, as it was known after 1949, occasionally displayed industrial artifacts from automobiles—"hollow, rolling sculpture"[19] according to Arthur Drexler—to space frames in the sculpture garden. Engineering that could aspire to sculpture would find favor.

The first of three postwar full-scale "houses in the garden" by which MoMA sought to persuade through a visitable building with its own public entrance from the sculpture garden, the 1949 butterfly roof design by Marcel Breuer, would arguably have the greatest impact on American residential architecture. The museum balanced the display of Breuer's exercise in synthesizing modern stylistic form and spatial arrangement using largely conventional means of American timber frame construction with exhibitions devoted to experiments in radical structure. In late August 1952, the press was invited to preview a display of scale models in *Two Houses: New Ways to Build*, returning Fuller—now with models of his geodesic domes—to the limelight, juxtaposed with Friedrich Kiesler's radically different "endless house." One of the earliest shows organized by Arthur Drexler, who would serve as the head of the department for more than three decades, the aim was "to demonstrate that two seemingly different approaches—the scientific and the aesthetic—can produce similar results in the architectural use of space."[20] It was clear that Architecture shows were meant to demonstrate and to persuade, not even to pretend to the neutrality of simply putting work on display for Kantian disinterested aesthetic enjoyment, as say, with the work of Jackson Pollock who was a mainstay of museum displays from the early 1950s. Fuller was described as "a well-known engineer," who believed that "[t]otal mechanization [...] would enable man's return to his earliest recorded home: the Garden of Eden."[21]

The denouement came in autumn 1959, when Fuller installed three enormous experimental structures in a vacant lot next to the museum's sculpture garden.[22] Billed as models for future architectures, *Octet Truss*, *Tensegrity Mast*, and *Geodesic Rigid Radome*, would remain on view for nearly a year and attract some of the greatest attention to the museum's architectural exhibitions since Breuer's house in the garden a decade earlier. This dramatic experiential display of full-scale environments—preludes to Fuller's imagination to take the scale to the enclosure of large parts of Manhattan under an enormous dome—was complemented by a contextualizing interior display of a more traditional gallery type. The dimensions were daunting: the 100-foot-long truss was cantilevered from a single asymmetrically placed support, projecting some 65 feet on one side, 40 on the other. The mast reached 45 feet into the air, the dome's apex reached 48 feet. Specially commissioned theatrical nighttime photography was featured in an exhibition brochure that unfolded from a single large sheet of paper folded in Fulleresque ways, and which was supplied to the press. *The New York Times* architecture critic, Ada Louise Huxtable, a former MoMA curatorial assistant who would prepare a MoMA traveling show on Italian modernist architecture that celebrated Pier Luigi Nervi as a formgiver, was effusive: "The world of tomorrow is here today at the Museum of Modern Art."[23] She continued to explain the significance far beyond the principle and calculations behind Fuller's work, describing how it represented, in essence, the very reconciliation between architecture and engineering that Hitchcock, Giedion, and Nikolaus Pevsner in his revised *Pioneers of Modern Design,* published by MoMA in 1949,[24] had all called for: "Mr. Fuller's space frames and enclosures represent the greatest advance in building science since the invention of the arch. Their building at full size in the heart of Manhattan, is splendid showmanship in the museum's tradition—a tradition that has seem a little tarnished lately. This is an exhibition with the museum's old flair; a superior blending of the startling and the significant, for a lively presentation of the latest frontiers of art."[25] Most importantly it represented a shift from objects to systems, from composition to invention, from individual buildings shaped to a bespoke function to open-ended principles that, in this case, "can be used wherever it is necessary to make large uninterrupted roof spans: concert halls, factories, museums, train sheds, airplane hangars."[26] Here Fuller and Mies van der Rohe—whose 1942 design for a concert hall inside a disused bomber factory by Albert Kahn had been included in his 1947 MoMA retrospective—converged.[27] The introductory wall label announced the museum's new architectural mission as one that aligned with Fuller, who "believes that the designer's real responsibility no longer is the creation of individual buildings or objects, but rather [...] the interrelating of physics, mathematics and [humanity's] well being." The show, Drexler noted, "suggests that we may ultimately learn to 'weave' enormous buildings that will differ in every way from what we now call architecture."[28]

This new mandate would be taken forward in two of Drexler's most ambitious curatorial projects of the decade, exhibitions on *Visionary Architecture* (1960)—"twentieth century projects considered too revolutionary to build"[29]—and *Twentieth Century Engineering* (1964). The latter, one of seven exhibitions in the *Art in a Changing World: 1884-1964* series, opened

---

22 For the best analysis of this exhibition see Maria Gough, "Backyard Landing: Three Structures by Buckminster Fuller," in *New Views on R. Buckminster Fuller*, eds. Hsiao-Yun Chu and Roberto G. Trujillo (Stanford, CA: Stanford University Press, 2009), 125–45.

23 Ada Louise Huxtable, "Future Previewed? Innovations of Buckminster Fuller Could Transform Architecture," *The New York Times* (September 27, 1959): 21. When Ada Louise Huxtable was a curatorial assistant in the Department of Architecture and Design, she first developed her interest in the work of Pier Luigi Nervi, explored in a traveling exhibition and book on the Italian engineer.

24 Irene Sunwoo, "Whose Design? MoMA and Pevsner's *Pioneers*," *Getty Research Journal*, no. 2 (2010): 69–82.

25 Huxtable, "Future Previewed?," 21.

26 *Ibid*.

27 See Claire Zimmerman, "The Base: Terrace and Podium of the Neue Nationalgalerie," in *Neue Nationalgalerie. Das Museum von Mies van der Rohe*, eds. Joachim Jäger and Constanze von Marlin (Berlin: Deutscher Kunstverlag, 2021), 140.

28 Quoted in Maria Gough, "Backyard Landing," 128.

29 MoMA Press Release, "Visionary Architecture," September 28, 1960, 1, MoMA Archives, viewable online: https://assets.moma.org/documents/moma_press-release_326200.pdf?_ga=2.247196676.1887772004.1633972257-338071719.1611330555. Accessed October 11, 2021.

BARRY BERGDOLL

simultaneously to celebrate the museum's expansion in two new buildings designed by Johnson, might be said to have undertaken for engineering what *Modern Architecture: International Exhibition* (1932) had done for architecture three decades earlier. Drexler set out to establish both a canon of major achievements of engineering with an international scope—including significant works from Latin America, a region entirely absent from the 1932 architecture show, with major works by Félix Candela in Mexico and Alejandro Pietri in Venezuela—and to create a typology of forms and programs from thin-shell vaults and tensegrity structures and from the buildings of Nervi, Fritz Leonhardt, and the Japanese Yoshikatsu Tsuboi to landscape-scale infrastructure of bridges, highways, and dams across the planet. The old chasm or rivalry of architecture and engineering was dismissed as outdated: "A more useful debate for the development of architecture in what is left of this century would have to do with the relevance of those forms engineers give us [...]. Engineering is among the most rewarding of the arts not only because it produces individual masterpieces but because it is an art grounded in social responsibility. Today we lack the political and economic apparatus that would facilitate a truly responsible use of our technology. But it may be that a more skillful and humane use of engineering depends on a more knowledgeable response to its poetry."[30]

Drexler followed up with another extravaganza in the sculpture garden, inviting Frei Otto to unfurl a huge translucent tent of polyester fiber to shade the garden for the summer of 1971, part of a monographic exhibition on the work of the German architect-engineer giving new formal expression to the idea of the programmatically flexible enclosure of vast spaces for use by masses of people. Engineering would also be given a major place in Drexler's swan song, the sprawling *Transformations in Modern Architecture*, which featured over 400 structures many in the large scale, almost walk-in photographs that Drexler had developed over decades as his exhibition style with the aim of giving general audiences something of the drama of experience of bold modern architecture and daring engineering experiments. Smaller follow-up exhibitions tracked new buildings: I. M. Pei and Partners' vast New York convention center "the largest exposition center under one roof in the U.S.,"[31] realized with Weidlinger as the engineer, and then in 1983 *Three New Skyscrapers* celebrating "three different responses to the questions of structure and organization of space."[32] These were Norman Foster's Hong Kong and Shanghai Bank building in Hong Kong, SOM's National Commerce Bank in Jeddah, Saudi Arabia, and Philip Johnson and John Burgee's International Place and Fort Hill Square in Boston. The latter was included, no doubt in homage to Johnson's continued influence at MoMA, as illustrated a new "manipulation of architecture as urban scenography."[33]

Transformations may be said in a way to have marked the end of an arc that had opened with the 1932 mission to bridge the canyon between architecture and engineering. If for Drexler the span was completed, it was soon to be overshadowed by the museum's attempts throughout the 1980s to grapple with architectural post-modernism, in which engineering stepped decidedly into the background. Scenography and engineering were not

30 Arthur Drexler, *Twentieth Century Engineering* (New York: The Museum of Modern Art, 1964), introduction.

31 Untitled, unnumbered Press Release for exhibition *New York City Exposition and Convention Center*, 1980, no. 16, 1, MoMA Archives, viewable online: https://assets.moma.org/documents/moma_press-release_327275.pdf?_ga=2.149653430.1887772004.1633972257-338071719.1611330555. Accessed October 11, 2021.

32 MoMA Press Release, "Three New Skyscrapers are subject of exhibition at the Museum of Modern Art," January 1983, 2, MoMA Archives, viewable online: https://assets.moma.org/documents/moma_press-release_327344.pdf?_ga=2.224559258.1887772004.1633972257-338071719.1611330555. Accessed October 11, 2021. Accompanied by a printed catalog. Arthur Drexler, *Three New Skyscrapers* (New York: The Museum of Modern Art, 1983).

33 MoMA Press Release, "Three New Skyscrapers," 2.

34 Published as Building Arts Forum/New York, *Bridging the Gap: Rethinking the Relationship of Architect and Engineer, the proceedings of the Building Art Forum/New York symposium held in April of 1989 at the Guggenheim Museum* (New York: Van Nostrand Reinhold, 1991).

35 Terence Riley, "Preface," to Matilda McQuaid, *Santiago Calatrava: Structure and Expression* (New York: The Museum of Modern Art, 1993), 6.

36 Guy Nordenson and Terence Riley, eds., *Seven Structural Engineers: The Felix Candela Lectures* (New York: The Museum of Modern Art, 2008).

37 Barry Bergdoll, *Rising Currents: Projects for New York's Waterfront* (New York: The Museum of Modern Art, 2010).

necessarily incompatible, but as imagistic Postmodernism increasingly dominated the discourse in the United States in the 1980s, Drexler's successors were often at a loss to chart the course of modern architecture and engineering.

A response to this new chasm came in an April 1989 symposium organized at Frank Lloyd Wright's Guggenheim Museum, "Bridging the Gap: Rethinking the Relationship of Architect and Engineer."[34] At MoMA, the arrival of Terence Riley in 1993 signaled a renewed appreciation of structural experiment, heralded in a small show on Santiago Calatrava curated by Matilda McQuaid. Riley resumed the task that had been handed down from Hitchcock and Johnson to Drexler. In the preface to the publication Riley noted "Throughout most of this century the practitioners of architecture and engineering have been sharply divided: the architect has been the designer and the engineer has been consultant and analyst. Calatrava's work in the last decade, however, has successfully transcended those boundaries, redefining the relationship between architect and engineer and between their respective disciplines. Perhaps more than any other, he has helped to revive the role of the engineer as proactive designer, in the tradition of John Augustus Roebling, Alexandre-Gustave Eiffel, and more recently [...] Robert Maillart, Pier Luigi Nervi, Eduardo Torroja, and Félix Candela."[35] *Light Construction* (1995), *Fabrications* (1998), and *Tall Buildings* (2004, with engineer Guy Nordenson) would mark this return, and even more so the "Félix Candela Lectures" inviting prominent engineers to speak at the museum.[36] *Tall Buildings* explicitly addressed the changes to the generation of form brought about by the computer revolution in calculations for architecture and for engineering, grappling anew with how to convey process as much as product in the display through the creation of dramatic didactic models. But as Drexler had argued in 1964, engineering was not confined to issues of structure alone. With rising attention to the challenges of climate change the holistic, regional approach of MoMA's *TVA* exhibition of 1941 seems all the more relevant. In 2009, together with Guy Nordenson, I invited five interdisciplinary teams of designers to explore forms of "soft infrastructure" to imagine and create images for the display of a New York City made more resilient to rising sea levels and storm surge.[37] The aim was at once to urge designers to think across specializations, blurring boundaries between architecture, landscape architecture, structural and hydraulic engineering, and to change the contours of the discussion on climate change in the city. Three years after the show opened at MoMA, Superstorm Sandy flooded the Brooklyn-Battery Tunnel. Engineering and its challenges were front-page news, even as the forms of future engineering would need to address a host of new challenges, and the museum could assume the role of instigator rather than simply archive.

EPFL – ROLEX
LEARNING CENTER

	LAUSANNE, SWITZERLAND
	2004–2010
ARCHITECT	SANAA
	KAZUYO SEJIMA
	RYŪE NISHIZAWA
ENGINEERS	MUTSURO SASAKI
	BOLLINGER+GROHMANN
	KLAUS BOLLINGER
	MANFRED GROHMANN

Built on the campus of the École Polytechnique Fédérale de Lausanne in 2010, the Rolex Learning Center is an experimental learning center. SANAA designed a spatial solution that creates a unified, fluid meeting place and environment for cultural exchange.

The building consists of two parallel rectangular surfaces alternating with a series of internal patios which, with their undulating, sinuous rhythm, create a topography of hills and valleys. The near-total absence of non-glass vertical partitions lends the interior visual and spatial continuity.

The lower surface in reinforced concrete is made up of two perforated shells supported by 11 arches, which are connected to the prestressed reinforced concrete ceilings of the parking lot below. The roof is a mixed wood-and-steel structure supported by slim tubular steel columns.

The structure was designed by the Bollinger+Grohmann studio with consulting by Japanese engineer Mutsuro Sasaki, one of the foremost experts in the use of calculation software for structural optimization.

← Walter Niedermayr
Bildraum S 240/2010, trittico.
Courtesy Ncontemporary
Milano, Galerie Nordenhake
Berlin/Stockholm, Galerie
Widauer Innsbruck

MEISO NO MORI MUNICIPAL FUNERAL HALL

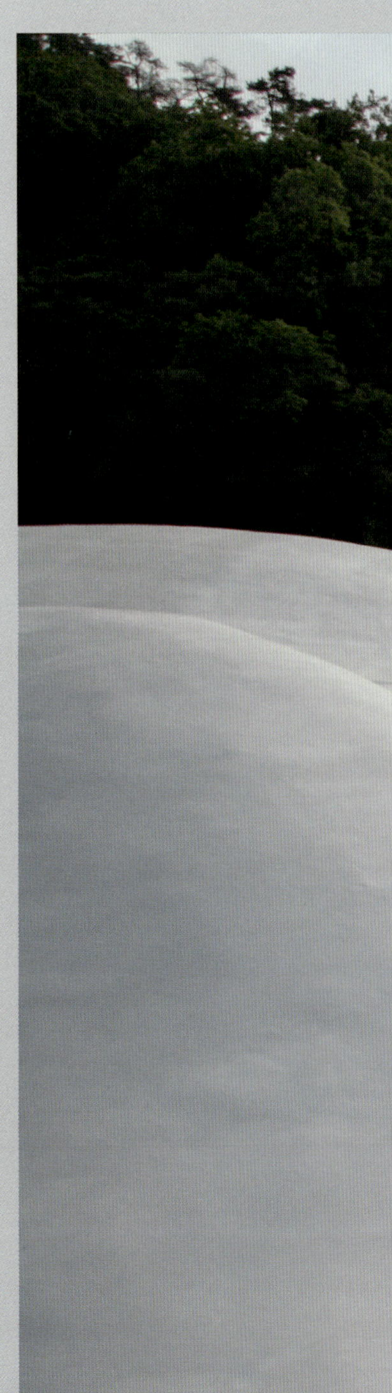

	KAKAMIGAHARA, JAPAN
	2004–2006
ARCHITECT	TOYO ITO
ENGINEER	MUTSURO SASAKI

On the bank of a small pond surrounded by gently rolling hills, the Kakamigahara Municipal Funeral Hall called "The forest of meditation" (*Meiso no Mori*), designed by Toyo Ito, is in keeping with his pursuit of architecture inspired by the landscape and natural elements.

A gently undulating 18-centimeter-thick reinforced concrete surface forms the building's roof, generating depressions in correspondence with the supporting columns, elements that also serve for rainwater drainage.

The extraordinary result is the fruit of the close collaboration between the architect Toyo Ito and the engineer Mutsuro Sasaki who, using calculation software and the "sensitivity analysis" method, determined the most efficient structural form by evaluating the conditions of least stress and least deformation.

Formworks built by specialized craftsmen also played a fundamental role, allowing for absolute precision in the realization of a complex surface.

↓   Meiso no Mori Municipal
Funeral Hall, Kakamigahara,
2006. Courtesy Toyo Ito
& Associates Architects

SICLI COMPANY BUILDING

GENEVA, SWITZERLAND

1966–1970

ARCHITECT	CONSTANTIN HILBERER
ENGINEER	HEINZ ISLER

The Sicli SA extinguisher factory is remarkable in terms of the complexity and size among its thin, free-form shells designed by Heinz Isler. Derived from his observation of natural forms, these structures were empirically generated by inverting the form assumed by a membrane hung on a priori positioned supports, and were continuously tested via scale models. The result is the most efficient form possible as, theoretically, it works strictly by compression. To take full advantage of the lot, Isler deduced the irregular perimeter of the building's layout, 33×54 m, and the positions of its seven supports. Although it can be perceptively read as a composition of two functional blocks—the larger one hosting the production hall and the smaller one with administrative offices on two floors—structurally it is a single asymmetrical shell, 10 cm thick on average and with no edge beams. The main block has a diagonal span of 58 m with a 6-meter-diameter polyester cupola at its center. A series of small circular apertures adorns the delicate point where the two blocks come together.

↑   Sicli Company Building,
     Geneva, 1970. Courtesy
     gta Archives, ETH Zürich,
     Heinz Isler

OPEN CHAPEL
IN PALMIRA

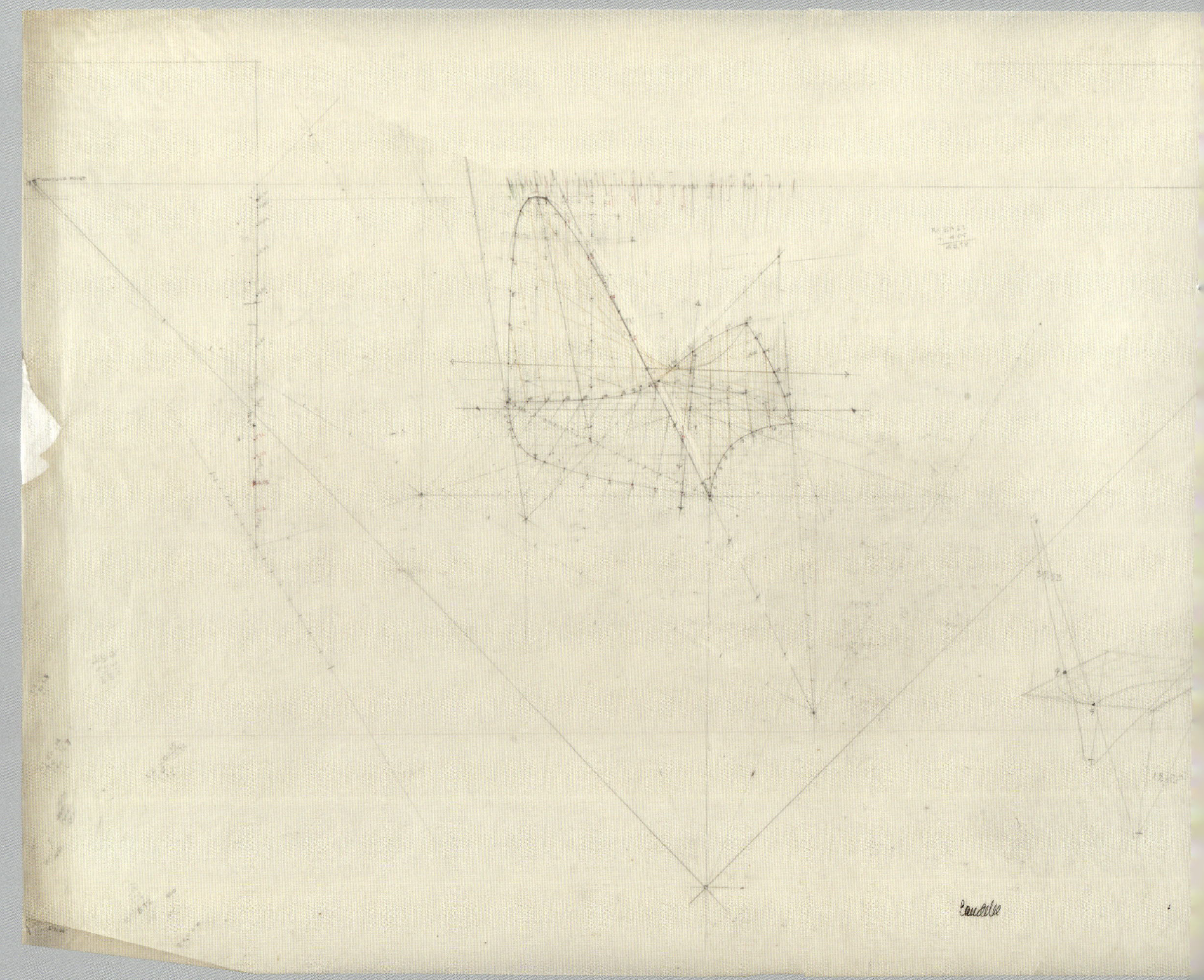

ARCHITECTS	FÉLIX CANDELA
	GUILLERMO ROSSELL
	MANUEL LARROSA

The Open Chapel is a sort of manifesto of the pursuits of Félix Candela, the Spanish architect commonly associated with thin reinforced concrete structures whose numerous experiments and built works consecrated him as a master of double-curved surfaces, in particular the hyperbolic paraboloid, in which the form is a direct expression of structural demands.

The Open Chapel is pure structure: a reinforced concrete saddle atop a hill that covers and defines a space of prayer. The double curvature guarantees structural resistance, allowing an almost-constant-4-centimeter thickness, and the geometric origin of the hyperbolic paraboloid, a ribbed surface, facilitated the pouring of concrete on formworks built of wooden planks. The surface thickens towards the edges, where it touches the ground and where there are apertures. The main one is 21.9 m in height, while the secondary one, with a stiffening beam along its edge, is 7.65 m.

The saddle slots directly into the terrain, to which it is anchored with curved foundation beams.

← Open Chapel in Palmira, project, Lomas de Cuernavaca, 1959. Courtesy Félix Candela architectural records and papers, 1950–1984, Avery Architectural & Fine Arts Library, Columbia University

CAN STRUCTURAL ENGINEERING STILL INVENT THE FUTURE?

Antoine Picon

QUESTIONING THE IDEA OF PROGRESS

Since the eighteenth century and the rise of the figure of the engineer as the embodiment of an inseparably technical and social progress, designing and building daring structures has been one of those areas where the future seemed to reveal its decidedly optimistic colors. Farther, higher, lighter: these imperatives were supposed to announce an era of limitless prosperity. The promise of structural engineering escaped the normal ideological divides. On both sides of the Iron Curtain, they appreciated the prowess of engineers who were enlisted at times under the banner of capitalism, at times under the banner of socialism.

This optimism does not seem altogether appropriate today. Certainly, large structural creations have not lost their evocative power. Bridges continue to break span records, towers are taller and taller, some lightweight structures seem almost intangible. But technical progress is far from being unanimously appreciated. The acceleration of climate change and the distancing from what some call the "world before," an expression which became popular in countries like France during the endless Covid-19 health crisis, often interpreted in light of the planet's urbanization upsetting the balance of nature, have heightened doubts. More generally speaking, engineering no longer seems capable of writing the future that is desired by entire segments of the population in developed countries, sensitive to the subjects of necessary energy transition and degrowth. Questioning its future, the future of structural engineering in particular, means to accept facing the question of the merit of progress, a question which was still unthinkable a few decades ago. In this regard, it is striking to note its weak place even within the exhibition *L'Art de l'ingénieur : Constructeur, entrepreneur, inventeur*, organized by the Centre Pompidou in 1997.[1] In twenty-five years, it has taken a crucial turn and is now a concern for young engineers who are currently completing their education.

A FIGURE IN CRISIS

Challenging the notion of progress goes hand in hand with the rise in questions regarding the figure of the engineer. Traditionally, the engineer still possessed something heroic insofar as it embodied the struggle of mankind against the elements. The boldness of structures designed by engineers was an expression of this heroism. The theme of progress, in the form that had progressively emerged during the Age of Enlightenment, referred to the idea of a nature tamed through science and technique. This process was apt to become violent—the elements were not so easily tamed—and this is the reason behind the often sublime aspect of the most daring works of civil engineering and construction.[2]

This attitude no longer goes without saying, as the ideal of protecting natural resources prevails more and more frequently over traditional development logic, with its procession of heroic intentions and technological violence. Along with this change in direction, we recognize the necessarily hybrid nature of the many responses to the challenges of this new age, which we have agreed to call the Anthropocene Epoch.[3] While the engineer's mission consisted of creating decidedly artificial works—bridges, viaducts, dams, buildings—which should effectively combat the effects of nature deemed undesirable, increasingly often it creates devices that allow human use to cohabitate with the natural elements, flora and fauna, more peacefully than in the past. There is an increase in preserved areas in close contact with infrastructures, animal crossings, fish ladders, and other devices to ensure the continuity of habitats and biosphere cycles of matter. Everything happens as if a successful engineering achievement is now a mix of artifice and nature, protected to a greater or lesser extent.

Leading to this change in direction, we must also look at a group of transformations that affect the very status of knowledge handled by engineers. These transformations are not only epistemological; they translate very concretely into an undermining of social legitimacy hardly won by the engineering profession at the turn of the eighteenth and nineteenth centuries. During this period, the relationship between cutting-edge science and engineering through institutions like the Parisian École polytechnique was asserted simultaneously with the eminently useful nature of engineers' work, whether in service of the state like the French or working in a predominantly private setting like the English.[4]

In the engineering design that prevailed uncontested until recently, engineers were responsible for taking charge of nature, for using its resources by relying on their scientific knowledge. In other words, they were tasked with converting scientific knowledge about nature into human use. Three a priori assumptions structured this project. The first depended on the existence of a clearly defined boundary between the natural world and the human world. It is along this boundary that the engineer worked, with the task of moving between the two worlds, natural and artificial. The science to which the engineer referred, on the other hand, was supposed to tell the truth about nature. At the same time, it seemed to be an authority linked to its total disconnection from the political and social sphere. Intervening, however,

1   *L'Art de l'ingénieur. Constructeur, entrepreneur, inventeur*, presented at the Centre Pompidou June 25–September 29, 1997, curator Alain Guiheux, catalog editor Antoine Picon.

2   For more on the sublime applied to engineering works, refer to Antoine Picon, *Architectes et ingénieurs au siècle des Lumières* (Marseille: Éditions Parenthèse, 1988); David Nye, *American Technological Sublime* (Cambridge, MA: MIT Press, 1994).

3   Christophe Bonneuil and Jean-Baptiste Fressoz, *L'Événement anthropocène. La Terre, l'histoire et nous* (Paris: Le Seuil, 2013).

4   See Irina Gouzèvitch and Peter Jones, "Becoming an Engineer in Eighteenth-Century Europe: The Construction of a Professional Identity," *Engineering Studies* 3, no. 3 (December 2011): 149–152.

between pure science, a system of theoretical statements about the physical world confirmed by experience, and techniques aimed at concretely transforming the conditions of people's lives, there was a layer of intermediate knowledge, often referred to as applied science. The strength of materials, for example, took a place between rational mechanics and the art of construction. The pioneering nature of the Parisian École polytechnique during the first decades of its existence held on precisely to this idea of applying science, an idea that was adopted in turn by the different polytechnical institutions that emerged thereafter, from the one in Milan to the one in Rio de Janeiro, from the ETH in Zurich to the Massachusetts Institute of Technology.[5]

For several decades, Science and Technology Studies, and the work of Bruno Latour and his followers in particular, have been shaking up this concept.[6] Their success in the academic arena is linked to quite concrete developments that, without the radical quality of some of the theories they helped popularize, contribute no less to shaking up the prevalent concept of engineering in a profound way. Science, first of all, lost much of its superb isolation. It no longer looks like a collection of theoretical statements confirmed by indisputable experiences, but rather it seems like a complex set of practices aimed at stabilizing phenomena, most often in the laboratory. Viewed in this way, science can no longer function on an absolute separation between nature and artifice, the physical world and society. The phenomena it studies are very often inseparable from the social practices and apparatuses, which ignore the distinction between nature and artifice. Above all, science is no longer external, a stranger to society and politics; on the contrary it seems to consist of the same substance, to the extent that it seeks to define a common world to the individuals and institutions to which it is directed. The engineer that lays claim to science can no longer at the same time insist on separating nature and society in order to better reassemble them through innovative works. As we noted earlier, engineers must assume the fundamentally hybrid character of their work and the results to which this leads. They can no longer remain above politics, overhanging

above social confrontations. Their projects can no longer claim the impartiality of humanity's real needs, which only they would be able to detect clearly. Under these conditions, should we be surprised by the increasing controversy concerning them? Debates about nuclear plants had paved the way, and the controversy has multiplied in recent years. From the tunnels in the Alps and the Pyrenees to the Notre-Dame-des-Landes airport, there was a whole series of such controversy in a country like France, despite its long tradition of valuing the role of the engineer, which, without question, was supposed to embody the common good.

Contemporary science, moreover, has new tools, digitalization in particular, that challenge traditional opposites, such as conceptualization and calculation. With the development of computers and simulation techniques, understanding, demonstrating, and calculating frequently seem to merge. With the progress of 3D printers and robotics, calculating and manufacturing are also becoming more and more closely linked. In this context, it seems that science can lead to processes and products more directly than in the past, rather than needing to establish the intermediate layer of applied knowledge equipped with a certain autonomy. This can be seen in key areas such as biology and materials science. Are engineers, in the traditional sense of the term, still needed in these areas? Wouldn't it be better to move on to a radical

5   Bruno Belhoste, *La Formation d'une technocratie. L'École polytechnique
    et ses élèves de la Révolution au Second Empire* (Paris: Belin, 2003).

6   See, for example, Sheila Jasanoff, Gerald Markle, James Petersen,
    Trevor Pinch, eds., *The Handbook of Science and Technology Studies*,
    rev. ed. (London, New Delhi: Sage Publications, 1995); Bruno Latour,
    *Science in Action: How to Follow Scientists and Engineers Through
    Society* (Cambridge, MA: Harvard University Press, 1987).

↑ John Lucas, *Conference of Engineers at Britannia Bridge*, 1850, ICE Portrait Collection. Courtesy Institution of Civil Engineers

redefinition of their skills and their role? The heroic figure of the modern engineer could be replaced, in the long term, by a different kind of scientist/entrepreneur figure. For the time being, this sort of development is only taking shape in very specific fields of scientific and technical activity, but it makes one wonder about the relevance of the figure of the engineer inherited from the eighteenth and nineteenth centuries.

STRUCTURAL UNCERTAINTIES AND THE "POSTMODERN CONDITION"

Along with fortification, civil engineering and construction are among the oldest areas of engineering. In many countries, the design of roads, bridges, canals, and buildings has allowed the figure of the civil engineer, distinct from its military counterpart, to come into existence. In France, the first corps of civil engineers, the Corps des Ponts et Chaussées, was created in 1716 in order to deal with roads and bridges.[7] In England, building transportation infrastructures also allowed civil engineers to establish themselves through the founding in 1771 of the Society of Civil Engineers and especially the creation in 1818 of the Institution of Civil Engineers. For the first civil engineers, building was also a key sector.[8]

Long considered a special branch of architecture, civil engineering progressively broke away, at the same time that it called into question the preponderance of geometric knowledge used in calculating works. This development, which led to the introduction of differential calculus to re-establish the engineer's knowledge, occurred at the same time as an equally fundamental transformation in the founding concepts of building art, which saw the modern notion of structure progressively emerge, setting itself apart from the decoration of buildings and works of art. Such a distinction was unthinkable within the framework of the Vitruvian theory of architecture and engineering that prevailed until the middle of eighteenth century, which instead thought that construction, like decoration, involved the rational use of proportions. Certainly, large-scale constructions were not lacking during that period, which extended from the Renaissance to the dawn of the Enlightenment, starting with the famous dome of the Florence cathedral by Filippo Brunelleschi, but their structural aspect, strictly speaking, was not always clearly distinct from the other building aspects, such as the harmony of proportions or even the delicacy of the ornaments. Above all, the construction performance was not valued as such, or at least when it was difficult to ignore, it was valued less than it would have been within the new conceptual framework that took shape in the second half of the Age of Enlightenment.

The rise of the modern notion of structure is tied to the rediscovery of Gothic building features and with these the possibility to envision a more complex circulation of forces within the material than the mainly vertical loads that had prevailed thus far. Fascinated by the Gothic device of the flying buttress, which could transfer the thrust of the vaults to the outer part of the building, engineers during the Enlightenment willingly opposed the direct forces of traditional construction in favor of the indirect or oblique forces of Gothic churches or the new works they imagined, inspired by their example. At the same time, while construction and decoration, long considered inseparable, had broken away from each other, the notion of technical performance gained new importance.[9]

Finally, we should note the close bond between modern structural thought and the idea of public utility. More than architecture, which by now was considered a separate discipline, engineering

7   Antoine Picon, *L'Invention de l'ingénieur moderne. L'École des ponts et chaussées 1747-1851* (Paris: Presses de l'École nationale des ponts et chaussées, 1992).

8   Hugh Ferguson and Mike Chrimes, *The Civil Engineers: The Story of Institution of Civil Engineers and the People Who Made It* (London: Institution of Civil Engineers, 2011).

9   Antoine Picon, "The Freestanding Column in Eighteenth-Century Religious Architecture," in *Things that Talk: Object Lessons from Art and Science*, ed. Lorraine Daston (New York: Zone Books, 2004), 67–99.

intended to serve indisputable needs such as crossing rivers or the possibility to house huge crowds in large halls. This line between structural thought and public utility would be confirmed with the development of new building materials such as iron, steel, and concrete in the nineteenth century. In the next century, it would form the backdrop for innovations, such as thin veils and hulls, lightweight, inflatable, or even tensile structures, which all intended to serve the indisputable needs of humanity.

The twentieh century marked both the triumph of the idea of structure and the start of the decline in its dominance. This decline was accelerated in recent years due to many factors, some of which refer to what was previously mentioned regarding challenging the idea of progress and the crisis of the figure of the engineer. Primarily, questions are emerging regarding the merits of technical performance in the name of the new ideas of preserving the planet. On this matter, it is worth noting the contradictory nature of the time in which we live. On one hand, very large works are multiplying giant bridges, towers hundreds of meters high, airport terminals seem more like cities than buildings; on the other hand, criticism against these structures is multiplying, accused of being excessive. Besides too much exclusive attention being paid, in their opinion, to the structural design, much of this criticism calls for taking certain factors into account, such as the grey energy involved during these works' life cycle.

In the area of building design, other factors contributed to the relative decline in structural ideas, a decline which, in the early 1990s, already alarmed Kenneth Frampton. His 1996 work, *Studies in Tectonic Culture*, was in fact a defense and illustration of these ideas, referred to as "tectonic culture," damaged, according to him, by the rise in digital technology.[10] Digital technology has effectively contributed to undermining structural codes long-held to be intangible. In the early days of computer drawing software, cutting-edge digital technologies had a tendency to spurn tectonic constraints for the benefit of exploring a geometry based on complex surfaces that graphic tools allowed to influence at will without worrying too much about construction issues. Parametric design later came to replace assembly logic with the establishment of more logical than constructive relationships between the parts of the structures.[11]

Digital technology is not the only cause of this weakening of structural ideas in building. We must also take into account the shift that seems to have taken place in numerous cases, from frame problems to issues pertaining mainly to the composition and performance of coverings, as if the skin of a building now took precedence over its skeleton. Environmental constraints contribute to this shift, which Spanish architect Iñaki Ábalos describes as a move from mechanics to thermodynamics and which Swiss architect Philippe Rahm tries to put into practice in his projects.[12] From an architectural point of view, digital technology also helped reinforce the importance of the periphery of buildings by providing tools that allowed the return of ornamental practices. In numerous contemporary projects, the ornament from which architecture had tried to break free, seems to have taken the place of the tectonic codes defended by Frampton.

Beyond building and architecture, this development could refer to a much more fundamental set of the sphere of techniques like the blurring of materials and structures which has been going on for several decades. Not only has materials science progressed in leaps and bounds, but it has also led to the multiplication of products whose complexity often has nothing to envy compared to that of structures. Composite materials and intelligent materials seem to proclaim that the structural complexity extends well beyond the levels to which engineers traditionally referred.

10   Kenneth Frampton, *Studies in Tectonic Culture: The Poetics of Construction in Nineteenth and Twentieth Century Architecture* (Cambridge, MA: The MIT Press, 1995).

11   Georges Liaropoulos-Legendre, *ijp: The Book of Surfaces* (London: Architectural Association, 2003).

12   Iñaki Ábalos and Renata Sentkiewicz, *Essays on Thermodynamics: Architecture and Beauty* (Barcelona: Actar, 2015).

13   Bruno Latour, *Nous n'avons jamais été modernes. Essai d'anthropologie symétrique* (Paris: La Découverte, 1997).

The tendency of contemporary technique to ignore the distinction between infrastructure and superstructure proves to be even more striking. Digital technology once again plays a key role in this development with phenomena such as platformization, where software often becomes more structural than masonry building and vehicle fleets, Uber being a noteworthy example of this development. It is true that many of the platforms develop along the lines of Amazon towards a hybrid model where physical installations and software layers are more and more closely connected. The fact remains that ways of interpreting technique, based on the opposition between infrastructural or structural elements and the devices supported by these, are powerless to account for the recent development of large technical systems.

At this stage, it's tempting to relate many previous comments to an even more general development, this exit from modernity tirelessly invoked since the 1980s, or if we believe Bruno Latour, the realization that this was never anything but an illusion since we were never modern.[13] Perhaps, even more than to Bruno Latour's work, we should first refer to the attempt to theorize the "postmodern condition" proposed by Jean-François Lyotard at the dawn of this surge in analyses about the end of the great tales of modernity, in order to grasp what connects the crisis of the figure of the engineer and the shaking up of structural thought to this large-scale cultural shift.[14]

Besides the dissolution of the frameworks of modernity, Lyotard's essay evokes a world where superficial effects, interface logic in particular, coding and decoding procedures, often take precedence over approaches which tend to rank causes and effects in a traditional way, by referring to a science that holds the truth. This "postmodern condition" now extends from the structuring of large globalized production and consumption apparatuses, starting with platforms, to individuals whose subjectivity seems to have extended to environments and networks in which they are integrated through a process that resembles crumbling, even if its defenders rather see it as a questioning of Cartesian dualism and especially of the separation between man and nature.[15] The questioning of structural ideas could refer to these modes of reading and organizing realities, which are different from those that prevailed in the second half of the eighteenth century. As for the crisis of the emblematic figure of the engineer, it seems paradigmatic of the blurring of the definition of human and of the generalized crumbling of the forms of subjectivity which we see today.

It is important to remember that Lyotard's essay was written in close connection with a series of questions about computerization and perspectives opened by cybernetic thinking. The direct descendant of this thinking, artificial intelligence, now seems at the point of further emphasizing the size and scope of the developments we see. For structural engineering alone, it seems to allow the possibility of calculating without necessarily understanding, that is to say, by dispensing with structural diagrams whose mastery has defined the engineer until now. The results to which this will likely lead could, at the same time, lose this constitutive intelligibility of the idea of structure, because the latter, in the sense that had been imposed since the beginning of the second half of the eighteenth century, was based on an interpretation by the designer of the progress of forces within matter. No structure without structural thinking. However artificial intelligence follow paths that are often inconceivable for the human spirit.[16] Is this situation expected to continue or will we instead witness the emergence of new patterns that allow a true dialogue between man and machine? The future of structural engineering could well depend on the answer to this question.

---

14   Jean-François Lyotard, *The Postmodern Condition. A Report on Kknowledge*, trans. Geoff Bennington and Brian Massumi (Minneapolis: University of Minnesota Press, 1984).

15   Sociologist Sherry Turkle has been dealing tirelessly with this fragmentation since her pioneer works *The Second Self: Computers and the Human Spirit* (New York: Simon & Schuster, 1984); *Life on the Screen: Identity in the Age of the Internet* (New York: Touchstone, 1995).

16   Mario Carpo, *The Second Digital Turn: Design Beyond Intelligence* (Cambridge, MA: MIT, 2017).

TOWARDS A DIFFERENT MODERNITY

Should we lay to rest, without further ado, the engineer's concept of science and art that we inherited from the first Industrial Revolution in the name of the advent of a "world after," which would be sensitive at once to environmental, "postmodern," and "posthuman" challenges? It is again striking to observe how contradictory our era is in its simultaneous pursuit of technical and economic development and its appeals to put on the brakes, or even for degrowth. Engineers continue to erect very large works. Speaking of very tall buildings, the 830-meter height of the Burj Khalifa Tower in Dubai should be surpassed by the more than 1,000 meters of the Jeddah Tower, if its construction resumes after the crisis. At the same time, some zealots are urging that they simply stop constructing in favor of an overall renovation of existing buildings. What should we think about this contradiction? What is the meaning today of an exhibition dedicated to the great engineering names of the past?

Perhaps we should start by taking a closer look at the modern heritage. Contrary to an opinion that is as widespread as it is simplistic, the concern with minimizing mankind's footprint on the planet, with building lightweight, even ephemeral, structures, exists strongly among engineers. The rise in metal construction in the nineteenth century and especially the development of lightweight structures in the following century, such as spatial structures, tensile structures, inflatable structures, and tensegrity systems, attest to the significance of this concern, even if monumental creations have had a tendency to eclipse experiments by designers like Konrad Wachsmann, Le Ricolais, or even Jean Prouvé. Let's also add that modern architecture attests to comparable trends. Frugality, a fashionable term nowadays, is one of the driving forces of many modern architectural works, starting with that of Le Corbusier.

Certain key aspects in the structural approach such as the desire to conserve material—the art of structures lies in the search for the recessed part rather than in the privilege that is granted to the filled part—resonate, on the other hand, with environmental imperatives. The same can be said for the multiplication of experiments on the use of materials other than steel and concrete. For example, we can mention the research of Philippe Block from the ETH in Zurich on thin vaults in masonry or even the works of Achim Menges, from the University of Stuttgart on the use of carbon fibers. Menges is also representative of one of the most fruitful trends in contemporary structural research, material computation, at the juncture of structural design, design, and digital production. Finally, the latter echoes the many contemporary questions about proper use of the reference to organic structures, biomimicry, in the area of engineering.[17]

Structural performance itself can be made compatible with better environmental efficiency. Without necessarily being a model, the Shanghai Tower in Pudong, in China, for example, uses its overall shape to limit wind effects and, as a result, to reduce the quantity of materials used to withstand them. Revealingly, the skyscraper also contains wind turbines which provide part of the electricity it needs to operate. The future of structural design will probably entail its pairing more closely than before with other areas in engineering, as well as the renewal of its thought patterns. With the spread of digital technology, it seems necessary, for example, to redefine tectonic codes, even if the "non-Cartesian" propositions of Cecil Balmond or the suggestions of Neil Leach, which consist of drawing inspiration from the swarming of insects and birds in order to rethink structural assemblies, didn't lead to anything.[18]

While waiting for this renewal, made even more necessary by the advance of artificial intelligence, we could multiply the examples of innovations that tend to prove that structural design retains its relevance today, as long as the point of

---

17 Achim Menges and Jan Knippers, *Architecture Research Building* (Basel: Birkhäuser, 2020).

18 Cecil Balmond, *Informal* (Munich: Prestel, 2002); Neil Leach, "Swarm Tectonics," in *Digital Tectonics*, eds. Neil Leach, David Turnbull, Chris Williams (London: Wiley-Academy, 2004), 70–77.

view under which it is considered changes. While historian David Billington could still envision structural engineering as a relatively independent art in 1980s–1990s, it is now fitting to abandon all desire for disciplinary purity, to rethink its link with the natural elements as well as with the desire for architecture, which is one of its most powerful allies.[19] We must also rethink the modes according to which it proves useful. Technical performance can no longer serve as a justification in itself; it must be related to social challenges that have become more complex. Above all, the question of materials' life cycle becomes paramount. The finished work is nothing more than a moment in a series of processes of extraction, shaping, and disassembly, which engineering must integrate more than it did before. This temporal nature could well form one of the most fruitful areas of exploration within the context of the renewal of structural engineering.

Beyond its strictly technical aspects, the future of structural engineering may speak to us about the possibility of continuing to be modern, but in a different way, preserving the enthusiasm but redefining the heroism, so that it no longer leads to the destruction of natural resources, without any demiurgic illusion but without the symmetrical illusion of being able to return to the past.[20] For better or for worse, we will never again live in that untouched nature, described to us in the art and poetry of ancient times, but we are compelled to preserve an irreparably hybrid techno-nature. Can structural engineering still invent the future? As long as we accept the drastic impurity of this future, a future made up of the inevitably unstable compromises between nature and artifice, non-human and human.

→ Achim Menges, ICD / ITKE Research Pavilion, University of Stuttgart 2016–2017, detail. Photo by Antoine Picon

ANTOINE PICON

---

19 David P. Billington, *The Tower and the Bridge: The New Art of Structural Engineering* (New York: Basic Books, 1983).

---

20 On the unrealistic nature of many suggestions to go back to the past and for the absolute need for energy transition, consult the stimulating essay by Pierre Veltz, *L'Économie désirable. Sortir du monde thermo-fossile* (Paris: Le Seuil, 2021).

ANTOINE PICON

MARKET (SOKO) LA KARIAKOO

DAR ES SALAAM, TANZANIA

1972–1974

ARCHITECT   BEDA AMULI

Born in the village of Machombe, Tanzania, Beda Amuli received a scholarship to attend the Israel Institute of Technology in Haifa, where he earned a Bachelor's Degree in Architecture in 1965.

After his initial professional experiences, he opened his own architecture studio, one of the first in Africa, in Dar es Salaam, then the capital of Tanzania. He designed the city's Kariakoo covered market, a reinforced concrete building that became an icon of brutalist modernism thanks to its roof, which was made up of 24 dendriform elements, columns supporting hyperbolic surfaces that terminate in a square at the top. Like a sort of funnel, each of these exposed reinforced concrete structural elements gathers rain water and provides shelter for the market, which is on three levels. The 16 perimetral structural modules are slightly lower than the 8 central ones, which creates an air space that facilitates natural air flow.

↓ Market (Soko) la Kariakoo,
Dar es Salaam, 1974. Photo
Benedikt Redmann. Courtesy
Benedikt Redmann

GARE TGV RAILWAY STATION

ENGINEER · MARC MIMRAM

The new Gare TGV railway station was designed by engineer and architect Marc Mimram, who lent particular attention to its Mediterranean context.
Natural ventilation and light are central to the architectural and structural choices, particularly with regard to the roof structure. It consists of five 18-meter spans created with curved V-section beams in UHPC (Ultra-High-Performance Concrete), a composite material of cement blends, reactive powders and fibers that guarantee ductility and high performance in terms of load resistance. These prefabricated elements, perforated to provide natural light, were designed for optimal response to structural demands, characteristics of the material and ease of assembly.
The roof shelters passengers and creates a pleasant, bright space for them to access the train platforms below.

← Gare TGV railway station under construction, Montpellier, 2017.
Photo Lisa Ricciotti.
Courtesy Lisa Ricciotti

ENGINEERS OF THE OCCUPATION

Jean-Louis Cohen

In 1923, in his manifesto, *Vers une architecture*, Le Corbusier praised the "engineer's aesthetic," reading therein a moral commitment which was tragically missing from the work of contemporary architects. That same year, the leader of the Deutscher Werkbund published *Die Ingenieurbauten in ihrer guten Gestaltung*, pointing to a list of figures suitable for many other projects than those of the industry. While they were celebrated by the opposing currents of architectural thought, engineers in the interwar period saw their sphere of influence expand well beyond technique. As demonstrated by Jeffrey Herf, they played a decisive role in conquering and wielding power by the Nazis.[1] If this history has been told, especially through biographical studies on important figures such as Ulrich Finsterwalder or Fritz Leonhardt, to say nothing of Fritz Todt, there is nothing about the presence of engineers in occupied France from 1940 to 1944.

In spite of its much shorter duration than the Reich's, which was meant to last a millennium, this period now appears to be a decisive one in the modernization of France, and the involvement of engineers from all disciplines was considerable. Beginning in the summer of 1940, following the Armistice of June 22 when all power was handed to Marshal Philippe Pétain, engineers were active in the main areas of public activity and even in the innermost circles of power. They took control of the essential administrative services for the "national revolution" undertaken by a regime that combined authoritarianism and technocracy, but which historians agree not

---

1   Jeffrey Herf, *Reactionary Modernism: Technology, culture, and politics in Weimar and the Third Reich* (Cambridge: Cambridge University Press, 1986).

2   Rémi Baudouï, "Les technocrates sous Vichy: Modernité productive et anti-modernité architecturale et urbaine," in *Architecture et urbanisme dans la France de Vichy*, ed. Jean-Louis Cohen (Paris: Éditions du Collège de France, 2020), 27–42.

3   Jean Berthelot, *Sur les rails du pouvoir (de Munich à Vichy)* (Paris: Robert Laffont, 1968), 117.

4   Jupp Grote and Bernard Marrey, *Freyssinet, la précontrainte et l'Europe* (Paris: Éditions du Linteau, 2000).

5   Eugène Freyssinet, "Une révolution dans l'art de bâtir. Les constructions précontraintes," *Travaux*, no. 101 (November 1941): 335–59. See also *Le Génie Civil* 61, nos. 25–26 (December 20–27, 1941): 261–66; Fritz Leonhardt, *Brücken: Ästhetik und Gestaltung* (Stuttgart: Deutsche Verlags-Anstalt, 1984), 98.

6   Fritz Leonhardt, letter to Lieselotte Leonhardt, July 1, 1944, saai | Archiv für Architektur und Ingenieurbau, Karlsruhe, quoted by Christiane Weber, "Freyssinet, Leonhardt et le béton précontraint," in *Interférences / Interferenzen: Architecture, Allemagne-France 1800-2000*, eds. Jean-Louis Cohen and Hartmut Frank (Strasbourg: Editions des Musées de Strasbourg, 2013), 364–69.

to deem fascist.[2] Recalling his experience with the government, the engineer Jean Berthelot uses repetition to describe the Vichy regime as being "technique, technique."[3]

In order to ensure it functioned, engineers were involved on all levels. Overall in their forties, they formed the framework of a plethora of administrations that remained in Paris, even though the ministers and state secretaries settled in Vichy, the spa town in the center of France. All engineers did not take refuge in the public sphere. Their three main fields of activity can be identified: firstly, the strictly technical work, which never stopped; then, supervising the reconstruction; and finally, the conduct of state apparatuses and the economy at the highest level. These engineers were trained primarily at the École polytechnique (the X) and at its application schools, such as the École des mines and the École des ponts et chaussées, or at the École centrale des arts et manufactures (the Centraliens). If building sites essentially stopped in the summer of 1940, the construction of works of art, from dams to bridges, continued, encouraged by a regime that was concerned with limiting idleness and despite the fact that the occupier was cornering building materials. Examining periodicals which continued to be published during the occupation, such as *Travaux* and *Le Moniteur des travaux publics et du bâtiment*, makes it possible to gauge both the quantity and quality of this activity.

STRUCTURAL RESEARCH AND BUILDING SITES

In this context, the great structural engineers continued their theoretical and practical work. The technique of prestressed concrete conceived by Eugène Freyssinet (X-Ponts) underwent continuous improvement. His connections to Germany were not non-existent, because he had built a bridge in 1938 with the company Wayss & Freytag for the Reichsautobahn in Oelde, in Westphalia, the first prestressed concrete work built in Germany. It was during the occupation that entrepreneur Edme Campenon, in order to take advantage of his methods, created the Société technique pour l'utilisation de la précontrainte.[4] He then worked on the Pont de Luzancy, a bridge spanning the Marne River, which was completed in 1946. In 1943 he received a visit from German engineer Fritz Leonhardt, whose archives preserve traces of a trip he took to France. The latter was then working for the Organisation Todt in Estonia, and he tells in his memoirs of how he decided to go to France after reading an article published in 1941 by Freyssinet on the "revolution" of prestressing.[5] He was interested in the bridge in Elbeuf-sur-Andelle and, during a second trip to inspect the Kriegsmarine submarine bases, he made sure to go see the great Plougastel viaduct on the Elorn, built in 1930. He returned for the last time, meeting Freyssinet during the summer of 1944, to discuss the resistance to the bombs of these bases' hangars.[6]

Among the great engineers of Freyssinet's generation, Albert Caquot (X-Ponts), stood out for the magnitude of his excellence and creativity, which extended from civil engineering to aircraft construction and from the planning to the management of large companies. He alternated between running the design office, Pelnard, Considère & Caquot, and administrative functions. Technical General Director of the Air Ministry between the

Reise von Russland-Nord nach dem Atlantikwall d

Kivióli - Reval - Berlin - St. Nazaire - Lorien

Blick von der Plougastelbrücke

Die Brücke bei Plougastel über

Drehbrücke in

satzgruppe West. November 1943

st u.zurück.

rts

den Meerbusen bei Brest

↑   Nicolas Esquillan, Auguste Perret, cover under
construction of the aircraft garage at Marignane
airport, Marignane, 1950, Fonds Delvert. SIAF/
Cité de l'architecture et du patrimoine/Archives
d'architecture contemporaine. Photo Ray Delvert

←   Eugène Freyssinet, Plougastel viaduct on the
Elorn, 1930. Photo Fritz Leonhardt. Courtesy
Südwestdeutsches Archiv für Architektur und
Ingenieurbau, Karlsruhe Institut für Technologie

↑ Bertrand, Dumont, Hommey, Rousselot, Olivier dell'Oflag VI D, project for a viaduct in Paris submitted to the competition of prisoners engineers of 1944, in *Travaux*, no. 133, July 1944

declaration of war and the armistice, he resigned because of his inability to maintain factory jobs. He worked on his own on numerous projects in the fields of construction, aerodynamics, and fluid dynamics, drafting a report on "Le rôle de l'ingénieur et la conception actuelle de l'habitation humaine" [The role of the engineer and the current concept of human habitation] for the Société des Ingénieurs Civils. He also planned strategies aimed at materials economy and tidal energy.[7]

Nicolas Esquillan (Arts et Métiers), stood out among business engineers, in particular at the company of Simon Boussiron, of which he became director in 1941 and for which he created the Coudette road bridge on the Gave de Pau, at that time the largest reinforced concrete work using the bowstring principle. In 1942, Esquillan, together with Auguste Perret, designed the twin shell aircraft hangars for the Marignane terminal, near Marseille, which would be completed after the war.[8] Centrale graduate Bernard Laffaille, the first to use cable structures, also designed an aircraft hangar in 1942 for Cherbourg. In 1941 he devised a construction process for a "hut with a self-supporting roof," while continuing more discrete designs on building craftsmanship.[9]

Also figuring among the great innovators was the Russian Vladimir Bodiansky (Moscow Institute of Civil Engineering), who had a great deal of experience in aeronautics and worked until 1940 with the firm of Eugène Beaudouin and Marcel Lods, for example, on the Cité de la Muette in Drancy and the Maison du Peuple of Clichy. Forced due to his stateless status to take refuge in Pau, in the unoccupied zone, he focused on designing scientific research instruments, in particular telescopes, one of which would be installed at the Pic du Midi Observatory in the Pyrenees.[10] Another remarkable inventor was the self-taught Robert Le Ricolais, who during the war continued to develop his space structures and lightweight metal shapes in Nantes, within the Air Liquide company.

Hundreds of engineers were held in German prison camps for the entire duration of the war. Following the model of what had been organized for their fellow architects, "competitions between prisoner-of-war building engineers" were organized between 1942 and 1944 by an action committee headed by Caquot. The seven topics included a suspension bridge over the Durance, a covered market in Valenciennes, and, in Paris, an Agriculture building at Porte de Versailles and a public road crossing at Porte de Vitry.[11] These educational exercises should not let us forget the larger building sites that continued during the war, which in general had a potential impact on the armament industry. This, for example, was the case with the large Génissiat dam on the Rhône, designed by Pierre Delattre (X-Ponts), whose construction was undertaken in 1939 and completed in 1946.[12]

SUPERVISING THE RECONSTRUCTION

Among Vichy's public policy areas in which engineers were mobilized, the most significant was the reconstruction of infrastructures and cities destroyed during the blitzkrieg of spring 1940. They were present at the local level, in departmental services and on Parisian administrative

7   Jean Kerisel, Thierry Kerisel, "Albert Caquot (1881–1976)," *Bulletin de la Société des amis de la bibliothèque et de l'histoire de l'École polytechnique*, no. 28 (July 2001).

8   Bernard Marrey, *Nicolas Esquillan. Un ingénieur d'entreprise* (Paris: Picard, 1992).

9   See the works of Nicolas Nogue, incl. "Bernard Laffaille," in VV.AA., *Jean Prouvé: La Poétique de l'objet technique* (Weil am Rhein: Vitra Design Museum, 2006), 226–29.

10 Christel Frapier, "The Career of engineer Vladimir Bodiansky," *Engineering History and Heritage*, vol. 65, no. 2 (May 2012): 113–21.

11 "Concours entre ingénieurs-constructeurs prisonniers de guerre," *Travaux*, no. 133 (July 1944): 175–80.

12 Pierre Delattre, "Génissiat," *Travaux*, no. 109 (July 1942): 179–84.

staffs. At a national level, two administrations presided over policy development: the Commissariat technique à la reconstruction immobilière (CTRI) and the Délégation générale à l'équipement national (DGEN), both infiltrated by engineers.[13]

Established in October 1940, the CRTI was run by André Muffang (X-Mines), now known for his career as a chess player.[14] The CTRI planned the building sites which opened without delay to clear and raise some 1,400 urban areas which were destroyed or damaged during the French campaign. X-Ponts graduate Jean Kérisel, soil mechanics specialist—and Albert Caquot's son-in-law—was the director of property reconstruction, which is different from industrial reconstruction; working under him, the town-planning group was led by William Palanchon, and the architecture group by Prix de Rome recipient André Leconte, while town-planner Jean Royer—also editor of the monthly *Urbanisme*, which acted as unofficial publication of the Commissariat—led the technical services.

Established in 1941, the DGEN was attached to the Ministry of Industrial Production and Labor and was responsible for leading the overall territorial planning and especially for immediately creating a common methodology within the perspective of an industrial decentralization. Briefly headed by François Lehideux (graduate of the École libre des sciences politiques), it was soon run by Henri Giraud (Chief engineer of the City of Paris) and Frédéric Surleau (X-Ponts). Leading the town-planning and property construction was engineer André Prothin (X-Ponts), along with Pierre Randet (X-Eaux et Forêts), Pierre Gibel (engineer of the City of Paris), and architect Roger Millet. Intellectuals such as Pierre George and Louis Chevalier also worked within the general delegation. The DGEN prepared a new town-planning law, enacted on June 15, 1943, which indicated the state's direct influence on the design of city plans, replacing the law of 1919 which only gave it a controlling role. The delegation also led the discussion about the layout of the Parisian region.[15]

The government's focus on the modernization of Paris crystallized in several programs aimed at de-industrializing the capital, transforming its road network, urban renewal, and the policy of open spaces and sports facilities. Engineers had their hands in all these activities: Maurice Baudot (X-Ponts) was the director of Architectural and Urban Planning Services at the prefecture of the Seine, while his classmate René Mestais, chief of Technical Services of Topography and Urban Planning, was in charge of planning the layout of Paris itself, which had not been prepared before the war.[16] Key in Vichy's political and social plan, which intended to develop physical culture in order to improve the performance of future soldiers, the program of playgrounds and sports fields was entrusted to Robert Joffet (Public Works engineer).

Within the overall system of the Vichy administration, which was complex to the point of being labyrinthine, other bodies were led by engineers. The Public Works and Building Organization Committee, responsible for overseeing production in 1940, was the scene of conflict between entrepreneurs from both domains. When it was created, it was headed by Centrale graduate Henri Garnier, president of the company Moisant-Laurent-Savey.[17] Within it, the Office of Standardization was directed by architect André Gigou who, after the war, would preface the French translation of *Bauordnungslehre*, written by Ernst Neufert while he was working with Albert Speer.[18] Among all the industries and professions, the French Association of Standardiza-

13 Michel Margairaz, "Les politiques économiques sous et de Vichy," *Histoire@Politique*, no. 9 (2009): 92–113.

14 To learn more about this organization, see Anne-Françoise Garçon, Bruno Belhoste, *Les ingénieurs des Mines : cultures, pouvoirs, pratiques* (Paris: Institut de la gestion publique et du développement économique, 2012).

15 Rémi Baudouï, "L'aménagement du territoire en France, antécédents et genèse, 1911-1963," in *L'Aménagement du territoire 1958-1974,* eds. François Caron and Maurice Vaïsse (Paris: L'Harmattan, 1999), 9–21.

16 L'Inspecteur général, chef des Services techniques de topographie et d'urbanisme, *Projet d'aménagement de la ville de Paris, La voirie parisienne*, typed, 1943. See Jean-Louis Cohen, "Le Grand Paris sous Vichy," in VV.AA., *Inventer le Grand Paris. 1919-1944* (Champs-sur-Marne: Collectif Inventer le Grand Paris, 2018).

17 Dominique Barjot, "L'industrie française des travaux publics (1940-1945)," *Histoire, économie et société*, vol. 11, no. 3 (1992): 415–36.

18 André Gigou, "Le rôle du bureau de normalisation du C.O. du bâtiment et des travaux publics," *Techniques et architecture*, no. 1–2 (1943): 44–45. André Gigou, preface to Ernst Neufert, *La Coordination dimensionnelle dans la construction: manuel de construction rationnelle* (Paris: Dunod, 1967).

→ Repertoire of reinforced concrete arches, page from *Techniques et architecture*, no. 2, 1944. Issue dedicated to "Béton." Please note, in addition to French structures, the presence of works by Robert Maillart, Pier Luigi Nervi and Owen Williams

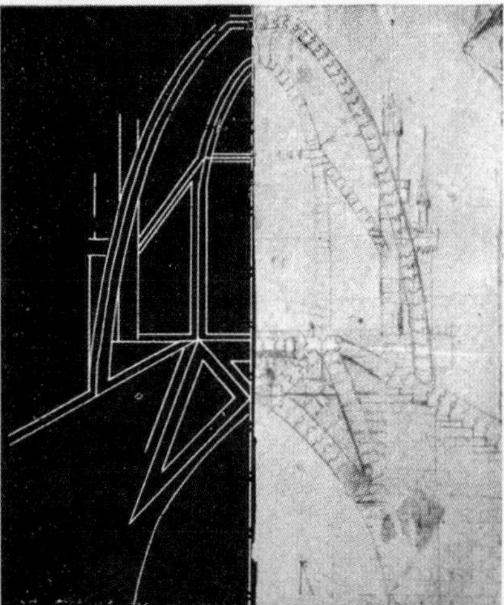

Arcs funiculaires en pierre.
(D'après Léonard de Vinci.)

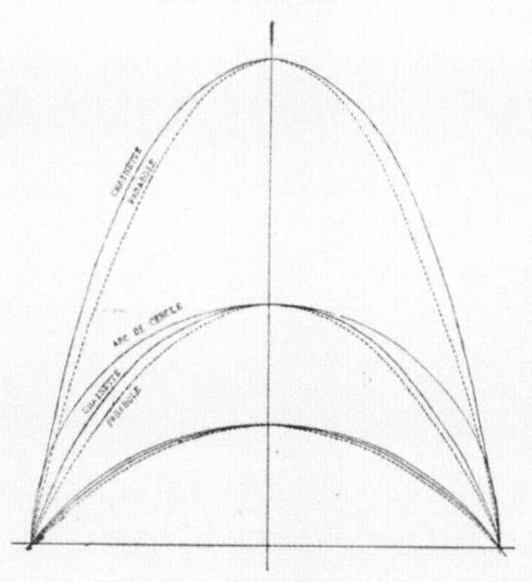

Arcs en plein cintre en béton armé,
Usines Esders. (A. et G. Perret.)

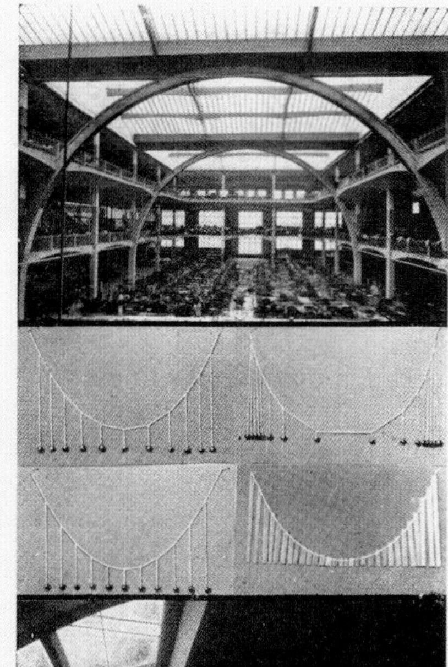

Détermination expérimentale du funiculaire :
chainette, parabole, plein cintre, charge proportionnelle à l'ordonnée.

Arcs en chainette. Piscine Blomet. (A. Sirvin.)
(Doc. C. C. I.)

(Doc. Reynes.)
Exemples divers d'arcs en béton armé. Dans la plupart des cas, le funiculaire des charges est polygonal et s'éloigne sensiblement de la fibre moyenne. Le béton armé permet de purifier la forme tout en exaltant la structure.

Hall de Piscine à Newington.
(Hobden et Porri.)

Arcs funiculaires.
(Doc. Fourré et Rhodes.)

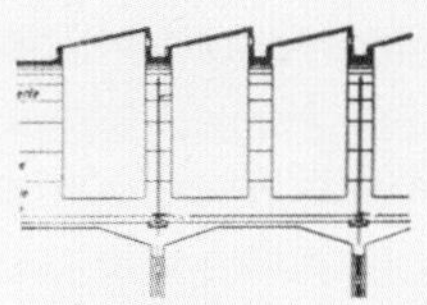

Hall de la gare de Reims à vitrages conoïdes.
(Doc. Limousin.)

Deux ponts de l'ingénieur Maillard : les formes expriment deux types de structures différents.

Hangar en béton armé (arcs diagonaux).

Portiques à trois articulations.

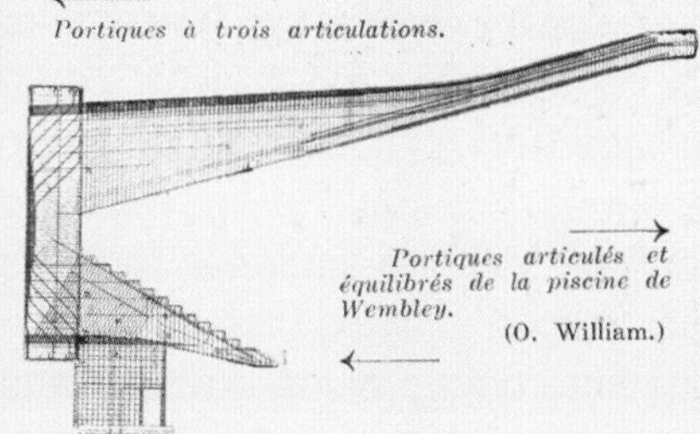

Portiques articulés et équilibrés de la piscine de Wembley.
(O. William.)

tion, created in 1926 and directed by Ernest Lhoste (École polytechnique and Artillery school), led to the creation of a Commissariat for Standardization, directed by weapons engineer Pierre Salmon.[19] Intense research activity was deployed during the occupation, which led to the formulation of a regulatory framework for postwar production. An amusing overview of this unrest was given in the novel *Vercoquin et le plancton*, by Centralien engineer Boris Vian, who soon after became a fulltime writer.[20]

COLLABORATION OR RESISTANCE?

Alongside their technical, or meta-technical roles, engineers were present in the more sensitive sectors of France's central administration, where they filled positions that the French Third Republic had reserved for the literati, jurists, political science graduates, and occasionally doctors. The most outstanding among these men who passed through large companies was undoubtedly the young prodigy Jean Bichelonne (X-Mines), who from April 1942 to March 1944 held the key position of state secretary, then minister of industrial production, making deals with his counterpart Albert Speer that solidified the role of French companies in the Nazi war effort.[21] A social-minded Catholic, Centralien graduate Georges Lamirand was State Secretary for Youth from September 1940 to March 1943. In 1932 he had published *Le rôle social de l'ingénieur*, a work whose title parodies a famous article by Marshal Hubert Lyautey,[22] and strove to moderate the most reactionary leanings of the regime.

Jean Berthelot (X-Mines), close to Radical-Socialist minister Anatole de Monzie, was named State Secretary of Transport and Communications in September 1940 and held that position until 1942, when Pierre Laval once again became the head of government. He was replaced by another X-Mines graduate, Robert Gibrat, who supervised the École polytechnique. Another influential engineer in this area was Frédéric Surleau (X-Ponts), who became inspector general of Ponts et Chaussées in 1942.

Many engineers refused to get involved in the collaboration and got involved in the resistance networks. Mines engineer Jacques Bingen, brother-in-law of industrialist André Citroën, fled to London and became one of the unifiers of the resistance, especially in creating the French Forces of the Interior. He committed suicide after his arrest so as not to talk. Raymond Samuel, called Aubrac, civil engineer from Ponts who went through Harvard and MIT, worked in a patent office in Lyon and played a decisive role in the creation of the Secret Army, becoming a legendary figure with his wife Lucie. Louis Armand (X-Mines) was the technical director of the Société nationale des chemins de fer français (SNCF) and created the Résistance-fer network, before assuming the direction, in early 1944, of the infiltration group called Noyautage des Administrations Publiques. Arrested, he was released near death at the time of the Liberation of Paris. Marine engineer Jacques Camille Louis Stosskopf was less fortunate. Stationed at the Lorient submarine base, he informed the Allies for a long time before being arrested and then shot at the Natzweiler-Struthof concentration camp. André Dewavrin, called Passy (École polytechnique and École du génie) created the Secret Service of Free France, which he continued to organize from Algiers.

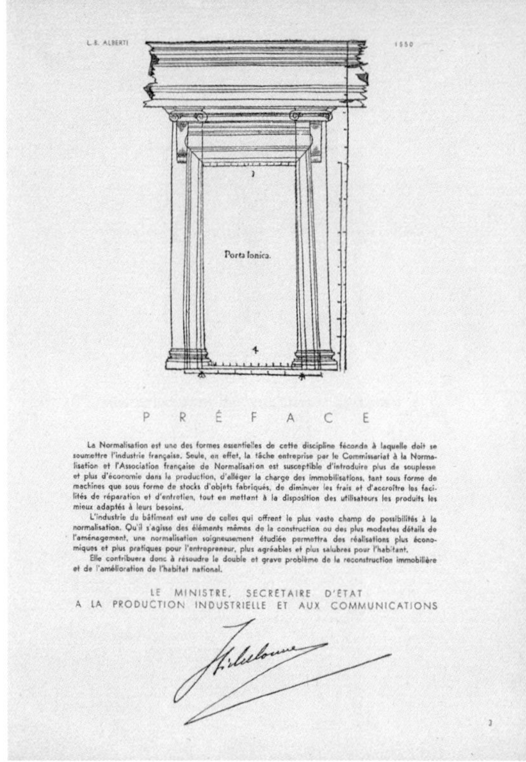

↑ Jean Bichelonne, preface to the *Techniques et architecture* special issue about normalization, January–February 1943

19 Pierre Salmon, *Le Problème actuel de la normalisation* (Paris: Éditions du Comité général d'organisation des industries mécaniques, 1942).

20 Boris Vian, *Vercoquin et le plancton* (Paris: Gallimard, 1946).

21 Limore Yagil, *Jean Bichelonne 1904-1944: Un polytechnicien sous Vichy. Entre mémoire et histoire* (Paris: Éditions SPM, 2015).

22 Georges Lamirand, *Le rôle social de l'ingénieur. Scènes de la vie d'usine* (Paris: Éditions de la Revue des jeunes, 1932). See Rémi Baudouï, "Du rôle social de la jeunesse dans la Révolution nationale, Georges Lamirand, secrétaire général à la Jeunesse, September 7, 1940–March 23, 1943," in *Être jeune en France, 1939-1945*, ed. Jean-William Dereymez (Paris: L'Harmattan, 2001), 141–42. Lyautey's essay was published as: "Du rôle social de l'officier dans le service militaire universel," *La Revue des Deux Mondes* (March 1891): 443–59.

23 Rémi Baudouï, "Raoul Dautry, la conscience du social," *Vingtième siècle*, no. 15 (July–September 1987): 45–58.

24 Barjot, *L'industrie française des travaux publics (1940-1945)*, 431–33.

25 Le Corbusier, François de Pierrefeu, *La maison des hommes* (Paris: Plon, 1942), plate opposite p. 116.

After the liberation, the post of minister of reconstruction and urban development was entrusted to Raoul Dautry (École polytechnique), who had been armaments minister in 1939–1940 and had withdrawn to the Lubéron during the occupation, taking part in the resistance from a wise distance. Basking in the success of his work in the railway networks before the war, he took charge of the reconstruction, heading an administration whose power stemmed from Vichy-created state centralization.[23] The purge struck the building and public works contractors who had worked too closely and visibly for the Nazis.[24] CTRI owner Muffang simply retired and resumed his career as chess champion, while Berthelot was sentenced to two years in prison. At the level immediately below this, many senior administration officials such as Prothin or Gibel enjoyed successful careers under the Fourth Republic founded in 1946.

In conclusion, it is worthwhile mentioning François de Pierrefeu (École polytechnique), director of the "Grands travaux hydrauliques" [Great Hydraulic Works] of Marseille in the 1930s and unwavering supporter of Le Corbusier as he tried to gain influence within Vichy's ruling circles. In 1942, he published with the aforesaid *La maison des hommes*, a work in which a book plate is dedicated to the "master plan," which equally associates "the spiritual man"—the architect—to "the economic man"—the engineer—in a two-tone graphic diagram.[25] Twenty years after he celebrated the engineer's aesthetic, Le Corbusier now pays tribute to their management ability, thus showing everything he learned from their multifaceted participation in Vichy's technical, industrial, and social program.

KIMBELL
ART MUSEUM

FORT WORTH (TX), USA

1966–1972

ARCHITECT   LOUIS KAHN

ENGINEER   AUGUST EDUARD KOMENDANT

Louis Kahn's design for the Kimbell Art Museum was planimetrically developed through the reiteration of 16 reinforced concrete modules with travertine cladding arranged in three parallel rows. The indented central partition and three patios interrupt the otherwise-strict rhythm, while the western spans lose their perimeter walls and become an entrance portico, almost as if to display the construction system. These 30.6-meter-long, 6-meter-wide modules owe their peculiar lowered-arch profile to August Komendant's geometrical-structural design. The engineer utilized a section with the shape of a cycloid, i.e., a curve traced from a fixed point on a circle that rolls along a direct line. Improperly called vaults, these shells, with skylights cut through their tops, work like curved beams in post-tensioned reinforced concrete, resting only on four corner pilasters. The narrow slots of light that separate the walls from the cupola clearly show the structural role of each architectural element.

KIMBELL ART MUSEUM

← Kimbell Art Museum, project, Fort Worth, 1972. Courtesy The University of Pennsylvania and the Pennsylvania Historical and Museum Commission

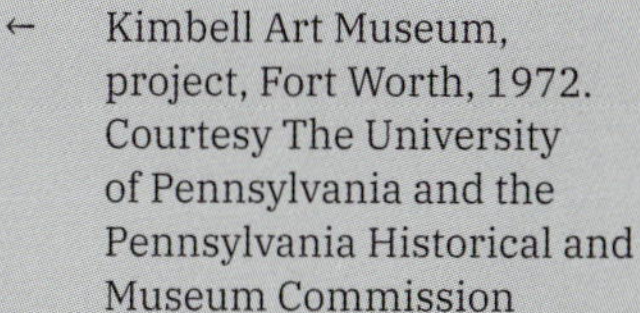

KIMBELL ART MUSEUM EXPANSION

	FORT WORTH (TX), USA
	2007–2013
ARCHITECTS	RENZO PIANO BUILDING WORKSHOP KENDALL/HEATON ASSOCIATES, INC.
ENGINEERS	GUY NORDENSON & ASSOCIATES BROCKETTE, DAVIS, DRAKE INC

Like the building opposite it by Louis Kahn and August Komendant, the expansion designed by Renzo Piano in 2007 is also planimetrically tripartite, reprising the former's axes, dimensions and materials.
The complete repetition of the trilithic construction system modulates the internal space, emphasizing its horizontality. Square, cast-in-place reinforced concrete pilasters run along the short façades, supporting 29 paired beams in glulam arranged longitudinally to cover the three functionally separate blocks. The double beams are joined by custom-made metal connectors and strengtheners, creating open spaces without interceding columns for the entire 31-meter width of the spans. Natural light from above, so important for Kahn's museum, is guaranteed here by a glass roof that extends beyond the perimeter of the building, incorporating an external aluminum sun-shade system covered with photovoltaic cells.

↓ Kimbell Art Museum Expansion, Fort Worth, 2013. Photo Nic Lehoux. Courtesy Renzo Piano Building Workshop Architects

DEEP DECORATION AS STRUCTURAL HOLISM

Nina Rappaport

In structural design as in nature, form, material, and behavior are inseparable, working together dynamically —and in many cases, sublimely. Structure is not just a prop to support buildings and bridges nor an additive element but is thoroughly embedded; it is not a feat to achieve, but a form to design. Structural design (as we see in this exhibition) is a creative endeavor in its own right, made evident in both standard and nonstandard—or nonlinear—structures created by engineers, architects, and designers both individually and collaboratively.

This essay investigates engineers as designers—one could say "whisperers"—of form-guiding structural design resulting in what I call "deep decoration."[1] First, it is important to define the differences between the terms "decoration" and "ornament" which will be described later, and to explain the concept of deep decoration in relation to tectonics, the expression of form

and experience, the marriage of construction and structure in which the engineer and the architect collaborate in ways that can elevate their activity to an artistic form. In featuring recent projects that also focus on issues of sustainable and renewable materials, deep decoration absorbs new technologies through form and structure, providing atmosphere that inspires human reaction, interaction, and emotion.

Structural geometry is the direct representation of how structural forces are distributed, and yields a type of elegance intrinsic to nature, one that minimizes material, is efficient, and is often considered beautiful. Neither the rational minimalization that follows the geometry, nor the forming of deep decoration, which is not an applied layer

---

1   I first wrote about "deep decoration" in the eponymous essay in *306090: Decoration,* eds. Emily Abruzzo and Jonathan D. Solomon (New York: Princeton Architectural Press, 2006), 95–105.

but part of the structure itself, is excessive. These subtle interventions can be intuitively felt and carry deep meaning for the participant or onlooker. Today's engineers and designers have united decoration and structure in new ways that both inform a space and provide what Heinrich Wölfflin's research on the psychology of architecture in 1886 concluded about tectonics: a form of empathy that can move us in different ways and can then create an atmosphere that merges structure, decoration, and society.[2]

ENGINEERS' INTUITION

While engineers often do not consider themselves to be designers, design happens through incremental adjustments to functional form and through maximizing structural performance through mathematical analysis. Engineering is an applied science and can be subjective because of engineers' diverse sets of knowledge and training, which attain a critical mass that becomes instinctive. Engineers recognize this aspect of their creativity, as French engineer Eugène Freyssinet emphasized: "[The structural task] will not be accomplished until the definitions of the forms has been unable to extract from the technical data at his disposal are revealed in himself. They will surge from his unconsciousness, at the behest of an instinct encapsulating all the accumulated experience inherited by man since the dawn of time, with that sense of inevitability which surrounds all instinctive creativity and satisfies it definitively."[3] Or, in the mid-twentieth century, Spaniard Eduardo Torroja understood this as a

method of practice and emphasized: "The process of visualizing or conceiving a structure is an art. Basically, it is motivated by an inner experience, by an intuition. It is never the result of mere deductive logical reasoning."[4] Their intuitions are also based on what they know from observation as scientists, especially observation of nature that informs their designs.

BIOMIMICRY

Engineers are inspired not only by forms in nature, but also by the behavior of natural systems which have become more essential today in terms of conserving and renewing natural resources. Engineers work with nature, not against it, so that all buildings must be designed to bear some combination of gravity (self-weight and occupancy loads), moving earth (seismic events), and moving air (windstorms). Since each natural organism has a performative logic, natural structures use material without extravagance for maximum performance, and in so doing are elegant. Structural biomimicry has a significant role to play in structural design, as we glean from Ernst Haeckel's *Art Forms in Nature* (1904) and D'Arcy Wentworth Thompson's *On Growth and Form* (1917). There is a creative and scientific interest in studying natural models—going beyond their theoretical examination as synergistic ecosystems—in terms of the sustainability of contemporary structures. Structural engineers are thus inspired by Radiolaria, spiderwebs, crystals, coral, honeycombs, nautilus shells, nests, soap bubbles, snowflakes, cellular arrays, mesh and nets, bats, leaves, palms, and Lily Amazonas, among other creatures and plant life, as guides for new types of nonlinear spaces and structural design in general.

Since my previous studies on larger-scale projects with characteristics of deep decoration in steel, glass, and concrete,[5] I have turned my attention to projects employing renewable resources including bamboo, wood, stone, and textiles, as well as efficiently-used materials such as thin steel plate. Engineers, in considering how

---

2   Ideas of tectonics and emotions have been analyzed by Wölfflin and more recently in the books: Daniel E. Snyder, *The Tender Detail: Ornament and Sentimentality in the Architecture of Louis H. Sullivan and Frank Lloyd Wright* (London: Bloomsbury, 2020) and Lars Spuybroek, *Grace and Gravity. Architecture of the Figure* (London: Bloomsbury, 2020).

3   Translation from Eugène Freyssinet, "Un amour sans limites," *L'Architecture d'Aujourd'hui*, no. 8 (November 1936).

4   Eduardo Torroja, *Philosophy of Structures*, trans. J.J. Polivka and Milos Polivka (Berkeley and Los Angeles: University of California Press, 1958), 313.

5   See Nina Rappaport, *Support and Resist: Structural Engineers and Design Innovation* (New York: The Monacelli Press, 2008).

to conserve materials and resources, underscore nature's significance. As we investigate basic earthbound materials, we must envision how, in the Anthropocene era, we can conserve resources. These natural materials come to be used as a *performative* deep decoration, inspiring engineers and designers to conserve and respect the environment through efficient structures that engage our imagination.

DEFINING ORNAMENT AND DECORATION

ORNAMENT

One of the challenges in this discussion is to precisely define *decoration* and *ornament*, as it has become unwittingly complex to discern the differences between them. In line with Kent Bloomer's theoretical discussions, ornament is that which is applied to buildings or objects and is separate from the object to which it is applied. It can be a motif, a detail that ornaments another form, generated in a pattern separate from the object itself, with the motif at its heart.[6] This is codified in Owen Jones's *Grammar of Ornament* (1856), as is the use of motifs such as the acanthus leaves in Greek and Roman temple cornices and ancient pottery border patterns, among countless other uses throughout history. Ornament in ancient times participated in a dialogue by bringing natural references into the artificial world, and recognizing the difference between ornament, which is additive, and its object. Ornament was a way of representing the cosmos using nature. So, for example, a vase was distinct from the key pattern along its edge; it could be delaminated, and each would remain unique. But the shape of the vase as a form moves into the realm of decoration through its holism and interiority as an object. Ornament also slips into the realm of decoration if there is interplay between the ornament and the constructed element. This is often seen in smaller constructions or parts of buildings rather than an entire volume, as in Louis Sullivan's cornices that fluidly emphasize the solid structure.

DECORATION

Decoration is slightly different from ornament, as it is that which can be seen as a holistic patterning animating a volume or surface; it informs the space more than ornament. Thus, decoration can lend meaning to structure, especially in contemporary architecture, which does not necessarily involve figural decoration. William Jordy described decoration as an arrangement (rather than a detail)—of all elements in an orchestrated composition especially in the work of Louis Sullivan.[7] This can also be seen in the works of French architect Auguste Perret, who imbedded concrete panel systems with foliated patterns intricately designed to fit the surface into façades, as well as in William Morris's wallpaper designs, which have an overall design imbued with symbolism and meaning that can be read. Decoration's subtle difference from ornament is the pattern's completeness and its ordering in a composition. Structural decoration absorbs the viewer with responsive meaning in an enveloping environment, as these things shape each other.

Decoration also relates to *decorum*, based on the ancient Latin definition, and is predicated on societal values and common social attributes. While the idea of decorum is associated with proper conduct and cultural norms, it also has a long history relating to the ancient orders of architecture—Doric, Ionic, and Corinthian. Perhaps the value of decorum today, which indeed seems antiquated, is to point towards a new social commons of visual stimuli, which relates to the idea of a building ethics that includes honesty of materials, structure, and decoration as well.

6   Discussion with Kent Bloomer, 2021, and see also Kent Bloomer, *The Nature of Ornament* (New York: W.W. Norton, 2000).

7   William Jordy wrote about the topics of decoration and ornament especially in reference to Louis Sullivan. See Wim de Wit, ed., *Louis Sullivan: The Function of Ornament* (New York: W.W. Norton, 1986).

8   Spuybroek discusses Ruskin's appreciation of the Gothic in these terms in Lars Spuybroek, *The Sympathy of Things: Ruskin and the Ecology of Design* (London: Bloomsbury Academic, 2016), 68.

9   See Robin Middleton, "The Iron Structure of the Bibliothèque Sainte-Geneviève as the Basis of a Civic Décor," *AA Files*, no. 40 (Winter 1999): 33–52; Martin Bressani, "Notes on Viollet-le-Duc's Philosophy of History: Dialectics and Technology," *Journal of the Society of Architectural Historians* 48, no. 4 (December 1989): 327–50.

DEEP DECORATION

Deep decoration reemerges as a part-to-whole relationship in engineering structures that I categorize here in a few forms: fluid lines, exoskeletons, and interior space-shaping holisms. The decoration is both on the surface and beneath it, and it engenders new spatial effects and atmosphere. The unity of deep decoration, from a structural point of view, influences a building's form, often with integrated patterns. Today, patterns generated by algorithmic formulae, such as fractals, as well as cellular and reticulated structures, are creating new relationships between skin (façade/cladding) and bones (structure), merging experience with complex and non-linear space. Asymmetrical space becomes an immersive environment through the performative combination of a structure's form and materiality. In Gestalt psychology, perception is understood as having laws of proximity, grouping, and closure, demonstrating that patterns have an innate appeal because of the visual continuity and relationship between things, wherein the knowledge of the pattern playing out continuously is comforting in its predictability; this is demonstrated by Islamic tile patterns or the continuity of a continuous grid on an infinite path. Deep decoration thus results from integrating structure, skin, and form in a holistic synergy between engineers and designers that creates a satisfying volumetric and visual play. In terms of fluid line, exoskeleton, and holism, deep decoration is evident in the following examples of recent built experimental projects.

ORNAMENT TO DECORATION – FLUID LINE

When ornament evolves from a line to decoration, structure as deep decoration is exposed—first, as a dominant and fluid sculptural line in the merging of the structure and organic forms, as seen in curved Gothic cathedral ribs articulated for structural support, and second, as ornament that when grouped together visually becomes decoration.[8] Figural lines seen in the exposed cast-iron arches punched with floral patterns in Henri Labrouste's Bibliothèque Sainte-Geneviève (Paris, 1838–1850) create the effect of lighter-weight supporting elements by concealing the industrial cast-iron material abhorred by the public. Likewise, Eugène Emmanuel Viollet-le-Duc, in his designs of structural columns for the Concert Hall, the Market Place, and foliated railings illustrated in his book *Entretiens* (1872), exposes cast iron with an intricate decoration, just as engineer Alexandre-Gustave Eiffel did in his cast-iron tower.[9] These instances were intended to appease viewers. Shortly thereafter, Art Nouveau designers Victor Horta in his Maison du Peuple (Brussels, 1899) and Hector Guimard in the Paris metro stations (1900) sculpted structural lines in three dimensions for cast-iron railings, window frames, and columns doubling as decoration. In the Modernist era engineers integrated curvilinear structural ribs using concrete, as seen in Giacomo Matté-Trucco's spiral ramps at the Lingotto Fiat factory (Turin, 1926), Pier Luigi Nervi's Palazzetto dello Sport (Turin, 1957) and the Gatti wool factory (Rome, 1951), to support floor slabs and form patterns, following structural forces that result in deep decoration.

Today, Masoud Akbarzadeh, an engineer, architect and director of the Polyhedral Structures Lab at the University of Pennsylvania's Weitzman School of Design, has done research on the traditional post and beam system of Le Corbusier's now-classic Maison Dom-Ino, questioning how to optimize it structurally. Rather than columns and beams, his team developed polyhedral structures generated by 3D graphic statics with funicular arch structure (one that achieves equilibrium through use of the "right" form) supporting floors of different patterns optimized through algorithmic designs. Expanding graphic statics analysis from 2D to 3D design by means of complex geometric computer calculations, 3D force diagrams were used with form-finding to direct the design. Not only is the floor pattern optimized, but the material follows the lines of force subdivisions and becomes decoration, integrating new structural computation and recalling both Gothic ribs and Nervi's ribbed concrete structures.

Similarly, in 2017 Steve Webb of London-based Webb Yates Engineers, with Fabric-Space architects, designed a rib pattern that follows the structural stress lines for a cast-iron mezzanine for a private residence in a former pump house. He and his team minimized build up by casting 0.7×1.15-meter panels with a monolithic stiffened underside and a solid upper surface that, when bolted together, form a continuous floor slab. Taking advantage of the malleability of ductile cast iron, the mezzanine floor is supported by the three walls with shear connections, making for equal stress distributions for each panel. Similar panels were used for the hand railing to generate a contiguous formal organization. The curvilinear vein pattern was optimized using finite-element analysis-driven topology optimization, with a traditional manufacturing technique of casting. Throughout, the team minimized material, reused the timber forms, and repeated the pattern, creating an elegant decoration.

In wood, engineer Martin Waters with HRW Engineers strove for a similar visible linear decoration for a house in Buckinghamshire, England, in 2019. Glulam beams describe the roof's curvilinear structural "lines of desire" and were intentionally exposed as a formal expression. The architect had wanted the timber structure to spring from the mullions like a Gothic fan vault, but the roof was to be flat. Thus, Waters could not work with wood members in compression; instead, he used bending reminiscent of the Lily Amazonas structure and Nervi's structures, which engineer Aldo Arcangeli worked on to "make explicit the isostatics of the principal bending moments in the slab."[10] Waters used continuous primary curved oak ribbing, single-laminated, and then accommodated

shorter secondary members. Two leaf-like curvilinear forms cross in the center and longer undulating wooden ribs cross perpendicularly to span to the roof edges.

EXOSKELETON

Another related structural system is the operative patterning of exoskeletons as the merging of structure and decoration visible as deep decoration, is seen in diagrids. In nature the exoskeleton is seen in sea urchins and the Radiolaria of protozoa, as their exterior structure supports their core body. Even exposed high-tech steel details such as fine stainless-steel joinery and glass

↓ Groupwork + Amin Taha Architects, Webb Yates Engineers in collaboration with The Stonemasonry Company, 15 Clerkenwell Close, London, 2017. Photo Agnese Sanvito

clamping systems by Anthony Hunt and Peter Rice are integral to a building's design and result in decoration. More contemporary exoskeletons include works by engineer Leslie Robertson and I.M. Pei for the Bank of China; Bollinger+Grohmann with Peter Cook and Colin Fournier for the Kunsthaus Graz; and Cecil Balmond with Arup and OMA for the CCTV in China. Glass and steel have been the dominant contemporary materials used to create exoskeletons, but renewable materials such as wood and stone are employed now as well.

In London, 15 Clerkenwell Close, a 7-story residential and office building designed by Groupwork in 2018 was to be an entirely concrete structure. However, focusing on concrete's negative environmental impact, engineer Steve Webb of Webb Yates Engineers found that stone is stronger than concrete and uses less energy to produce as it is quarried and then transported directly to the building site. The embodied energy of the limestone that he used was 3,600 kg CO_2 versus 14,300 kg CO_2 for the same volume in concrete. While the building has a concrete core and slab construction, the stone provides a solid load-bearing exoskeleton of columns and lintels. The column dimensions and strength were determined via the loads with parametric modeling that then sized the stones. The stone finishes —drill holes, saw grooves, machine cuts, and split faces—were left not as a direct aesthetic choice but as the most pragmatic way to cut out the stones to minimize the shaping for construction, an accidental design effect. The variety of textures that serve to reveal the stone's nature expresses a deep decoration in an exoskeleton that contributes to a new urban atmosphere.

In Düsseldorf's Media Harbour district, the INTERBODEN Gruppe built a 6,600-square-meter office building with Cradle to Cradle requirements: at the building's end-of-life, the materials are to be deconstructed and reused. Thorsten Helbig of Knippers Helbig with HPP Architekten designed the six-story building with an outer bracing structure of diagonal wall frame segments of glue-laminated columns. Rising above the concrete ground-floor base, the rhombic structure is a supporting wall that shifts in density according to solar orientation. Rather than the typical post and beam system, the columns support the floor slabs and the horizontal bracing. With Cross-Laminated Timber (CLT) developed in the mid-1990s and new mass timber systems, the structure manifests a new formal expression exposed in an exoskeleton wood diagrid that envelops the building's concrete core. The structure's depth and façade create larger or smaller windows in relation to the building's solar orientation. Zigzag patterns are highlighted depending on shadow and light, with some sections open for terraces and others glazed. This gives the building depth and support rather than just cladding, following a lineage of the exoskeleton and decoration as patterning in the form of an exterior array in wood.

INTERIORITY

Perhaps the most expressive designs are considered to be a deep decoration found in nature which are nonlinear structures and topological forms such as crystals, the structural intensities of sponges and bones, and the forms of knots and tubular intertwining. An open meshwork often results from an interior pattern projecting a space and an enveloping array in an overall network of distribution, rather than the classical, hierarchically organized—or Cartesian—buildings comprised of trabeated columns and beams. The interior structure holistically fills the building as the space frames become decoration. The lightness of Richard Buckminster Fuller's geodesic domes, Konrad Wachsmann's Airplane Hangar of multiple gridded three-dimensional space, Robert Le Ricolais' tensile structures, and Frei Otto's curvilinear meshworks based on the structures of soap bubbles—all balance intricate form. In contrast, dark cave-like spaces also envelop us in an atmosphere of ritual, as seen in the nonlinear spaces of the Mayan underground temple caves of Belize, where roofs, walls, and structure are one in a womb-like setting, and walls basically do not exist.[11]

10   Discussion with Martin Waters, 2021.

11   See discussion of wall-less caves in Vilém Flusser, "Bare Walls," in Vilém Flusser, *The Shape of Things* (London: Reaktion Books, 1999).

In 2020, Akbarzadeh and his lab at the University of Pennsylvania explored how to translate force flow into a volumetric design in the prefabricated concrete project Saltatur, in which a series of concrete linear elements seemingly float, much like a spatial bone structure connected with transfer nodes. The rigid elements are in compression and tension so that the steel connections effectively transfer the tensile forces between the concrete elements. The structural geometry is a spatial funicular form (an equilibrium state free from bending stresses) created using 3D graphic statics that influenced a twist in the geometry, which reduced customized linear element production and allowed for a more compelling asymmetrical design. In this way, the armature patterns create an overall decoration that is also structure. The grooved-surface geometry merges with the concrete, resulting in ribs, or creases, along the direction of the members; these marks and methods of the fabrication instruments at detail-scale, and the way the parts combine to form a whole, are also visible as decoration. The interior becomes a deep structure in the way the diagonals, special nodes bolted through the concrete, and cross pieces interact structurally and formally. An ultra-thin, 4-mm glass tabletop was designed as a three-hinged arch, with the structure as a long span with special connectors, similar to furniture joints. The use of discrete spatial systems minimized material consumption so that the volume of concrete is 0.06 cubic meters distributed in 4.44 cubic meters of space.

For the TRUMPF Smart Factory in Chicago in 2017, Thorsten Helbig of Knippers Helbig worked with Barkow Leibinger to design a façade and roof that was more expressive than the typical factory shed. Harnessing TRUMPF's laser-cutting technologies, Helbig designed 11 44-meter-long and 3.6-meter-high Vierendeel trusses of laser-cut steel sheets placed in parallel for the girder to support the roof. The patterning creates a through-vista perforated mesh in which people can walk on a mezzanine platform resulting in occupiable deep decoration that shapes the vast space within.

The structure is an interpretation of Arthur Vierendeel's 1896 truss system that used moment joints rather than riveted trusses, and rectilinear elements instead of diagonals, but yielded imprecise calculations. At TRUMPF, Helbig worked to calibrate the static forces so that the truss shape related to the distance and thickness of verticals and horizontals from the understanding of the force flow of the beam. The laser-cut, extra-thin, steel-plate girders minimized the welding and concealed the bolts. The vertical sheet extends over the horizontal with a fillet weld so that the shaping results from the assembly. While the girders look heavy, the space frame is only 75 kilograms per square meter. The variation in the forms resulted from the way the forces flow from the verticals and the chords from the upper and lower beams, with the largest bending moments in the center where the horizontals and verticals are connected. The asymmetrical organization also supports a spatial idea in which the engineer's decision arose from an understanding of the force flow, intentionally forming a holism as decoration in space.

INTERIORITY – INSIDE IS OUTSIDE

Gottfried Semper's concept of *Bekleidung,* or the idea of cladding as a dress that reveals the body or structure beneath, runs parallel to the idea of draping material to reveal an object's essential form.[12] But with deep decoration, those aspects that unify as a whole are neither interior nor exterior, but merge so that inside is outside, and vice versa. A holism between surface and structure-like weaving is seen in baskets as holistic forms, and in concrete shells such as Félix Candela's restaurant at Xochimilco, Mexico City (1958), and Heinz Isler's small concrete-shell petrol stations in Switzerland (1950s and 1960s). Cubic concrete as folded plate is visible in Owen Williams's mushroom columns for the Sainsbury factory in

12 Gottfried Semper, *The Four Elements of Architecture and Other Writings*, trad. Harry Francis Mallgrave and Wolfgang Herrmann (Cambridge: Cambridge University Press, 1989).

13 Discussion with Neil Thomas, 2021.

14 Discussion with Jenny Sabin, 2021.

London (1932), and in the Church of the Pilgrimage at Neviges, Germany (1964–1972), by Gottfried Böhm and engineer Felix Varwick. The folded concrete interior is like the inside of an origami form in which creases and flat planes play off each other in mountain-like geometric compositions.

This relationship between structure and volume is perhaps most satisfying when the interior and exterior react and interact. Japanese engineer Jun Sato often collaborates with Kengo Kuma & Associates, as he did for the GC Prostho Museum Research Center in Kasugai, Japan (2010), a 102-square-meter building featuring a mesh grid comprised of perpendicular units of wooden sticks. Inspired by Japanese traditional joinery and the *Cidori* concept, the meshwork both envelops the building and also seems to grow from within, similar to Sato's pavilion—also called Cidori—for the 2007 Salone del Mobile in Milan. For SunnyHills bakery, built in 2014 in Minami-Aoyama, Japan, Kuma used a new interpretation of *Cidori* with a four-point joinery, like traditional *Jigoku-gumi* joinery, in a deep progression of lattice mesh sticks of cedar combined in three-dimensional space, not just two-dimensional. Sato, using 2D spectra, combines this forest-like feeling with a structural design based on a digital rendition of the Japanese concept of *Komorebi*, or the way sunlight falls through leaves. This effect he said, is inspired by a Pampas grass field and fleecy clouds in terms of the quality of light that he is seeking. SunnyHills has 5,000 meters of wood elements assembled in diagrids of 30- and 60-degree angles for the stick-based structural apertures that merge from floor to ceiling to the building exterior, like intertwined fingers opening and closing. The wood diagrid is both the structure and the decoration, which mimics the spatial depth of a forest.

Bamboo inspired Atelier One engineers, working with bamboo expert Jörg Stamm and designer Ibuku, for the design of the Arc, a community wellness space and gymnasium for the Green School in Bali. In 2003 when Atelier One founder Neil Thomas designed a structure for the Singapore Arts Centre, he was inspired by the local durian fruit for the shading device's form—spiked on the outside and smooth on the inside. For the Bali project, Thomas studied bamboo's inherent qualities. It is an anisotropic composite material with a hollow structure wound in a spiral fiber, which also makes it an ideal model for new carbon fiber tubes. Bamboo can even withstand earthquakes, but to become a structural material it must be stiffened. The use of palm fronds and fruit bat-inspired ribbing with double curvatures resulted in a weaving of structure and form as deep decoration.

The Green School also required a structure to enclose an odd geometry formed by a combined basketball gym and tennis courts. The structure spans 19 meters and reaches 14 meters high. Jorg Stamm imagined the project as a natural shape, like many of the other buildings on the site. The calculated structural form became a series of interdependent bamboo arches stitched together by anticlastic gridshells with intensive form-finding analysis that eliminated interfering trusses. Similar to a dramatic Frei Otto tent structure, but in bamboo, the double curvature of the parabolic arches in tension provides strength. The thin arches and their shells have an intricacy resulting from the material and the form. As Thomas notes, "The two systems together create a unique and highly efficient structure, able to flex under load allowing the weight to redistribute, easing localized forces on the arches."[13] The consequence of the synergy between materials, forms, and geometries is deep decoration through holistic interiority, like being enveloped in a tightly woven nest that symbolizes the celebration of humanity.

NINA RAPPAPORT

Jenny Sabin, an architect and designer with her own studio and lab at Cornell University, works with knitted fabrics and textiles, innovating with material performance and structural systems. Patterns in her installations "begin as a mathematical mosaic that becomes thickened in a hierarchy."[14] She works from a material-driven generative process, starting with simple parameters that are often based on biological systems. As the design evolves, it becomes more mature and brings in other constraints, which start to productively contaminate the process, incorporating dynamics of scale and human interaction. As engineer Clayton Binkley, who collaborated with Sabin on earlier projects with Arup, emphasized, "We wanted to achieve the design in a seamless way so that it is not an armature but a shape. [Jenny] has a lexicon with formal components of her work—fiberglass rods, knit cone shapes, nylon webbing tensile networks— and we take steps within that language."[15] Sabin's *Ada* installation embraces an embedded decoration that is threaded through the forms holistically.

Knitting is complex and difficult to control, so working with Microsoft Research, Binkley and Sabin collaborated on *Ada*, named after scientist Ada Lovelace. The project followed in the footsteps of *Lux*, a 2018 project at the Smithsonian Institution that featured fiberglass tubes, and *Lumen*, an installation with hanging knitted tube forms, winner of the 2017 Young Architects MoMA PS1. *Ada*, the next iteration of Sabin's design thinking, was composed of a double-knitted seamless net form in three dimensions made with SHIMA SEIKI circular CNC Wholegarment knitting machines to create hundreds of digitally knit cones and cells as tensile structures. A few years earlier, working with Binkley on tensile stress tests, they realized that the location of holes globally impacts the structures. This followed from the observations of French engineer Robert Le Ricolais, who studied bones and taught at the University of Pennsylvania in the 1950s and 1960s. In bones he found that the strength is in the voids, and the organization of structure lies in where and how to put the holes rather than the structure itself. He also discovered that Radiolaria are perforated membranes working in tension within a framework.[16] This biological structural analysis inspired Sabin, who

realized that placing larger holes in the fabric stiffened it, because of the knots dispersed throughout the net, thereby increasing the performance of the tensegrity structure within its own internal systems.

Binkley's analysis resulted in the manifestation of the inner tensile surface as netting and the outer surface as a diagrid structure with fiberglass rods, similar to those used in earlier projects.[17] The 3D-printed nodes were a way to address the geometry and make a two-way symmetrical form with 150 unique elements. It became a shell structure because the diagrid on the outside is a compression shell, and the tensile surface on the inside hangs from the ring at the top in tension with rings weighting the bottom. The equal and opposite forces working between the exterior semi-rigid exoskeleton, which is formed with 3D-printed components and fiberglass rods in compression, and its structural opposite in the tensile interior, create one form. Suspended in a public atrium space, the installation incorporates integrated AI (Artificial Intelligence) to interact with the viewers through the use of photoluminescent fibers.

In the synthesis of structure and form as deep decoration in linear, exoskeletal, and holistic constructions, space is shaped in an evolving structural theory. Nontraditional structures and environments, which incorporate sustainable and renewable materials—wood, stone, and bamboo, among others—and are inspired by complex natural structures, can contribute to new experiential and responsive space. Buildings and structures react and interact in immersive environments that move beyond the space frames of Konrad Wachsmann and Richard Buckminster Fuller and reengage structural engineers through empathetic and architectonic relationships with an inclusive design approach that expands ideas of decorum for today. The interaction between structural performance, materials, natural forms and decoration can transform our interactions with and relationship to the built environment as we dwell, work, play, gather, and move in a deeply decorated three-dimensional space that renews itself as attentive biological systems, often sublimely.

← IBUKU, Atelier One, The Arc at Green School Bali, Abiansemal, 2021. Photo Tommaso Riva

→ Jenny Sabin Studio, Ada, Redmond, WA (USA), 2019. Courtesy Microsoft Research. Photo Jake Knapp

15   Discussion with Clayton Binkley, 2021.

16   Robert Le Ricolais discussed these concepts in "Structures Implicit and Explicit," *Via*, vol. 2 (1973).

17   Discussion with Clayton Binkley, 2021.

MENIL COLLECTION

Although Piano & Rice Associates had recently disbanded, in 1981 Renzo Piano brought Peter Rice in to work on a design for a primitive and modern art museum in Houston. The request on the part of the commissioner, Dominique de Menil, had one significant design requirement: natural light from above, but not direct. Rice merged this requirement with his desire to experiment with two materials: ferro-cement, borrowed from the shipbuilding industry, and ductile cast iron, more malleable than steel in the casting phase. With the former, 300 25-millimeter-thick white "leaves" were created to filter and diffuse sunlight thanks to their S-shaped section, which allowed for subtle illumination and protection from the sun's heat. The latter is the material used for both the beams that support the "leaves" and the truss beams perpendicular to it. Piano's initial idea to have the sun shading contained within the truss beam was transformed in the final version by Rice's suggestion to separate the two elements, confirmed by their work with prototypes and physical and virtual models.

→ Renzo Piano, Peter Rice and others around the prototype of an element from the Menil Collection, Houston, 1987. Photo David Crossley. Courtesy Fondazione Renzo Piano

1981–1987

ARCHITECT	PIANO & FITZGERALD
	RENZO PIANO
	SHUNJI ISHIDA

ENGINEER	OVE ARUP & PARTNERS
	PETER RICE
	TOM BARKER
	ALISTAIR GUTHRIE
	NEIL NOBEL
	JOHN THORNTON

BROADGATE EXCHANGE HOUSE

LONDON, UNITED KINGDOM

1987–1990

ARCHITECT   BRUCE GRAHAM
SOM

ENGINEER   WILLIAM FRAZIER "BILL" BAKER
SOM

Broadgate Exchange House is the result of a successful synergy of functional needs and engineering solutions, structural expressiveness and architectural sensibility. The office building stands near Liverpool Street station, rising above the tracks in a spot that entailed the challenge of reducing to a minimum points of contact with the ground. The solution was a hybrid between the structures of a ten-story building and a bridge.

Four parallel steel arches overcame the problem of the 78 meters required for the train tracks, allowing the building's structure to be "suspended" and minimizing anchoring points. Two of the four arches are on the façades, highlighting the building's static workings and lending it an iconic look through meticulous attention to construction details.

The arch on the façade clearly highlights the division between the steel columns below, designed to withstand tension, and those above, subject to compressive loading, which require horizontal stiffeners.

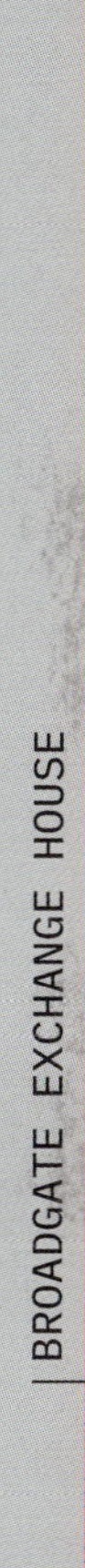

↑ Broadgate Exchange House under construction, London, 1990. Photo John Davies. Courtesy SOM. © John Davies | Davenport Association

BURGO
PAPER MILL

ENGINEERS   PIER LUIGI NERVI
                   MARIO DESIDERI
                   GINO COVRE

The need to contain large-scale paper-making machinery was the basis of the design for Nervi's innovative building, which required a single 250-meter-long space and a 160-meter-long uninterrupted façade to allow for future expansion and additional production equipment.

The design has its roots in the sphere of infrastructures, specifically the suspension bridge. Two massive reinforced concrete frames created by the Nervi e Bartoli firm support cables from which the metal roof designed by Gino Covre is suspended. Each 50-meter-high frame is made up of two Y-shaped pylons connected by a 35.6-meter-long transversal beam. The structural and architectural innovation was made possible by Nervi's years of experience as a builder, via the use of disposable formworks, elements prefabricated on the ground, ribbed slabs and mobile scaffolding.

The real functional block is the long reinforced concrete base, detached from the rest of the structure, which supports the production machinery.

The complex also includes a warehouse with an orthogonal-ribbed slab system patented by Nervi.

← Burgo Paper Mill, Mantua, model, 1964. Courtesy Collezione MAXXI Architettura, Pier Luigi Nervi Archive

THE TWENTIETH-CENTURY ITALIAN SCHOOL OF ENGINEERING: BETWEEN NATURE AND TECHNIQUE

Tullia Iori

In the 1950s and 1960s, Italian engineering garnered international attention with a number of highly original structural works. From World War II through the economic miracle period, there were many opportunities to build: the reconstruction of thousands of bridges destroyed during the conflict, the Autostrada del Sole Milan-Naples highway, the 1960 Rome Olympics, the centennial of the Unification of Italy celebrated in Turin in 1961, hangars for the first international airports, and skyscrapers in Milan and Rome. In this fervent period, a real School of structural engineering took shape, and soon garnered admiration around the world. In fact, the exhibition held in the summer of 1964 at the Museum of Modern Art in New York reserved a place of honor for Italy, generously displaying Pier Luigi Nervi's roofs, Riccardo Morandi's cable-stayed bridges, Silvano Zorzi's prestressed structures, and the gigantic arches of the Autosole highway, as well as the monumental dams Claudio Marcello built using his "hollow gravity" technique.

These feats of "Italian Style" engineering were the culmination of a long period of experimentation that had begun with the advent of reinforced concrete in the early twentieth century and continued uninterrupted through the difficult years of Fascist autarchical prohibitions and the war. The experiments went on without fanfare in the open-air laboratory of postwar reconstruction, and became a torrent in the euphoric boom years. Then, just after the economic miracle, the School suddenly waned. There were several reasons: the national economic crisis, worsened by the international energy crises of the 1970s; the increasing cost of labor after the strikes and protests of Italy's "hot autumn" (1969/70); changes at universities, which decupled the number of matriculants, and in the business world, with a shrinking number of family businesses. An attempt to resist the general homogenization with a series of "posthumous masterpieces" failed; the end was marked by one of the most beautiful bridges in the world, the bridge with the "nameless form" designed by Sergio Musmeci in Potenza. Then the School died out, like the fireflies in Pier Paolo Pasolini's 1975 "corsair writing," and was gradually forgotten, even by historiography. It is true that a few of its leading figures became famous: Nervi is still today one of the best-known structural designers in the world, and Morandi also enjoyed significant international popularity, long before the dramatic collapse of the bridge over the Polcevera river in Genoa in 2018. But the School was a collective adventure that involved two entire generations of scientists, architects, entrepreneurs and builders, and left its valuable heritage throughout Italy.

To bring this story out of the shadows of archives and into the light, the SIXXI research project was launched in 2012, financed by an ERC Advanced Grant and led by Sergio Poretti and Tullia Iori. For a complete bibliography of all the volumes published as the research progressed and a sample of the information available, readers can see the SIXXIdata database, which gathers tens of terabytes of archival documents. Thousands of drawings, calculation reports, letters, cost breakdowns, patents, business indexes, publicity videos, entire libraries, and magnificent construction-site photographs: delving into that "magical library" has made it possible over the past decade to immerse ourselves in the glorious history of twentieh-century Italian engineering, and thus to recognize its originality.[1]

At first glance, Italian structures do not present particularly innovative traits from the scientific or technological points of view. On the contrary, they fit perfectly into well-defined typological categories of modern structures, so at first, they appear familiar: appropriate, with no particularly local or vernacular elements. And yet, in this context, they are also highly recognizable, introducing their own unmistakable tone, and are distinguished by a specific architectural physiognomy. This balanced polarity between orthodoxy and national identity is the truly characterizing trait of the Italian School of engineering—its fingerprint, we might say.

So, as we explored the characteristics of a world-class engineering formulated by a country that was struggling to achieve complete modernity, two contrasting questions guided us through the labyrinth of the past: what foundations formed the basis of the conformity of Italian structures to the international context? And at the same time, what factors in the country's history generated its uniqueness?

Let's start by asking: was it always like this? Has Italian engineering always told a special story? In ancient times, certainly yes, but not in the nineteenth century.

In the nineteenth century, metal construction came to the fore: bridges and roofs in cast iron, and then in wrought iron, and towards the end of the century, steel. This type of construction was extraneous to us; we remained an agricultural land that had been skipped over by the first industrial revolution, with no iron mines and no coal. Compared to the rest of Europe, our iron and steel industry was irrelevant in the nineteenth century.

But in terms of structures, we were orthodox; we did what everyone was doing. Suspension bridges, trusses and reticular arches—types invented abroad, where they mainly served the development of railroads and consequently of industry. We imported them, copied them, built them by the thousands throughout the nineteenth century. But there was no "Italian way" of building suspension bridges (while there was an English way, with chains, and a French way, with wires); Alfredo Cottrau's wrought iron lattice trusses, and Jules Röthlisberger's truss arch bridges, which dotted Italy at the end of the nineteenth century, were repetitions of types that had already been successfully developed elsewhere.

But we did make an original contribution in that period, a theoretical one. It was the Italian approach to developing hyperstatic structures, which we did not yet know how to calculate in the mid-nineteenth century; even a load distributed along a continuous beam with multiple supports generated stress that were still mysterious. Federico Menabrea first and Alberto Castigliano later contributed to

1   This essay, which should have been written by Sergio Poretti (1944–2017) as well, is the result of research carried out within the sphere of the *SIXXI – Twentieth Century Structural Engineering: the Italian Contribution* project, ERC Advanced Grant 2011. For details, see the series of volumes *SIXXI. Storia dell'ingegneria strutturale in Italia*, specifically: *SIXXI 1* (2014), *SIXXI 2* (2015), *SIXXI 3* (2015), *SIXXI 4* (2017), *SIXXI 5* (2020), edited by Tullia Iori and Sergio Poretti and published by Gangemi, and monographic issues of the magazine *Rassegna di architettura e urbanistica*: from *La Scuola italiana di Ingegneria* (no. 148, January-April 2016) to the pioneering *Ingegneria italiana* (no. 121/122, January–August 2007).

solving the problem by proposing an "energy approach." Other theories from German spheres would eventually rise to the fore, but the Italian way was central to debate on the question for quite some time. Menabrea said: "When a system attains equilibrium under external forces, the elastic energy is a minimum." Menabrea presented the principle, and Castigliano demonstrated it scientifically. At the base of it was a philosophical position, a way of viewing reality and the role of the architect. To simplify: the laws of nature are determined by criteria of minimum effort and maximum effect; if we let nature do its work, equilibrium is achieved with minimal effort. Hence, the idea that nature knows how to find the ideal solution on its own and it would be better to let it do so conditioned the Italian School of engineering in one way or another.

With the advent of reinforced concrete, everything changed. The new technique spread rapidly at the start of the twentieth century, partly because we had plenty of cement and the raw materials to make it. Moreover, compared to iron, reinforced concrete was more compatible with the artisanal state of Italian construction. But even in the pioneering phase, bridges with arches cast *in-situ* by patent holders or, after the Great War, by the first builders to be liberated from paying royalties, remained orthodox

with regard to international developments. François Hennebique himself was directly responsible for changing the course of the history of reinforced concrete, overhauling the design for the Risorgimento Bridge which Giovanni Antonio Porcheddu built over the Tiber in Rome; Eugenio Miozzi learned from Eugène Freyssinet how to perfect the "systematic cracking" technique for the bridges of Venice, and openly acknowledged his indebtedness. To begin to recognize characteristics of a specifically Italian identity, we must look to the experimentation of the autarchic period, and then, especially, the postwar period, when the School finally achieved maturity.

Spurred by restrictions on the use of certain materials imposed by Fascist propaganda after Italy became subject to international sanctions for the invasion of Ethiopia (in 1936 reinforced concrete was accused of being not Italian enough, and thus prohibited), experimentation began that would lead to the definitive physiognomy of our structures. The obligation was to save steel, which was reserved for the war industry and which no other country was authorized to sell us. We thus moved in two directions, which were once again common to experimentation taking place around the world, confirming our School's inclusion in the great family of modern engineering.

On one hand, the decision was made to diminish reinforcement, reducing weight and taking advantage of shape-based resistance: we became enthusiastic about thin vaults, which marked an international shift in structures in the mid-1920s, from Dischinger and Finsterwalder's Zeiss-Dywidag planetarium domes and cylindrical thin shells to Eduardo Torroja's hyperboloid canopy roofs and Bernard Lafaille's hypars. On the other, we were early adopters of prestressing, introduced in 1928 by Freyssinet, which led to more efficient use, and thus savings, of the two materials in play, concrete and steel.

In Italy, however, these two lines of thought became veritable ideologies, and their opposition is palpable in texts that sometimes ingenuously sought to support and endorse one over the other. In any case, this sort of virtuous competition is how maturity is achieved.

Two of the interpreters and guides along the way in this process were Arturo Danusso and Gustavo Colonnetti, professors of Theory of Structures at the Polytechnic schools of Milan and Turin, respectively, who influenced the entire School until the boom years (nearly the same age, they died a few months apart in 1968). With a shared passion for reinforced concrete, both were aware that the classical theory of elasticity, developed for iron and hastily adapted to the new material during the pioneering experimentation phases, was absolutely insufficient to justify its behavior.

Colonnetti was certain that it was possible to formulate a new mathematical theory that could predict the true functioning of structures, even beyond the elastic phase: the long-awaited, but never elaborated, "general theory of coactions." This faith in theory and thus in calculation was accompanied by the conviction that engineers must play an active role: in Colonnetti's view, structures had to be "trained" to respond to stress in the best possible way. And this could be done by impressing on bodies forces or coactions, precisely established through calculation and capable of correcting the natural state of equilibrium of the structures themselves. Colonnetti thus urged architects and engineers not to passively wait for a bridge or roof to find its own equilibrium, but to balance, compensate and equilibrate its forces, ensuring more favorable distribution of internal tensions. The most brilliant concrete application of this logic is prestressing: does it not mean, precisely, teaching concrete to resist forces of traction? That is, to do something that by nature it would not be able to do?

Danusso, on the other hand, referring back to Menabrea, maintained that it was not necessary to teach structures how to behave, but rather to allow them to spontaneously adapt to loads, making up for any gaps or design errors in the project. So, he had unconditional faith in the intrinsic resources of works. In Danusso's view, the engineer's job is to observe and interpret nature and facilitate its intervention, so complex and often hyperstatic solutions are good, although very difficult to theoretically predict through calculation. In his articles, he constantly mentioned the host of restrictions that theory must impose in order to reduce ordinary structures to calculation schemes, noting the consequent lack of validity. Skeptical of the possibility of mathematically predicting a structure's response via analytical calculations, he relied on a "stress calculating machine," i.e., a reduced-scale model on which to perform load tests in the laboratory.

← Riccardo Morandi, roof of the Alitalia hangar, Fiumicino, 1961–1964. Photo Sergio Poretti

The model simulated, showed and anticipated the work, and, if correctly stimulated, would deform just like its real full-scale duplicate. In short, the model could come closer to nature than the calculation. Hence, in 1931 he founded a model testing laboratory at the Milan Polytechnic, and later, after the war, the famed ISMES, the Institute for Experimental Models and Structures. (On a parallel track, Colonnetti founded the Center for Study of elastic coaction states in Turin, which oversaw precompressed reinforced concrete constructions authorized in Italy beginning in 1950.) Italian engineers of these generations were all either Danussians, like Nervi and Musmeci, or Colonnettians, like Morandi, Zorzi, and Giulio Krall. But all architects and engineers, including current ones, might ask themselves which side they are on: the side of "going with the flow" of natural behavior (as in form-finding experimentation, and in Mutsuro Sasaki's "Flux Structures") or correcting and enhancing it through technological means (as Santiago Calatrava, Peter Rice and Jürg Conzett, for example, have always done)?

In the postwar period, the two lines of thought, sketched out during the autarchy, gave rise in Italy to a structural engineering that stood apart in the international panorama. Our School was completely different from the Anglo-Saxon one, for example. The underlying reason was that Italian engineering developed in an environment that was literally dominated by humanistic culture and Catholicism, allied in combating the supremacy of the scientific and technological culture that was accompanying modernization in other countries. On the secular side, Benedetto Croce's neo-idealism was utterly hegemonic; there was no other country where a philosopher influenced the totality of cultural development as it did in ours. On the religious side, where Catholicism held sway, the key was the compatibility between faith and science. In this cultural climate, there was no recognition of the autonomy of the scientist, but rather an acknowledgement of the need to bring scientific knowledge under the *aegis* of a superior spiritual truth.

This should not have facilitated the development of engineering; on a path towards modernity, the dominance of philosophical/literary and spiritual views should have been an obstacle. In the modernization of Anglo-Saxon countries, the situation was the diametric opposite: there, positivism was more prevalent than ever. In fact, the scientific approach extended to the humanities and social sciences. Engineers were considered stars, heroes—the builder of bridges was an exemplary model for all other disciplines.

The Italian engineer, however, was constantly subjected to a process of "humanization." The paradoxical thing was that the engineer, rather than defending himself, i.e., defending the autonomy of applied science from the dominion of humanistic culture, became one of the latter's most fervent supporters. Theoreticians were among the most dogged defenders of the superiority of the spiritual view, as we need only read a few lines of their most popular writings to understand. In 1943, Colonnetti wrote: "I think that the Apostle's adage *Adjutores Dei sumus*—we are collaborators with God—applies to scientists and technicians in a very special way. Devoting oneself to science or technology means agreeing to collaborate with God in the fulfilment of a divine design [...]. It means freely accepting a mission in which every activity, in the sphere of thought as well as that of action, in the dominion of ideas as in that of life, must be oriented towards this supreme purpose of collaboration with God for the realization of good; a supreme purpose that is neither weakened nor diminished by the fact that the field in which God wants us to practice is modest and limited." Danusso, for his part, in the celebrated article "Le autotensioni" published in 1934, as well as in successive reworkings, recognized parallelisms between divine justice and the plastic deformation of bridges: "Under the glare of a higher light, the effort of experimentation is ennobled, because it is first and foremost an encounter with nature, considered the great revealer of the harmonies and purposes that God has put in place to govern the world. They should be drawn from fully, profitably studying the material world, which might otherwise seem arid [...]. In particular, in constructions elastic deformability tends to distribute strains in harmony with resistant tendencies; and when in spite of that the strains in certain parts worsen, corrective plasticity comes into play to improve the situation [...]. So, the construction behaves like an orderly society, which is based on the distributive, integrated and perfect justness of charity."

In addition to its impact on theoreticians, humanistic culture also influenced engineers who designed large structures, who

more secularly set above all else any mystical sort of understanding of correctness. It is no wonder that in this context, Nervi entitled his first article in the first 1947 issue of the magazine *Strutture* "Corretto costruire" [Correct construction], accompanying it with a conceptual map in which social values, human values, art, science and technology merged, and later gave a nearly identical title to his 1955 book *Costruire correttamente* [Constructing correctly]. The principle of the "structural minimum," which had always been present in the engineer's experimentation, goes beyond the specialistic bounds of science to take on a universally ethical value.

In the end, what practical consequences did the humanistic propensity have on the characteristics of built works? What differentiated the Italian School was above all their pronounced architectural value, and the consequences of the cultural climate are easily identified in the languages of these structures. The Italian "humanist" engineers were, first and foremost, history lovers. The dogma of modernity that imposes a break with the past did not prosper in our country. Nervi, like many of his colleagues, looked at the monuments of antiquity with sincere admiration. He thoroughly studied and consulted on the stabilization of the cupola of Santa Maria del Fiore in Florence, auscultating its increasingly labored breathing as a doctor would a patient's lungs. He had a true sense of devotion with regard to the artifices of grand cupolas, in masonry or concrete. After all, isn't his Palazzetto dello Sport a Pantheon in reinforced concrete, as Bruno Zevi defined it? The "Nervi system"—a means of construction based on ferrocement and structural prefabrication, with a large wooden model and a sequence of "grandmother, mother, daughter" matrixes thanks to which workers, beneath a covered loggia, molded small pieces to be put together like a gigantic three-dimensional puzzle—seems a direct imitation of the worksite of a Gothic cathedral. (We know from his grandchildren that Nervi kept Jean Gimpel's book *The Cathedral Builders* on his nightstand for a long time.) His nostalgia for the pre-scientific era when architecture and engineering were not yet distinct and separate from one another was shared by all of his colleagues.

And that was not all: the engineers of the boom years were trained in art and were particularly sensitive to avant-garde movements like Futurism. Futurism fed on engineering: it was based on positivism, scientism and technolatry. Antonio Sant'Elia's drawing are filled with endless skyscrapers, hovering streets and dams filled with energy. What engineering absorbed from Futurism, for its part, was a certain lyricism and visionary tendency. These themes are evident in Morandi, for example, who was an early Colonnettian: he was capable of stabilizing his bridges by adding strength in the form of tie rods or cables; compensating for thrust by using struts that constantly refuse vertical direction; setting up worksites where temporary prestressing brought about beneficial alterations in the functioning of entire pieces of the structure, which only reached their final positions after significant turning. Morandi even declared himself a Futurist in terms of his designs, with their very high antennas that seems to rival airplanes in perspective images. But above all, his works, with their jointed, hinged elements, look like automatons ready to spring forward with Boccionian velocity. Thus, the underground pavilion in Turin for Italia '61 seemed the perfect setting for an aerodance.

Coming out of the war and heading towards the miracle of the boom years, Italian engineers were in perfect harmony with the world of design. They designed structure as if they were landscape-scale pieces of furniture. The elective affinity with this sector of architectural culture was largely due to the co-habitation between engineers and designers in Swiss university internment camps, during the World War II exile of many Northern Italian students and young professors in Lausanne, in particular Colonnetti and his favorite apprentice Silvano Zorzi. Zorzi, a very young major player in the reconstruction and the boom years, was one of the few who tried to stop the decline during the crisis. He did so by transforming work sites, without capitulating to prefabrication. He invented, and imported from other worlds, machines with futuristic names: "self-launching formwork" or "little by little" balanced system allowed him to continue to shape his made-to-measure bridges, using an elegant, minimalist approach not unlike that of the great names in fashion. The affinity with design was also in part based on an "anthropological" resemblance; after all, a bridge is an object for everyday use, like a lamp, a bookcase, a bicycle or a coffee pot. And a bridge is much more similar to a table than to a house.

History, art, design: these were the foundations of postwar Italian engineering. But in all honesty, it was not just the different humanistic climate that distinguished our structures in the international panorama. The Italian School also sprang from particularities with the production system that were lost when the crisis hit. In fact, the history of modern construction followed a unique path in Italy in the twentieth century. While industrialization was sweeping the rest of the world, Italy tiptoed quietly into modernity, without violent breaks with the past, and without industrial revolutions. It was a slow modernization, and the country seems frozen, suspended in a sort of chronic "protoindustrialization" for quite some time.

What were the repercussions of this for construction, and in particular the construction of large structures? In lagging yet successful Italy, the construction sector, in every phase of the period, had a specific task: to deal with unemployment. That meant that technical progress was slowed and at certain moments completely blocked. The construction site was the junction in the passage of manual labor from agriculture to industry. Hence, highway construction sites, which included hundreds of bridges, were filled not with equipment, but with men: they revolved around the worker and his potential to build "by hand" enormous artisanal objects, unique sculptures in the landscape. Philosophical humanism was thus joined by humanism in practice. This artisanal character, which favored unique, unrepeatable works, was the first to suffer the effects of the crisis: when the workers realized they had not enjoyed the benefits of the boom as others had, when they understood that these works were the fruit of their laboring without guarantees, without disability insurance, without vacation days, without a pension and without overtime, they began to go on strike. They demanded their sacrosanct rights, which would be recognized by the Workers' Statute of 1970, but which effectively led to the depopulation of work sites, and to the drastic reduction in manual labor, replaced by machines and above all by the use of conventional prefabrication. This was what led to the sudden disappearance of the reinforced concrete arch, unquestionably a mainstay of the Autosole highway, but built with Innocenti tube scaffolding, which had to be assembled solely by hand, by acrobatic workers. Its place was taken by bridges with extremely tall pilings and rectilinear trusses, which can be put up without propping up with Zorzi's timid machines, or with beams, all exactly the same, produced in the workshop. And so, the smaller firms, those that could handle only one worksite at a time, and not too far from their operational center, succumbed to the crisis and were swallowed up by larger enterprises that no longer had names, but that had internal technical offices and were more inclined to invest in the means required to win tenders than in technological innovation and dedicated design professionals.

Another effect of the "humanism" that imbued Italian engineering in the boom years was the development of the figure of the designer of large structures, the creator. He was a multifaceted figure who opposed specialization in the field, personally combating it on various fronts. He was more than just a hybrid engineer-architect or architect-engineer.

↓ Silvano Zorzi, Teccio viaduct for the highway Torino-Savona, 1973–1976. Photo Sergio Poretti

→ Sergio Musmeci, ceiling of the San Carlo church, Vicenza, 1959. Photo Sergio Poretti

This traditional interdisciplinarity was enhanced by another, special sort of flexibility: the capacity nimbly alternate between high culture and material culture, between theory and practice, between research and handiness, between laboratory and building site. A visionary figure, he vanished along with the fireflies when Italian universities were transformed from elite to mass institutions and the decision was made to teach the crowded classes only calculation rules and methods, omitting the element of innovative conception.

Exemplary creator-engineers of their time, a time of change during the short century, were Nervi, Morandi and Zorzi. And Musmeci, who died too young to see the era when his visions would come to fruition. At the beginning of the 1970s, he wrote that he wished for the advent of the computer to help him not in the banal phase of calculation verification, but in the truly useful one of conception: in his imagination, he skipped over an entire generation of software to arrive directly at the most recent genetic optimization algorithms in the sphere of artificial intelligence. And in practice, his bridge of the Basento anticipated by decades the form-finding engineering and parametric engineering of the new millennium. Musmeci predicted a new era—ours—in which engineering, like architecture, has lost its strictly functional role, but is instead called upon to amaze, to attract attention with new, complex forms that are repeatable yet astounding. The rigorous principles of maximum economy typical of engineers of previous generations, assimilated directly from Gothic construction sites, were replaced by new principles much closer to those of Baroque construction. Musmeci was the element of transition in this process: with his exceptional mathematical-scientific abilities and his pursuit of optimized but certainly not economic forms—which were in fact intended to astound—he embodied the transition towards "Pop Structure" engineering, the engineering of Instagram.

This congenital impurity of influences sheds light on another characteristic of the Italian-born structural idiom that may be the most distinctive of all: its historical weightiness. Rarely have works of engineering, as opposed to architectural idioms, demonstrated such a capacity to reflect their historical context. Structural language usually limits itself to saying something about the universal value of scientific progress. But in this sense, the structural architectures created by Nervi, Morandi, Zorzi, Musmeci and the others constitute a striking exception. Their strict adherence to the tenet of sincerity notwithstanding, they also tell us a great deal about some sensational vicissitudes of Italy's singular modernization phase (especially in terms of the ways in which they were built). For this reason alone, engineering structures should hold a place of honor in a museum of all things Made in Italy, in the grand showcase of "Italian Style" products, alongside objects by the most famous industrial designers and clothing by our most sophisticated fashion designers.

TURIN: AN ENGINEERING CITY

Cristiana Chiorino
and Mario Alberto Chiorino

INTRODUCTION

The Turin school's contribution to scientific and technological advancements in the field of structural engineering between the eighteenth and twentieth centuries can with good reason be called extraordinary. Fundamental contributors to the great successes of Savoy construction engineering were theoreticians like Joseph-Louis Lagrange, who in the mid-eighteenth century established the analytical bases of modern mechanics as a whole, and the equally sophisticated mathematical models of Vito Volterra, who in the early twentieth century further developed some of its features. But extraordinarily important contributions also came from other figures who left their mark on the history of Piedmontese structural mechanics, like Federico Menabrea and Alberto Castigliano in the nineteenth century,[1] and Gustavo Colonnetti and Franco Levi in the twentieth. They were responsible for the development of instruments for analytical interpretation and the establishment of criteria for testing construction processes and techniques like steel construction, reinforced concrete and, later, pre-stressed concrete.

Some of the most important works built in this historical period embody the results of advancements in knowledge and express a constructive art and acumen that was often far ahead of the theoretical framing of their underlying structural mechanisms and construction techniques.

The distinguishing characteristic of the Piedmontese structural engineering development process from the Enlightenment on is that it

1   Danilo Capecchi, Giuseppe Rupa, eds., *La scienza delle costruzioni in Italia nell'Ottocento. Un'analisi storica dei fondamenti della scienza delle costruzioni* (Milan: Springer, 2011).

2   Richard Pommer, *Architettura del Settecento in Piedmont. Le strutture aperte di Juvarra, Alfieri e Vittone*, translation and new expanded and updated Italian edition by Giuseppe Dardanello (Turin: Allemandi, 2003).

3   Giuseppe Dardanello, ed., *Giovanni Battista Borra da Palmira a Racconigi* (Turin: Editris Duemila, 2013).

4   Thomas Le Seur, François Jacquier, and Ruggiero Giuseppe Boscovich, *Parere di tre mattematici sopra i danni, che si sono trovati nella cupola di S. Pietro sul fine dell'anno 1742. Dato per ordine di nostro signore Papa Benedetto XIV* (Rome: 1742).

5   Giovanni Poleni, *Memorie istoriche della gran cupola del tempio vaticano, e de' danni di essa, e de' ristoramenti loro, divise in libri cinque. Alla santità di nostro signore papa Benedetto XIV* (Padua: Stamperia del Seminario, 1748).

unfolded amid early elaborations of absolutely groundbreaking mathematical theories and analytical models that later became particularly fruitful interpretative instruments for structural applications, or, vice versa, amid precocious, pioneering constructions of extraordinary vitality, true cornerstones in the history of construction techniques that incentivized successive theoretical systemization.

THE SCIENCE AND ART OF BUILDING IN SEVENTEENTH AND EIGHTEENTH-CENTURY PIEDMONT

In Piedmont, at the dawn of the Enlightenment, the extraordinary artfulness found in seventeenth and eighteenth-century Baroque architecture, frequently distinguished by configurations of significant static-structural ambition, did not seem to be accompanied by an adequate codification of technical-scientific knowledge of modeling and mechanical interpretation of those constructions. Nor were there any noteworthy contributions to the debate on these questions, which, particularly after Leonardo and Galileo, the scientific world had begun to contemplate with increasing fervor.

L'Architettura civile by Guarino Guarini, published posthumously by Bernardo Vittone in Turin in 1737, contains sophisticated, elegant geometric constructions, but provides no useful instructions on the configuration of mechanical-structural problems, particularly with regard to vaults and cupolas, static figures that the author had taken on with extraordinary results.[2] The same can be said of Vittone's contribution on the same matters: in his *Istruzioni elementari per indirizzo de' giovani allo studio dell'architettura civile* (Lugano, 1760) he merely reprised and examined the empirical dimensional rules of a geometric nature, linked mainly to maintaining harmony and proportions among parts, already dictated by Carlo Fontana at the end of the previous century.

But even when treatises were more attentive to elements more strictly concerned with construction and the resistance of materials, as in the case not only of Vittone but especially of Giovanni Battista Borra who used an extensive mathematical apparatus in his *Trattato della cognizione pratica delle resistenze geometricamente dimostrato* published in Turin in 1748, the contribution to scientific advancement was meager or inexistent.[3] In particular, there was no echo of the debate on the mechanical interpretation of vaults, and especially cupolas, triggered in the 1740s by concern regarding the stability of the great cupola of Saint Peter's and the need to repair it. A debate in which the three principal protagonists were the "Tre Mattematici" [Three Mathematicians] Tommaso Le Seur, Francesco Jacquier and Ruggero Giuseppe Boscovich, with their 1742 treatise,[4] and the Marquis Giovanni Poleni, the actual architect, along with Vanvitelli, of the consolidation intervention using tension hoops, with his 1748 treatise.[5]

In light of this absence of Piedmontese participants in the scientific debate on the beginnings of a rational approach to the structural problem, the daring and construction knowledge of the great Piedmontese architects seems all the more surprising. One emblematic case in point was the conception and 1732 construction by Francesco Gallo of the audacious elliptical cupola for the Sanctuary of Vicoforte, envisioned in the late sixteenth century by Ascanio Vitozzi as a grandiose Savoy mausoleum and then left for many years an incomplete cathedral in the desert. The cupola, despite stability problems like those of St. Peter's, is still today the larges elliptical cupola in the world.[6]

LAGRANGE AND ANALYTICAL MECHANICS

While the art of building, with a combination of empiricism and intuition of the mechanical phenomena that regulate the responsiveness of constructions, allowed for the creation of extraordinary, bold structures between the seventeenth and mid-eighteenth centuries in Piedmont, the new century of enlightenment also saw a blossoming in Turin scientific and academic spheres of theoretical schools of thought dedicated to the mathematical interpretation of statics problems.

The major figure to whom we owe this scientific revolution in Piedmont is Joseph-Louis Lagrange.[7] His *Mécanique analytique,* published in Paris in 1788 but conceived in an earlier period he spent in Berlin, is the crowning achievement of all eighteenth-century efforts geared towards developing an organized and unified corpus on the dominion of mechanics. Lagrange's fundamental tool was the calculation of variations, the branch of mathematical analysis that deals with determining maximums and minimums of variable quantities, presented in the form of functionals. The new unifying principle underlying *Mécanique analytique* was the more general and fertile principle of virtual work. This principle, to which Lagrange normally referred as "principe des vitesses virtuelles," had already had a few earlier formulations, as has been documented: for example, a quite general, although in some ways not yet completely perfect one was found in the famous 1717 letter from Johann I Bernoulli to Pierre Varignon. But all of the grand importance that Lagrange attributes to it was by no means grasped or even vaguely intuited. The systemic application of the principle of virtual work to the more limited field of statics opened the door to a new way of approaching this discipline, which underlies modern structural mechanics.

All of the power and applicatory fertility of the principle of virtual work concerning questions of structural mechanics would be demonstrated only later, particularly in conjunction with the study of deformable bodies and the development of the mathematical theory of elasticity, of which it would become the fundamental operative tool. This theory, the early foundations of which date back to earlier authors like Robert Hooke and Edme Mariotte and to which Leonhard Euler (better known as Eulero) and Lagrange

↓ Annibale and Giorgio Rigotti, New Exhibition Palace under construction, 1956–1961, Turin. Archivio Impresa Guerrini

6   VV. AA. , "Modeling Strategies for the World's Largest Elliptical Dome at Vicoforte," *International Journal of Architectural Heritage. Conservation, Analysis, and Restoration* 2, no. 3 (July–September 2008): 274–303.

7   Mario Alberto Chiorino, "La Meccanica strutturale da Lagrange a oggi: il contributo della scuola torinese," in *Lagrange matematico europeo. Atti del Convegno di studi, Accademia delle scienze, Comando per la formazione e Scuola di applicazione dell'esercito, 14–15 novembre 2013*, ed. Livia Giacardi (Turin: Centro Studi Piemontesi, 2014).

both contributed themselves, would be developed in all its complexity in the following years with the fundamental contribution of some of Lagrange's students at the École polytechnique, including Siméon-Denis Poisson and especially Augustin Cauchy.

This process led from theoretical bases to practical developments in engineering science through the progressive systematization of the theory of elasticity and its applications to various structural forms, to an initial recognition of the theory's limitations and reflections on material fatigue under repeated loading, and finally to the analysis of technical issues typical of construction engineering such as earth pressures on walls.

Lagrange's role in the promotion of science in Piedmont cannot be overestimated, in particular in the 1757 founding of the Società Privata Torinese, which in 1783 became the Reale Accademia delle Scienze [Royal Academy of Sciences]. Lagrange was certainly the main driving force of this institution, particularly in its early period, even after his 1766 transfer to the Academy of Berlin and 1787 move to the Académie royale des sciences in Paris.

The group of French scholars that was among the foreign members of the Turin Academy between the 1830s and 1850s played a central role in the development of the new science of materials and construction. Their research led to the development of tools and models for modern structural analysis, particularly regarding the development of the mathematical and technical theory of elasticity.

Lagrange's efforts brought various members into the Turin Academy from the outset, including Eulero, Jean-Baptiste Le Rond d'Alembert, Marie-Jean-Antoine-Nicolas de Caritat de Condorcet, Pierre-Simon de Laplace, Gaspard Monge, and Charles Bossut.

THE DEVELOPMENT OF ENGINEERING SCIENCE

The "science of engineers" began to develop in Piedmont in the first decades of the nineteenth century and gained vitality in the second half of the century in constant contact with the French sphere, in parallel with major transformations of cities and the surrounding territory and important associated construction efforts. The fact that in Piedmont in particular, technical and scientific progress looked often and attentively at cultural and development models from more advanced European countries—particularly, but not only, France—does not seem to have been a limitation, either. In fact, the expressly pursued understanding of those models is proof of the strong Europe-wide integration within which that progress moved forward.

For example, we can consider the Parisian education and training of figures like Carlo Bernardo Mosca (from 1809 to 1812; Mosca, as we will see, played a part in our story), and of prestigious mathematicians and physicists like Giovanni Plana (1800 to 1803) and Francesco Faà di Bruno (who studied with Cauchy for many years until he obtained his doctorate and was in Paris in 1849–51 and 1854–56), and the scientist and politician Quintino Sella (1847 to 1850), who would play a fundamental role in the creation of training institutions for engineers in Turin and Milan that eventually developed into modern polytechnical schools, taking celebrated French schools as models. Piedmontese culture's strong ties with France also brought about the sojourn in Turin of Cauchy, who in 1832 and 1833 held the post of "sublime Physicist" at the University of Turin.[8]

Within this scenario, periods of study abroad were undertaken by a few important figures from the Piedmont political and intellectual sphere (in particular Des Ambrois, and Menabrea) with the dynasty's financial support (Carlo Alberto initially and later Vittorio Emanuele II): Mosca's 1834–35 journey to France to study construction techniques for suspension bridges, railways and related works; the Belgian sojourn from 1846 to 1848 of Germain Sommeiller and Sebastiano Grandis, future creators of the Frejus tunnel along with Severino Grattoni; Sella's 1851–52 trip to see mines in various European countries; and Alessandro Mazzucchetti's 1853 journey to France to study its great railway stations.

Thus, Mosca's 1822 re-proposal for the Dora River of the innovative *arche tendue* stone bridge, conceived in 1788 by Jean-Rodolphe Perronet to cross the Seine at Melun but never built, became the occasion for the creation of an extraordinary work in Turin.

In 1859, mainly on the initiative of Quintino Sella, the establishment of the Regia Scuola di Applicazione degli Ingegneri [Royal School of Engineering Applications] in Turin, modeled on the école polythecnique and other French superior technical training institutions, was an important step in this process, as young Piedmontese talents no longer had to go to Paris to study.

MOSCA'S BRIDGE, PART OF THE HISTORY OF CONSTRUCTION SCIENCE

Carlo Bernardo Mosca, a brilliant and ingenious young man from Biella, spent time in Paris during the period of Napoleonic annexation of Piedmont to France, studying first at the École polytechnique and then at the École des ponts et chaussées.

The former school, established during the revolutionary period, was intended to provide the scientific foundations, particularly in physics and mathematics, to deal with typical engineering design issues at the latter school (which was older, founded by Jean-Rodolphe Perronet in 1747).

In his last designs, Perronet had begun to introduce two very innovative technical developments: the substitution of the traditional profile of the *anse de panier* arch (i.e., one that follows a polycentric curve) with a circular arch that was significantly lowered with respect to the flood level, and the creation of a vault with stone blocks cut perfectly and fit together practically without mortar. Initially adopted for a small-span bridge in Nemours (completed by Louis-Charles Boistard in 1805), these innovations constituted the essence of the design Perronet proposed for the Melun bridge. It was a single, 49-meter-span arch with a span/deflection ratio of 10.3:1.

Back in Turin, in 1823 Mosca proposed a design for a bridge over the Dora Riparia that was very much inspired by the Melun bridge. In this case as well, it was a single, constant-radius arch with a span initially planned as 50 meters, but reduced to 45 by the project's approvers, and with

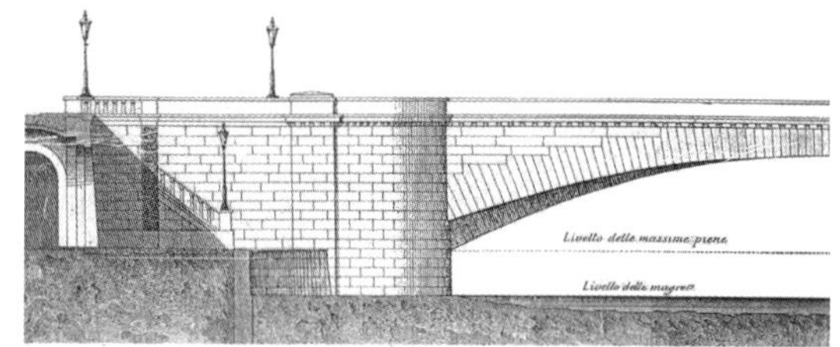

↑ Mosca bridge, in Giovanni Angelo Reyoned, *Il Ponte Mosca sulla Dora Riparia presso Torino ed il Murazzo del nuovo Corso Napoli* (Turin: Tip. e Lit. Camilla e Bertolero, 1880)

8 For further discussion see: Alessandro Terracini, "Cauchy a Torino," *Rendiconti del Seminario Matematico dell'Università e del Politecnico di Torino*, 16 (1956–1957): 159–203 and "Postilla su 'Cauchy a Torino'," *Rendiconti del Seminario Matematico dell'Università e del Politecnico di Torino*, 17 (1957–1958): 81–82. See also: Clara Silvia Roero, ed., *La Facoltà di Scienze Matematiche Fisiche Naturali di Torino 1848–1998*, IX, X (Turin: Deputazione subalpina di storia patria, 1999).

a span/deflection ratio of 8.2:1. The new bridge, linked with Rue d'Italie as it headed out of the city towards Milan, was intended to be a prestige work for the reborn Savoy state.

Mosca's ingenious intuition lay in the fact that in order to re-center the thrust line upon removal of the shoring, he inserted cuneiform mortar connectors into the springer and keystone areas, oriented so as to increase the compressibility of the springer stones at the intrados and keystones at the extrados. The rapid removal of shoring when the mortar was still deformable, which Mosca decided to carry out in the face of understandable diffidence, actually augmented the effect.

The Turin bridge, which long stood as an unsurpassed example of constructive audacity, also became the object of repeated studies and analyses by illustrious specialists in structural mechanics, starting with Castigliano, who took Mosca's bridge as one of the structures to which to apply his own theorem.

TWO GLORIOUS THEOREMS OF STRUCTURAL MECHANICS

The second half of the nineteenth century was the heyday of Piedmontese contributions to the history of the development of structural mechanics.

The figures involved were the Piedmont natives Luigi Federico Menabrea and Alberto Castigliano. These two scholars were responsible for the development of two of the three most celebrated theorems of the nascent theory of elasticity, which marked fundamental stages in the progress of structural mechanics, and their importance was immediately recognized internationally.

A modern reading of Menabrea and Castigliano's contributions to the theory of the elasticity of structures necessarily led to the framing of the theorem of least work (Menabrea) and the theorem on derivatives of strain energy (Castigliano) within the sphere of variational methods initially conceived by Lagrange. However, we must acknowledge that this now-consolidated approach—which allows us to trace a fascinating line of direct continuity between Lagrange's conceptual and methodological innovation and the formulations devised by Menabrea and Castigliano a century later—was substantially absent from the work of the latter two.

One of the most interesting applications of Castigliano's theorem concerns the elastic analysis of Mosca's bridge. The mortar blocks Mosca inserted into the springer and keystone areas of the arch to obtain a recentering of the thrust line, taking advantage of their high level of initial deformability at the moment of rapid removal of the shoring, were simulated by Castigliano with elements that had a lesser modulus of elasticity than stone blocks.

→ Camillo Guidi, *Lezioni sulla Scienza delle Costruzioni* (Turin: Vincenzo Bona, 1929)

→ Gustavo Colonnetti, *Scienza delle Costruzioni* (Turin: Einaudi, 1957)

MATHEMATICAL FOUNDATIONS OF NEW STRUCTURAL PROBLEMS – VOLTERRA AND SOMIGLIANA: HEREDITY AND DISTORTIONS

In the introduction, we acknowledged that the Turin school's contribution to the progress of structural mechanics was marked as much by phases in which the search for instruments to interpret pioneering construction techniques that still lacked theoretical systematization prevailed as by phases in which early mathematical elaborations began to bud, later proving to be particularly fruitful means of interpreting and resolving structural problems eventually dealt with using new techniques.

Two illustrious Italian mathematicians working in Turin in the nineteenth and twentieth centuries, Vito Volterra and Carlo Somigliana,[9] certainly pertained to this second category. Volterra, one of the greatest mathematicians in the world at that time, was an instructor of rational mechanics and advanced mechanics at the University of Turin from 1893 to 1900, then went to the University of Rome to become the chair of Mathematical physics. Somigliana was a professor of Mathematical physics in Pavia initially and then, from 1903, in Turin, where he remained until his retirement in 1935.

Volterra's best-known contribution, developed during his years in Turin, concerned functional calculus and its use in the study of hereditary phenomena, with the organic formulation of the theory of heredity associated with his name.[10] It became the basis for modern structural analysis in the field of viscoelasticity for aging materials like concrete. Castigliano had already taken into consideration stress states originating in the absence of external forces. In particular, he had examined the case of stress states induced in reticular structures by inserting additional rods of a length that did not correspond exactly to the distance between the nodes they connected and were thus subject to strain.

The study of such conditions of applied stress, for which Gustavo Colonnetti later coined the term "states of coaction," was systematically picked up by Volterra in the early twentieth century, taking cues from an idea originally expressed by the German mathematician Julius Weingarten. One particularly important result Volterra achieved in this sphere was a theorem of reciprocity between two systems of distortions and the corresponding systems of stress.[11] A generalization of Volterra's approach was proposed by Somigliana, who suggested extending the concept and the term distortion to all states of elastic equilibrium that are established in the absence of external forces, regardless of the degree of connection of the solid, and that can be considered to have been generated via a completely arbitrary path (in terms of form and position) cut through it, and imposing relatively small displacements on the two faces.

9 On both figures' contributions in the specific sector of mathematics see: C.S. Roero, *La Facoltà di Scienze Matematiche Fisiche Naturali di Torino 1848–1998*, and Vito Volterra, "Sulle equazioni integro-differenziali della teoria dell'elasticità," *Rendiconti Accademia Nazionale dei Lincei*, s. 5, 18 (II semester 1909): 295–301.

10 Volterra, *Sulle equazioni integro-differenziali della teoria dell'elasticità*.

11 Vito Volterra "Sur l'équilibre des corps élastiques multiplement connexes," *Annales scientifiques de l'École Normale Supérieure* 24 (1907): 401–517.

THE CONSOLIDATION OF CLASSICAL THEORY AND THE DAWN OF REINFORCED CONCRETE

As we have seen, at the turn of the nineteenth/twentieth century, in the sphere of mathematics the theoretical roots of what would become the new structural mechanics were being planted and embryonic interpretative models that would prove useful for the revolutionary construction techniques of the next few decades were being formed. At the same time, schools of engineering, and in particular of construction science, were experiencing a period of consolidation.

On the threshold of a new century, this approach to engineering science was suddenly confronted with an extraordinary technical innovation in the art of construction: reinforced concrete.
Turin was fully immersed in the successes and the contradictions of this epoch, shifting between the enthusiasm and innovative upheavals of the technical sector and the objective need in the scientific sphere for an assimilation of the extraordinary conceptual baggage of the "theory of elastic systems" —to use Castigliano's definition—to which the Turin school had already contributed significantly.
Thus reinforced concrete developed in Turin amid intense experimental curiosity and prudent theoretical framing.

A central figure in this complex period was Camillo Guidi. With a solid theoretical and experimental background developed in close contact with the major European research centers, Guidi wrote, in his *Lezioni sulla Scienza delle Costruzioni*, published in several successive editions in the first decades of the twentieth century, what Colonnetti would deem a masterful summary of the contributions of various European schools to the theory of elasticity.
Guidi and his school, the most distinguished figures of which were Modesto Panetti and Arturo Danusso, also had the merit of focusing on experimental aspects and on the codification of construction standards, and above all, particularly after the tragic 1908 Messina earthquake, of giving the first significant attention to questions of the dynamic response and anti-seismic safety of buildings.

GUSTAVO COLONNETTI AND HIS SCHOOL: CONTRIBUTIONS TO CURRENT STRUCTURAL MECHANICS AND INTERNATIONAL ROLE

With Gustavo Colonnetti and his students, the Turin school of structural mechanics became a central presence in the international development of contemporary structural mechanics, and in the worldwide debate on the transfer of both theoretical and experimental knowledge acquired in the scientific sphere to technical guidelines and the codification of standards for construction, in particular the structure of reinforced and prestressed concrete.[12]

Colonnetti's most important contributions concern:[13] Definitive clarification of Menabrea's theorem through a variational type of procedure, once again representative of Lagrange's innovative approach to theoretical mechanics; the second principle of reciprocity, which asserts the existence of reciprocity between the system of internal stresses produced by a given external load and the system of movements determined in the elastic body by a given distortion of Volterra or Somigliana; his generalization to states of tension induced by given distortions that were anything but ordinary, and the connected definition of the state of elastic coaction; the generalization of the concept of elastic coaction and the clarification of the theorem of least work regarding deformation in the presence of imposed deformations; elasto-plastic equilibrium and phenomena of adaptation in solids and structures; the theoretical foundations of the new prestressed reinforced concrete construction technique, which was developing towards the end of the first half of the twentieth century.

Colonnetti's student Franco Levi and his research group earned the merit of having continued his legacy, in terms of innovations and international standard-building.[14] Under Levi's guidance, the Turin school made a name for itself worldwide[15] thanks to contributions to numerous questions that have been the focus of international debate in recent years, including—to name just the main—onesprobabilistic formulation of safety, scalable non-linear boundary analysis as an alternative to excessively schematic theoretical approaches based on general theorems of plasticity, fracture mechanics and the theoretic bases and operational procedures for the analysis of structural response to the deferred deformability of concrete based on Volterra's hereditary integral expression.[16]

All of the history reported here indicates that the contribution of the Turin school to the advancement of scientific and technological culture in the field of structural mechanics over the two centuries from Lagrange to today can, with good reason, be defined as extraordinary.

12 Franco Levi, Mario Alberto Chiorino, "Concrete in Italy. A review of a century of concrete progress in Italy, Part 2: Contribution to a modern theory of structural concrete and to international codification," *Concrete International* 26, no. 10 (October 2004): 38–43; Mario Alberto Chiorino, ed., *Moderni orientamenti di ingegneria strutturale e geotecnica. Omaggio a Franco Levi nel 90° compleanno* (Milan: FrancoAngeli, 2006); Franco Levi, *Ibid.*, 13–20.

13 Mario Alberto Chiorino, *Testimonianze su Gustavo Colonnetti – Pubblicazioni Scientifiche e Altri Scritti* (Occhieppo Superiore: Ecomuseo Valle Elvo e Serra, 2000).

14 VV.AA., *In ricordo di Franco Levi, Docente, ricercatore, code maker, progettista* (Turin: Politecnico di Torino, 2010), 72 pp.

15 Franco Levi's authoritativeness on the international scene is evidenced by the exceptional duration of his presidency of the two standard-setting bodies at the European and international levels for structures in reinforced and prestressed concrete, respectively: the CEB – Comité Européen du Béton (1957–1968) and the FIP – Fédération internationale de la précontrainte (1966–70). The international notoriety of Levi and his school were further confirmed by the Honorary Membership in the American Concrete Institute awarded to him in 1965, and to the author of these notes in 2014.

 An important role Franco Levi played during his long presidency of the CEB was that of promoter, at the start of the second half of the twentieh century, of a fruitful dialogue and debate between the western structural concrete scientific community on one hand, and on the other, the most advanced scientific bodies in that sphere in Easter Europe and the Soviet Union. The advanced research carried out in those environments—an eminent figure of reference of which, among others, was the Russian scientist Alexei A. Gvozdev—were in fact leading to the development of innovative formats that could be incorporated into international calculation standards and technical guidelines then being drawn up for the testing of limit-state reinforced concrete constructions and their long-term behavior taking into account the hereditary viscoelastic behavior of concrete itself.

↓ Gustavo Colonnetti in his library in Pollone, 1966. Archivio Privato Margherita Colonnetti

MASP – MUSEU DE ARTE DE SÃO PAULO

Designed in 1957 and built between 1960 and 1968, the MASP is a lucid expression of a design limitation transformed into a strength. Lina Bo Bardi was asked to design a museum that would not block the panoramic view from the Terraço do Trianon over Avenida Paulista. The solution was simple and clear: a partly raised, partly sunken structure that freed up the street level for a granite plaza, with two pools of water at the feet of two coupled red, exposed prestressed reinforced concrete "bridges": structural expressionism and a graphic element at the same time. The lower part is made up of three levels, while the upper part, 8 m off the ground, has two floors and a completely glassed-in façade. The suspended "box" structure is more complex than it seems from the outside, hiding a second pair of hollow beams—the same section, 2.5x3.5 m, and span of 74 m—that traverse the first floor. As he could not use the Freyssinet cable anchorage system, José Carlos de Figueiredo Ferraz developed and patented a specific prestressing system, the "Ferraz system."

→ MASP – Museu de Arte de São Paulo under construction, São Paulo, 1968. Photo Hans Gunther Flieg. Courtesy Hans Gunter Flieg, Instituto Moreira Salles Collection

	SÃO PAULO, BRAZIL
	1957–1968
ARCHITECT	LINA BO BARDI
ENGINEER	JOSÉ CARLOS DE FIGUEIREDO FERRAZ

MAM – MUSEU DE ARTE MODERNA DO RIO DE JANEIRO

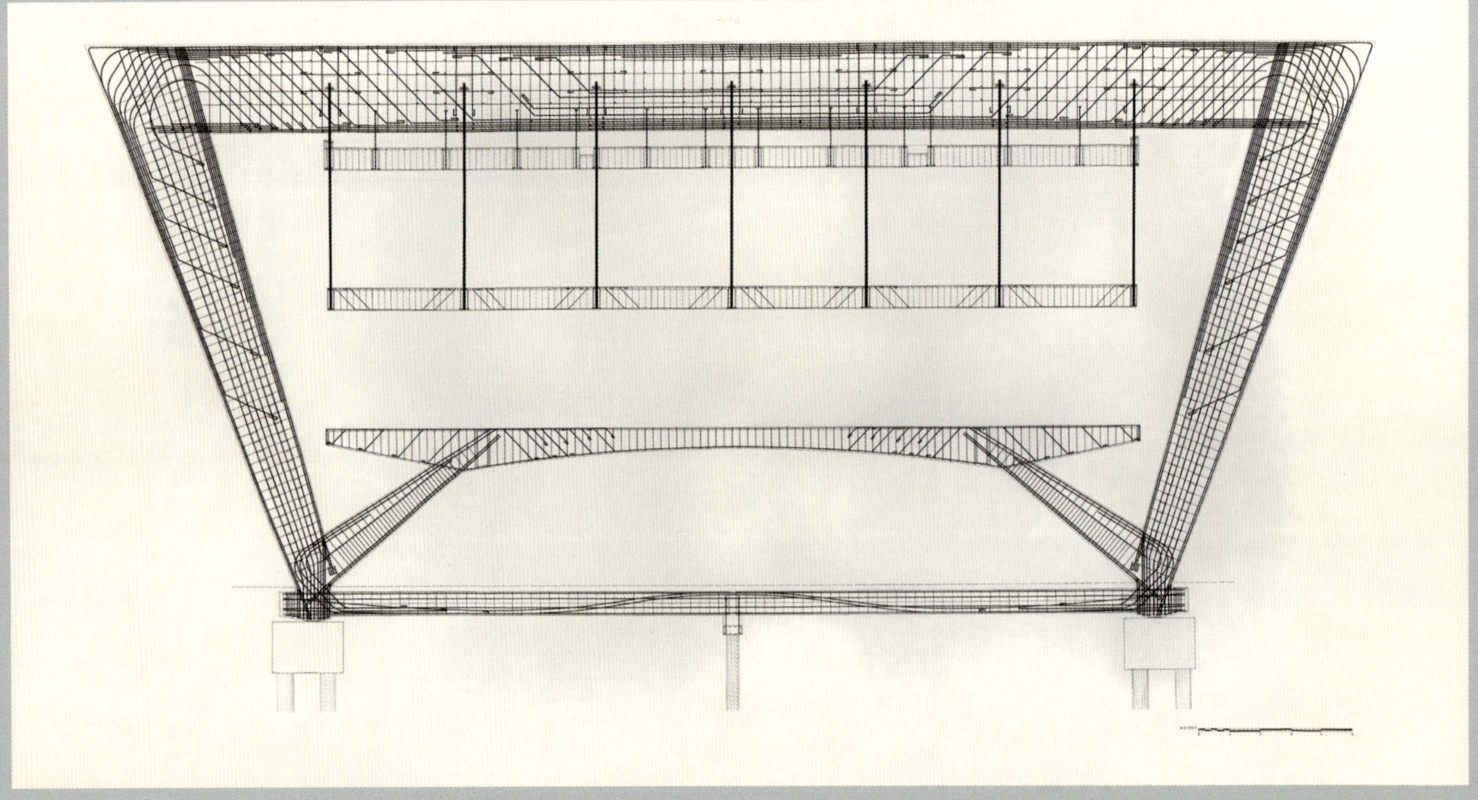

RIO DE JANEIRO, BRAZIL

1953–1967

ARCHITECT   AFFONSO EDUARDO REIDY

ENGINEERS   CARMEN VELASCO PORTINHO
                 ARTHUR EUGENIO JERMANN
                     SERV. ENG. EMÍLIO BAUMGART LTDA

Surrounded by the bay of Rio and a landscaping area by Roberto Burle Marx, the complex designed by Affonso Eduardo Reidy is dominated by the long, 130×40-meter museum building, punctuated by 14 trapezoidal exposed reinforced concrete ribs every 10 m. The larger base of the overturned trapezoid is the extrados main beam—60×275 cm—that holds up both the roof, arched and shaped to contain the skylight, and the second floor, suspended via stay cables. The first-floor slab is raised off the ground by tapered slanting convergent columns, which share the same point-loads as the diverging columns of the ribs. The result is a space with no visual obstacles on the ground and a completely free, flexible floor plan for the first-floor gallery, which is either 3.6, 6.4 or 8 m in height depending on the point sectioned. Carmen Velasco Portinho, the only woman on the worksite with more than 450 workers, was in charge of all construction decisions. Arthur Eugenio Jermann dealt with the structural calculations.

← MAM – Museu
de Arte Moderna do Rio
de Janeiro, Rio de Janeiro,
1967. Courtesy MAM Rio
Collection

NOTHING ESCAPES TECHNOLOGY. CONCRETE WORKS ITS "MAGIC" UNDER THE LOGIC OF *DESARROLLISMO*

Patricio del Real

When it's time to use a certain
beam, we shouldn't be thinking
that it's American, German,
or French.
If it is, in itself, a good
way of using a material there's
no sin in using it in any part
of the world.[1]

EMILIO DUHART

A double curvature inverted shell known as "la Teja," the tile, appears to float. Its thin shallow concave curve opens to the sky like a feather poised on two cantilevering beams. It extends, horizontally, with a graceful bend over the entrance of the CEPAL building, the Comisión Económica para América Latina y el Caribe (Economic Commission for Latin America and the Caribbean), in Santiago, Chile. This canopy—which also functions as an updated porte-cochère—served as a symbol for this temple of *Desarrollismo* which translates to, Development Theory, a philosophy that bifurcated the road to modernity after World War II. By the late 1940s and early 1950s, the concept of "development" displaced earlier notions of "progress" and "civilization." Securing a productivist paradigm of unfettered and unlimited growth, it was underwritten by an economic imperative that placed technological innovation at its center.[2] The message of *Desarrollismo*, embraced by governments across Latin America, is embodied in the wondrously thin reinforced concrete shell of the headquarters of the CEPAL, the United Nations branch created in 1948 as part of a regionalist impetus to spur economic growth and lead the social modernization of the

1 Damián Bayón and Paolo Gasparini, *The Changing Shape of Latin American Architecture: Conversations with Ten Leading Architects* (New York: Wiley, 1979), 124. I want to thank Marcelo Sarovic and Jeannette Plaut for their insights on the CEPAL building and help with obtaining images.

2 Maristella Svampa, *Debates Latinoamericanos: Indianismo, desarrollo, dependencia y populismo* (Buenos Aires; Edhasa, 2016), 137–38. Diego Martín Giller, *Los años dependentistas. Algunas cuestiones en torno de Dialéctica de la dependencia* (Buenos Aires: CLACSO, 2016), 8.

3 See for example Arturo Escobar, *Encountering Development: The Making and Unmaking of the Third World* (Princeton: Princeton University Press, 2012).

4 Henry-Russell Hitchcock, *Latin American Architecture since 1945* (New York: The Museum of Modern Art, 1955), 26.

5 On the early period of *Desarrollismo*, see Jorge Francisco Liernur, "Vanguardistas versus expertos: Reconstrucción europea, expansión norteamericana y emergencia del 'Tercer Mundo:' para una relectura del debate arquitectónico en la segunda posguerra (una mirada desde América Latina)," *Block*, no. 6 (2004): 18–39.

region in the second postwar era. Today, *Desarrollismo* is highly criticized, and correctly so.[3] Yet, its message lives on through the canopy, and the building as a whole. As one walks under this levitating lyrical form, one cannot but think: All is possible. All is buildable. Nothing escapes technology.

Desarrollismo renegotiated the contract between society and nature in Latin America. The theory explored a controversial belief in technology and science, demanding a social and spatial reorganization that prompted a new scale in building with which to imagine the future of the region. Firm believers of reinforced concrete technology, architects and engineers from across Latin America responded to meet the challenges. The CEPAL headquarters was designed and built between 1961 and 1966 led by Chilean architect Emilio Duhart with engineers César Barros and Hartmut Vogel and their team. The building continues to serve as an entry point to a time when the hopes, yearnings, and purpose of progressive architects and engineers were bound by the spell of Development to the international economy of technological innovation, as expressed by Duhart himself in the opening epigraph. Many of the region's buildings, that today have entered the canon of modern architecture and the iconography of "progress," were bound by the dynamics of dependent development.

The CEPAL's inverted shell is a statement of a techno-topia, of a place, a *topos* that—in accordance with its Greek etymology—constructed a territory. In short, concrete thin shells became part and parcel of the form-image of Latin American architecture. Conceptualized as a localized artisanal technology, they revealed, for architectural historians such as Henry-Russell Hitchcock, a "tradition of masonry vaulting" dating back to colonial times.[4] Vaults were architectural signs of civilization. These arching forms underscored the sustained presence of Western technical reason updated by continued European immigration with the likes of the Spanish-Catalan Antoni Bonet in Argentina and Uruguay, and the Italian Mario Bianco in Peru, just to name two of many architects and engineers who, escaping the horrors of European fascism and World War II, found new homes in Latin America. The development of thin shells offered a new lyrical and technological symbol. Their best-known promoter remains the Spanish-Mexican architect Félix Candela. Duhart's inversion of this culturally charged form becomes a powerful symbolic statement that, resting between the empirical and objective dimension of technology and its cultural justifications, is caught between a magic trick and a delirious dream.

The CEPAL headquarters in Santiago, Chile, presents a selection of architectural forms and techniques refined since the late 1940s by architects, engineers, and builders across the region—including thin shells, tapering pillars, umbrella columns, cantilevers, hanging slabs, and more—that collectively embody the search for ever-larger clear spans that would not fully materialize until the late 1950s and early 1960s under the imperatives of *Desarrollismo*.[5] The determinant factor was the pursuit of the unobstructed open plan that led to an alliance with engineering and what is known as structural expressionism across the globe during this period. Based on the traditional courtyard house typology, the CEPAL building is unambiguously structural: a 96-meter-square ring of uninterrupted office space hovers over the site, on the embankment of the Mapocho River. Its 14-meter-wide open-plan ring surrounds an internal patio in which special programs, housed in distinct expressive forms, emerge from the landscape. In the patio, the conical helicoid of the main assembly chamber, known as "el Caracol," the Snail, recalls the Andean peaks that traverse the landscape in the background. Its form conjures up the telluric forces that shaped this continental landform. The Snail rises to form an outdoor mirador that links the ideological space of transnational economic and social planning to a phenomenological experience that unveils the scale of the development enterprise. This play between what is near and what is distant turns the Snail from mere platform for the contemplation of nature into a vessel for its domination. Such is the contract between architecture and nature under the logic of *Desarrollismo*. Acts of rhetorical and formal poetics, which summon the mysterious forces of nature or call upon the symbols of the region as magical amulets to give meaning to this building, can't renegotiate the contract of development underpinned by the extractive economy of modernization in Latin America.

The exploitation of natural resources bonds the region to the international circulation of industrial products and knowledges, shaping both its natural and built environments. Eight post-tensioned perimeter master-beams are lifted by 28 tapering pyramidal columns and connected transversally by secondary pre-stressed prefabricated beams to form the square superstructure, from which the offices and the bureaucracy of the CEPAL literally hang. This allows for a complete open plan and for the site to flow below. The unimpeded stream of technocratic ideas occurs above a liberated landscape, opened to be reshaped. Traditional post-and-lintel construction was updated with technological equipment and expertise from the West German construction company Philip Holzmann AG and the firm Maschinenfabrik Esslingen, which developed the all-important seismic joints between the columns and the perimeter beams that allows for circulation and flows.[6] If the Caracol emerges above the horizontal datum set by the ring as a symbolic reminder of the forces of nature, the joint between the master-beams and the columns mediates the actual seismic telluric ritual that ever-so-often castigates modernity in Chile.

In the CEPAL building, the living force and magnitude of nature is captured and controlled in the joint—a system composed of high-resistance steel rings and half-inch steel bearings mediated by neoprene elements.[7] Such technological fearlessness was the objectification of a techno-sphere, of the space of an established technical and social order that structured a place under the regime of *Desarrollismo* and unfolds the full meaning of techno-topia at the time. This techno-topia was based on the dialectics between place and space and undergirded by a social order seeking to industrialize the region. This is evidenced by the feverish scientific discourse in diverse disciplines from the social sciences to engineering, economics to architecture. As an institutional space of scientific social research, the CEPAL incorporated technical advancements in building construction. Prefabrication emerged at the CEPAL in a plethora of reports, congresses, meetings, and more, as an imaginary and objective technological problem to be solved.[8] The use of 14-meter-long, pre-stressed, prefabricated beams in the building's ring megaform embodies the new techno-social order of postwar modernity under *Desarrollismo,* geared toward the transformation of the physical territory and of society.[9] The confluence of CEPAL ideas and architectural production is a fertile field of research. The institution's many efforts created a transnational community, a technical and social intelligentsia, working together within development paradigms.

The aim of the CEPAL was to bring Latin America into full modernity by industrializing it. Cepalinos, as those associated with the institution became known, unfolded the center-periphery model—first theo-

6   The technical information on the CEPAL building is presented in: Jeannette Plaut and Marcelo Sarovic, "Entre el imaginar y el construir: Construcción del edificio para las Naciones Unidas, CEPAL, 1961-66," in *CEPAL 1962_1966: United Nations Building, Emilio Duhart Arquitecto*, eds. Jeannette Plaut and Marcelo Sarovic (Santiago: CONSTRUCTO, 2012), 50–73.

7   *Ibid.*, 58.

8   See for example: "Documento a ser apresentado ao Seminário Latino-Americano sobre Pre-Fabricação de Habitações por Saul Fuks, do Escritório de Pesquisa Econômica Aplicada (EPEA), do Ministério do Planejamento e Coordenaçao Geral," *Documento Informativo No. 13: Comisión Económica Para America Latina. Seminario Latino Americano sobre Prefabricación de Viviendas*, Copenhagen, August 13 to September 1, 1967, viewable online: https://repositorio.cepal.org/handle/11362/18057. Accessed March 24, 2022.

9   On the relationship between megastructures and a new territorial scale in architecture see: Ana María Rigotti, "Fósiles de futuro: megaestructuras," *Block*, no. 9 (2012): 18–31.

10   This peripheric condition structured foreign commerce, technology, and capital accumulation. See: Eduardo Devés Valdés, *Del Ariel de Rodó a la CEPAL (1900-1950) (El pensamiento latinoamericano en el siglo XX, entre la modernidad y la identidad)* (Buenos Aires: Editorial Biblos y Centro de Investigaciones Barros Arana, 2000), 291.

11   Xavier Tafunel, "On the Origins of ISI: The Latin American Cement Industry, 1900-30," *Journal of Latin American Studies* 39, no. 2 (2007): 309.

12   On the notion of artisanal value in the work of Candela see: María González Pendás, "Fifty Cents a Foot, 14,500 Buckets: Concrete Numbers and the Illusory Shells of Mexican Economy," *Grey Room*, no. 71 (2018): 14–39.

El acceso se encuentra destacado por una colosal marquesina cóncava de doble curvatura: la "teja".

su escala. La circulación le da su forma y circunscribe un gran tranque que refleja, arquitectura, montañas y cielo. Al avanzar hacia el edificio se rodea el "Árbol de las Naciones" y ese movimiento hace aparecer el conjunto en todas sus dimensiones. Se puede también acceder a pie, en cuyo caso se elige el camino más corto por una calzada que parece flotar sobre el tranque y cuyo ángulo destaca la tridimensión del edificio. Se penetra entonces bajo el volumen por el Porch al Gran Patio de entrada donde pueden darse reuniones públicas o exposiciones. Se llega así al corazón del conjunto, el Hall Central, cuyas circulaciones verticales relacionan todas los niveles.

El espacio propio del edificio con sus patios interconectados se comunica por la prolongación del eje central hacia el sector norte del terreno, cuyo uso se puede reservar a los miembros de la N.U. o a los invitados. Este último sector, cuyo gran prado tranquilo se asemeja a los pastizales del Valle Central de Chile, está regado por el sistema de acequias de agua limpia que se prolonga en sentido inverso hacia el Sur a través del Edificio y desagua en el gran tranque de entrada; el cual es utilizado además para el funcionamiento del aire acondicionado.

Además, hay una intercomunicación entre el sector Sur y Norte por el costado Oriente que los une en una perspectiva rematada por un muro de cerámica. Este forma parte del futuro edificio, que es una de las ampliaciones eventuales.

Al poniente, hacia el río el barranco, se organiza a todo lo largo del sitio en un sistema de muros de contención de concreto con agregado de bolones del Mapocho que aparecen en sus paramentos. Su carácter pedregoso y robusto sugiere la proximidad del río y de sus materiales. Estos muros cierran y controlan el sitio hacia el río.

La totalidad del terreno y las vistas del valle de Santiago se captan desde las cubiertas en terrazas, especialmente en su parte culminante situada sobre la Sala de Conferencias.

El Edificio mismo se presenta en contraste con su zócalo como una estructura de concreto armado robusta y ligera a la vez, semejante a la de los puentes cuya buena resistencia a los terremotos ha sido comprobada. Sus luces están en proporción con la altura de las grandes vigas de borde de la cubierta. El concreto se acusa claramente y se dejó aparente tanto en el cuadrado como en los órganos centrales.

donde comienza el debate

AUCA.— Permítasenos establecer una pauta para esta conversación. Aún a riesgo de separar artificialmente categorías que están integradas en la obra como una unidad, tendremos que enfocarlas de manera aislada como medio de ordenar el debate.

32

↑ View of the "la Teja" during the construction of the CEPAL Headquarters, Santiago de Chile, in "Edificio de las Naciones Unidas en Vitacura," in *AUCA*, no. 3 (1966): 32

rized in 1948 by the Argentinian economist Raúl Prebisch who headed the institution—as a structural socio-economic condition of the region's development that needed to be overcome with new concerted efforts on Import Substitution Industrialization. The region's position in the international division of labor needed to be changed by ceasing to be a supplier of food products and natural resources to the industrial centers, principally Western Europe and the United States.[10] By disarming the linear telos of Modernization Theory that called upon peripheral nations to follow the stages of development outlined by industrial countries and tied the region's modernity, CEPAL's *Desarrollismo* and later Dependency Theory, which refined and developed the center-periphery model, sought to remedy the dialectics of development under capitalism. The close relationship between economics, social sciences, and development projects in architecture is obscured by the few showcase buildings that have penetrated the global history of architecture. Yet, canonical works, such as the CEPAL, reveal key contradictions in developmental schemes. Architects, for one, did not abandon the earlier notion of progress tied to humanist civilization that had been foundational to the discipline in Latin America and the Western world. As both a practice and discipline, architecture was key to a progressive spiritual conversion throughout the material transformation of the nation, and reinforced concrete technology was imagined as its ultimate trump card. After all, most countries in the region had developed robust national cement industries; Chile as early as 1908.[11]

At the CEPAL, architecture's alliance with engineering was not smooth; visible in the refusal to accept the raw finishes of engineering, its matter-of-factness. Its architects gambled on the artisanal value of reinforced concrete.[12] There's a wealth of buildings in the region that can be enlisted in this defense of the art of building—brought to the point of symbolic excess in the CEPAL with the hands of the construction workers and technicians (as well as politicians) imprinted on cement tiles and set on the south wall under the Teja. The ring megastructure, however, makes clear the renegotiated contract of the historic relationship between architecture, engineering, and labor underwritten by a new quest for industrialization under late *Desarrollismo*.

The CEPAL building embraced multiple forms of knowledge—from local building expertise to technological advancements in reinforced concrete construction first attempted in infrastructural works under the supervision of local engineers.[13] The on-site prefabricated beams that incorporated German pre-stressed technology were a means to integrate local technical know-how and construction techniques with the international circulation of technological knowledge. Such forms of appropriation and exchange underpin capitalist exploitation by subsuming uneven temporalities embodied in the processes of production as an introduction to their future levelling.[14] This process of synchronization frames the use of prefabrication across the region. Duhart recognized that this new regime of labor had serious implications. There was a deep social and production contradiction in the use of prefabrication—a technique aimed at both reducing and intensifying labor—and other technological innovations that required a more qualified labor force at CEPAL. In developing countries, Duhart argued, architecture needed to act as a force of social development: "[W]e should be able to think up solutions of our own that will use the maximum amount of labor, not in order to maintain it in a subservient state," he stressed, "on the contrary, making it evolve 'within' that work that needs to be done."[15] The work of architecture was thus to transform the laborer into a subject of industrial modernity.

13 Jeannette Plaut and Marcelo Sarovic, "Entre el imaginar y el construir," 58.

14 On the question of temporalities of production and their synchronization see: Massimiliano Tomba, *Marx's Temporalities*, trans. Peter D. Thomas and Sara R. Farris (Chicago: Haymarket Books, 2013), particularly 135–50.

15 Damián Bayón and Paolo Gasparini, *The Changing Shape of Latin American Architecture*, 119.

↓ CEPAL Headquarters under construction, aerial view, Santiago de Chile, ca. 1964, in Jeannette Plaut, Marcelo Sarovic, *Cepal 1962_1966: United Nations Building: Emilio Duhart Arquitecto, Constructo*, Santiago 2012. Courtesy Enrique Albertz, CEPAL

Reinforced concrete construction in many Latin American countries—its innovation, structural audacity, and creativity, as well as *savoir-faire* in building—embodied the processes of development under dependency. The alliance between architecture, construction, and engineering had clear social implications as the production of reinforced concrete construction and its eloquent and value-laden finishes was dependent on cheap labor; on a labor force that was generally housed in the sprawling urban slums. The projects that symbolized dreams and hopes of modernity could not emerge without its dark side, as Brasília and its satellite slum cities testified. The technoscape of *Desarrollismo* was supported by the survival tactics of millions. The sin of technology, which Duhart attempted to absolve, did not rest in its universal laws but rather in the ways these laws, once applied, exploited local conditions of production: the superabundance of labor, transforming it into a natural resource to be extracted, used, and discarded, to serve the functions of local and global capitalist development.

Technological transfers unfold processes of translation —both objective and conceptual —that activate local innovation; processes of appropriation that trigger scalar adaptations, and of discovery that prompt changes in use.[16] The center-periphery model challenged the passive reception of ideas and techniques by opening up the concept of technology to a critique of postwar development. The work of Uruguayan engineer Eladio Dieste exemplifies this critique.[17] Dieste, along with a team and group of engineers, architects, and builders, advanced a localized constructive logic of architecture. His work upheld the activity of acquiring empirical knowledge through the act of building, over a rationalist paradigm of architectural production based on the primacy of calculation and intellectual abstract work.[18] "We were always faced with the limits of what we could calculate," Dieste noted, "and for an engineer, to conceive of something meant to be able to calculate it."[19] The construction site was a key well-spring of construction knowledge. The primacy of empirical construction knowledge is evidenced in every test structure built to observe the behaviors of complex forms—from the Baseball Stadium in Cartagena, Colombia (1948), to the National Art Schools in Havana, Cuba (1961–64), to shell constructions across the region—that escaped a rationalized industrial logic. The overall polemic was against the structural cage, that migrated to reinforced concrete from steel construction. The persistence of what effectively was a nineteenth-century technology, rationalized in the twentieth century to advance a capitalist industrial mode of production, hampered the development of reinforced concrete under the aegis of shell and laminar tile vaults. These "estructuras rebeldes" or "rebellious structures," as Dieste called them, required the tried-and-true method of trial and error.[20] Faith was of the essence and its revelation could come only from the construction site. While Duhart symbolically gestured to the process of construction through realist representations—such as the imprint of worker's hands—Dieste objectified it. He materialized it without romanticism, without the idealization that today envelops his work—for in the end the quest was the adaptation of brick construction to industrial modernity. We must not forget that the companion to the "cerámica armada," or reinforced ceramic tiles, that allowed for large clear spans with laminar vaults, was the "molde móbil," the reusable formwork that increased the speed of building, reducing labor and material costs.[21]

The price of industrialization was the loss of empirical knowledge that emerges in and from the construction site, mystified as "traditional" because of the difficulty of adjusting them to an ever-increas-

16	On the question of technological transfers in the region see: Eden Medina, Ivan da Costa Marques and Christina Holmes, eds., *Beyond Imported Magic: Essays on Science, Technology, and Society in Latin America* (Cambridge, MA: MIT Press, 2014).

17	See for example: Eladio Dieste, "Técnica y subdesarrollo," *CEDA: Revista del Centro de Estudiantes de Arquitectura* 34 (February 1973): 1–5.

18	Juan Pablo Bonta, *Eladio Dieste* (Buenos Aires: Instituto de Arte Americano e Investigaciones Estéticas, 1963), 9–11.

19	Eladio Dieste, "Some Reflections on Architecture and Construction," *Perspecta*, no. 27 (1992): 191.

20	Cited in Juan Pablo Bonta, *Eladio Dieste*, 10.

21	Juan Pablo Bonta, *Eladio Dieste*, 25. See also: "Eladio Dieste en la V Bienal," *CA: Revista Oficial del Colegio de Arquitectos de Chile*, no. 42 (December 1985): 72–76. "Uruguay. La Arquitectura de Eladio Dieste," *Periferia*, no. 8/9 (December 1988): 27–37.

PATRICIO DEL REAL

ing speed of production concomitant with the rationalization of architecture and the standardization of construction. Signature buildings, such as the CEPAL, embraced hybrid processes of construction, acknowledging the difficulties in industrializing the construction industry. Yet, such buildings guided by the logic of *Desarrollismo*, served as test sites in which to manage the erasure of empirical knowledge and renegotiate the contracts of a modernity bound by technological transfers under the different phases of Import Substitution Industrialization, an economic process that can be traced back to the consolidation of Latin American states in the late nineteenth century.[22] Such management of diverse knowledge, which included its appropriation, is clear in the CEPAL project in the rationalization of the construction site to incorporate an unevenly qualified labor force alongside cutting-edge technology.

Duhart's inverted vault turned canopy strikes as a reminder of the perils of development. Gestures of structural inversion create symbolic forms that suspend the logic of the world. These help us recover the function of utopia and argue for its place in the techno-topia that dominates the world. Utopia's function is not that of being "no-place," but of "having no-place" in the built environment while, at the same time, existing in the world. This is of special significance in countries bound by uneven exchanges, by systemic dependency, and continued scarcity; in places which are generally considered as serious parts of the world where "play"—conceptualized as a luxury—should be deferred, if not banished. Under the regimes of development, utopia—the function of creating alternative possibilities—is left to those who can afford it. This form of epistemic domination through the expropriation of wonder is part and parcel of capitalist exploitation and domination. Emphasis on the symbolic character of architecture helps us recover its utopian function, no matter how many times critics inform us of the complicity of the activity of building with the forces of capitalist development. Architecture can and must still be constructed as a force of change if it is to remain a socially valuable progressive practice.

In the CEPAL, one finds a solid constructive solution. It allowed the building to be within budget, which was modest, and on time, which was tight. Overall, the building may be a sound answer to the imperatives of the site and the times, but to literally hang the program in a seismic country is also a playful and joyful solution. Occasionally, bureaucracies need a good shakeup and these shocks—like those proposed by neoliberal priests—should not remain in the world of abstraction but be fully felt, as they transform people's actual lives. In Chile—and other Southern cone countries—there is a popular expression: "por fin le cayó la teja," which translates to "the roof tile finally fell on their head," in other words that one has finally reached a realization or understanding of something. Today, it seems, and one hopes, that amid our developing climate crisis and impending ecological disaster the *teja* has finally fallen on our present techno-topia.

↑ An example of *neotopflager (neoprene-topflager)*, a structural joint fabricated by Maschinenfabrik Esslingen, West Germany, as shown in a corporate catalog of the 1960s. Courtesy Marcelo Sarovic

22 Xavier Tafunel, "On the Origins of ISI," 300.

On site fabrication of the 14-meter-long prestressed beams for the ring megaform of the CEPAL Headquarters, Santiago de Chile, in Jeannette Plaut, Marcelo Sarovic, *Cepal 1962-1966: United Nations Building: Emilio Duhart Arquitecto, Constructo*, Santiago 2012. Courtesy Enrique Albertz, CEPAL

WOMEN ENGINEERS IN BRAZIL: AT THE CROSSROADS OF FEMINISM AND FEMININITY

Anat Falbel

INTRODUCTION

In Brazil, women gained access to higher education in 1879. Nevertheless, it would be almost half a century before these new privileges were available to a significant number of the country's female population. In fact, until almost the 1930s, the women who attended university, enjoyed a career in the liberal professions, or were prominent participants in the country's cultural and political life, came mostly from the economic and intellectual elite of Brazil's major urban centers.

While there were already practicing female doctors in the late nineteenth century, the military origins of a career in engineering and the institutions that preceded the Escola Politécnica, established in 1874, were far removed from young women's aspirations. The abovementioned Escola Militar, influenced by the French model, was responsible for training the first Brazilian engineers, who were mostly involved in the construction of the country's railway network, essential infrastructure for the coffee industry. Meanwhile, the Politécnica was organized in the style of the German Technische Hochschule, displaying a practical teaching method that valued technological research and innovation. The same model guided the establishment of the Politécnica in São Paulo (1894) and in Recife (1895), the Escola de Engenharia in Porto Alegre (1896), and the Politécnica in Bahia (1897), as well as the country's first private engineering school, the Escola de Engenharia of Mackenzie College (1896), which followed the syllabus of the University of the State of New York School of Civil Engineering and Architecture.

1   Raymundo Teixeira Mendes, *A Preeminência Social e Moral da Mulher* (Rio de Janeiro: Igreja do Apostolado Positivista do Brasil/Empreza Brasil Editora, 1920).

2   Griselda Pollock, *Vision and Difference: Feminism, Femininity and the History of Art* (New York: Routledge, 2003), XVII.

Despite the positivistic atmosphere that surrounded the creation of these schools and Auguste Comte's assumptions regarding women's place in society, as translated in Brazil by Raymundo Teixeira Mendes' article "A Preeminência Social e Moral da Mulher,"[1] between the late nineteenth and early twentieth century one may still identify a few women enrolled as listeners at some of these institutions.

Notwithstanding, the first generation of Brazilian women engineers who graduated in the 1920s were drawn into the feminist atmosphere created by the international spread of suffragism, particularly after World War I. The committement to the women's emancipation movement and their feminist militancy led most of those young professionals to question their role in society at large,[2] leading them to become involved in progressive movements.

Effectively, despite the emergence of feminist initiatives and leaders in Brazil since the beginning of the twentieth century, the movement achieved more recognition under the leadership of Bertha Maria Júlia Lutz. The daughter of the physician and epidemiologist Adolfo Lutz of Swiss origin, Bertha studied Natural Sciences in Paris before returning to Brazil in 1918. After being admitted to the National Museum in 1919, she began to organize the Liga de Emancipação Intellectual da Mulher, with the support of organized European and American (including South American) feminist movements and figures. By 1922, the league was replaced by the Federação Brasileira pelo Progresso Feminino (FBPF), which headed the Brazilian suffrage movement from the Federal District—a struggle that only achieved its goal in 1932—and aimed to guide the advancement of women's culture, encouraging their presence in the public, intellectual, and political spheres. Lutz was flanked by the FBPF's treasurer, the young engineering student Carmen Velasco Portinho, married to Lutz's brother, who brought her fellow female polytechnic students into the movement, a couple of whom were already civil servants in the capital's administration, with Portinho herself joining them there in 1926. This was the case of the active Maria Esther Corrêa Ramalho (1894–1974), who graduated in 1922, the engineer Amelia Sapienza, who graduated in 1928, and the first civil engineer to graduate from the Politécnica, namely Edwiges Maria Becker Hom'meil. The FBPF's intention of promoting higher education among women led to the creation of the União Universitária Feminina in 1929. As president of the União, Carmen Portinho continued to mobilize her abovementioned polytechnic colleagues, including Elza Pinho Osborne. In 1937, all those intrepid young women would accompany Carmen in the creation of the Associação Brasileira de Engenheiras e Arquitetas/ABEA, the only exclusively female professional organization that aimed to offer legal apparatus to guarantee the rights of women in the professional field. In the mid-1940s, their militancy would continue, as the first women to be accepted initially into committees and then into boards of professional and scientific societies in the Brazilian capital, such as the Clube de Engenharia, the Sindicato de Engenheiros e Arquitetos, and the Conselho Regional de Engenharia e Arquitetura (CREA).

↓   Carmen Velasco Portinho at the MAM – Museu de Arte Moderna do Rio de Janeiro, ca. 1960. National Archives of Brazil, Rio de Janeiro - BR RJANRIO PH.0.FOT.39233(36)

FEMALE ENGINEERS IN THE BRAZILIAN PRESS IN THE 1920S AND 1930S

The loud noise made in the local press by the FBPF was very likely due to its members' solid standing within the circles of the capital's elite, as was the case of Bertha Lutz, but also Carmen Portinho, whose father Coronel Francisco S. B. Portinho was a superintendent in the capital's administration and close to the mayor. Indeed, a couple of decades later, the powerful position of her brother José Velasco Portinho at the influential daily newspaper *Correio da Manhã* would also prove crucial, not only regarding her role as executive director of the Museu de Arte Moderna in Rio de Janeiro (since 1951), but also concerning the development of the new museum designed by Affonso Eduardo Reidy.

In her autobiography, Portinho describes press support during the 1920s, mentioning the *Jornal do Brasil* (RJ), as well as the pro-State newspaper *O Paiz* (RJ). It is interesting to note that newspapers with a wide circulation showed great sympathy for female engineers, praising their accomplishments in a traditionally male profession.[3]

As a feminist engineer, Portinho herself was particularly attractive to the press. In 1929, *O Paiz* published an article entitled "Mulheres Engenheiras," underscoring the efforts of the first female engineers working in the Federal District, and the achievements of the young Carmen Portinho.[4]

Nevertheless, one could suggest that the perception of the essentially feminine character of their work, in the sense suggested by Pollock,[5] was only recognized in 1949 by the perspicacious writer and journalist Yvonne Jean in her column "Presença da Mulher," published between 1948 and 1958 in the *Correio da Manhã,* in which she used to examine the issue of women professionals. A Belgian exile, with a substantial modern and profound humanist background, who found a place for herself in the intellectual and progressive "carioca" milieu after arriving in Brazil in 1940, Yvonne Jean presented the engineer Berta Leitchic as a professional who despite important concrete structure designs in the city of Rio de Janeiro, including bridges, viaducts, tunnels, and even the Botafogo pier,[6] "remained a true woman: happy, pleasant… feminine!"[7] In her article, Jean observed the fundamental development of concrete structures in Brazil, also mentioning the presence of more than one hundred women engineers and architects working in the city, mostly as civil servants. In the following edition, Jean presented the acclaimed Pedregulho social housing complex designed by Reidy and constructed by the recently created Departamento da Habitação Popular, directed by his life partner Carmen Portinho between 1947 and 1958. Ahead of her time, Jean implied that the accomplishments of those female engineers were the consequence of their feminist and feminine positions, a substantial assumption used to explain, among other things, Portinho's initiatives since her first engagements within the FBPF, her efforts at the *Revista Municipal de Engenheira*, in the Departamento da Habitação Popular, and at the Museu de Arte Moderna (1951–66), and later at the Escola Superior de Desenho Industrial (1967–88).[8]

ANAT FALBEL

3   See *Revista da Semana*, no. 12 (April 27, 1918): 35; *Jornal das Moças*, no. 151 (May 9, 1918): 11.

4   "Mulheres Engenheiras," *O Paiz*, no. 16212 (March 10, 1929), 4.

5   Pollock, *Vision and Difference*, XVII.

6   See Berta Chnaiderman Leitchic, "Viaduto da Estrada da Canoa," *Revista Municipal de Engenharia* 15, no. 3 (July–September 1948): 108–11.

7   Yvonne Jean, "O Viaduto de Canoas," *Correio da Manhã*, no. 17131 (January 22, 1949): 12. See also "Berta Leitchic. A engenheira de saltos altos," *Correio da Manhã*, no. 21059 (November 19, 1961): 61.

8   Carmen Portinho, *Por toda a minha vida* (Rio de Janeiro: EdUERJ, 1999).

→   Affonso Eduardo Reidy, Prefeito Mendes de Moraes Housing Complex (Pedregulho) built under the coordination of Carmen Velasco Portinho, Rio de Janeiro, 1948–1952. Photo Flavio Salazar. Acervo Arquivo Geral da Cidade do Rio de Janeiro

Revista da Semana

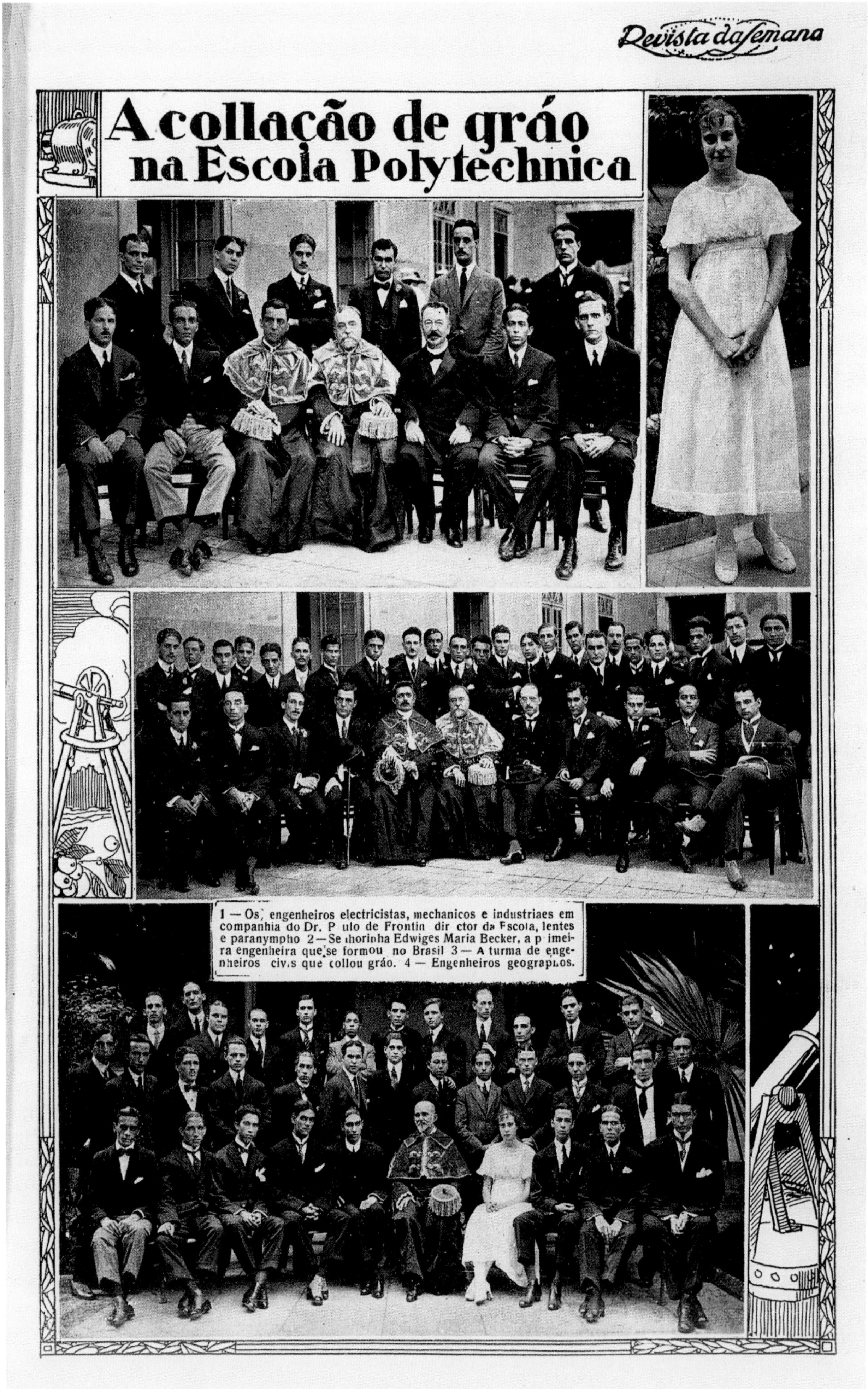

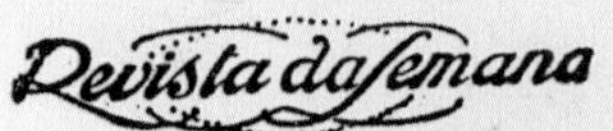

A collação de gráo na Escola Polytechnica

1 — Os engenheiros electricistas, mechanicos e industriaes em companhia do Dr. Paulo de Frontin director da Escola, lentes e paranympho 2 — Senhorinha Edwiges Maria Becker, a primeira engenheira que se formou no Brasil 3 — A turma de engenheiros civis que collou gráo. 4 — Engenheiros geographos.

FEMALE ENGINEERS IN PUBLIC AND PRIVATE OFFICE

The first generation of Brazilian female engineers who graduated between the 1920s and 1930s, found a place for themselves in public service, just at the end of a long campaign that gave women access to positions in all state ministries in 1918.

The public administration was a traditional destiny of male Politécnica graduates from all over the country, notably Rio de Janeiro's political, administrative, and economic elite. It also became the destination of pioneering female engineers from the same social stratum that defined the initiatives of a state eager to present itself as a promoter of modern culture, including industrial and urban infrastructures. The professionals who witnessed and sometimes partook in the iconic achievements of Brazilian "state" architecture included the previously mentioned Edwiges Maria Becker Hom'meil, who found a position at the Ministério da Viação, together with Maria Esther Ramalho, who would be a vigorous voice within various engineering professional organizations and unions from the 1930s onwards, as well as being involved in progressive movements and the Brazilian Communist Party in the early 1950s; Amelia Sapienza, who occupied a position in the Comissão das Estradas de Rodagem within the same ministry, which was one of the state's priority programs, continuing the "rodoviarismo" that began in the 1920s; Carmen Velasco Portinho, invited by mayor Alaor Prata himself to a position in the capital's Diretoria de Obras e Viação, where she had the opportunity to develop both architectural and urban projects, reinforcing their social character through her own militancy. In the early 1930s, two more highly active engineers from the Politécnica found a place as civil servants in the capital: the abovementioned Berta Chnaiderman Leitchic and Elza Pinho Osborne. The former, a Russian immigrant, began her career as a structural designer in the municipality's Departamento de Planejamento e Projetos, which she would later direct. In the late 1940s, she worked alongside Reidy in the new Departamento de Urbanismo, while during the 1950s she took on a managerial position within the municipal agency SURSAN and was responsible for one of its construction sites, the Aterro do Flamengo designed by Lota de Macedo Soares.[9] In turn, Elza Pinho Osborne, who graduated in 1933, was admitted to the Inspetoria de Águas e Esgotos, going on to direct its water and sewage analysis and treatment laboratory. Over the next two decades, the engineer and playwright would take on the role of administrator in charge of the Campo Grande peripheral district, the Department of Parks and Gardens, and later on the neighborhood of Santa Teresa, seeking to intervene in the socially disrupted local communities through the introduction of gardens and/or cultural activities. The engineer Clara Perelberg Steinberg, born in Brazil into an immigrant family who had arrived in Rio de Janeiro in the early 1920s, followed a different path from her fellow students at the Politécnica. After graduating in 1946, as both a civil and industrial engineer, by as early as 1949 she and her husband had started their own engineering firm called SERVENCO, with Clara having a written document signed by her husband authorizing her to "engage in a commercial activity." Perelberg was responsible for all the company's feasibility studies, design, and construction activities. In fact, despite the country's economic and political crises, half a century later SERVENCO had completed 247 buildings in different neighborhoods of Rio de Janeiro. Introducing new housing programs alongside new management practices that favored female professionals, the company also developed a social program for its construction workers, usually migrants fleeing from poverty in the north-east of the country.[10]

↑ Berta Leitchic, the Canoas viaduct (1949) and the Pasmado tunnel (1948), in "24 horas na vida de Berta Leitchic," in *Correio da Manhã* (June 25, 1959): 9. Courtesy National Library, Rio de Janeiro

← Edwiges Maria Becker Hommeil with the graduates of the Escola Politécnica do Rio de Janeiro, 1918, Rio de Janeiro, in *Revista da Semana*, ed. 012 (April 27, 1918). Courtesy Biblioteca Nacional, Rio de Janeiro

9   Berta Leitchic, "Berta Leitchic," in *Capítulos da Memória do Urbanismo Carioca: Depoimentos ao CPDOC/FGV*, eds. Américo Freire and Lúcia Lippi Oliveira (Rio de Janeiro: Folha Seca, 2002), 40–47.

Alongside her colleagues, Perelberg's militancy continued in profession-al organizations such as the Clube de Engenharia, where she created the women's department in the 1970s, as well as in the Associação Brasileira de Engenheiras e Arquitetas, which she chaired twice.

WOMEN ENGINEERS AND ADVANCES IN REINFORCED CONCRETE IN BRAZIL

In her memoirs, Leitchic recalls the privilege of having been a student of the engineer Antonio Alves de Noronha and starting work alongside the experienced structural concrete design engineers Feliciano Pena Chaves and João Gualberto Marques Porto.

Effectively, despite the innovative structural design and technology employed by the engineer Emílio Baumgart (1889–1943) in the iconic Ministério da Educação e Saúde (1937–45),[11] reinforced concrete was not seen as a field of specialization in the engineering curriculum until the early 1940s, instead being distributed among other disciplines. Although the subject was covered by manuals and local professional and technical publications from the 1920s onwards, the first courses on the issue were given by the Associação Brasileira de Concreto (ABC), established in 1930, in Rio de Janeiro.[12]

Nevertheless, the evolution of concrete construction following its introduction by foreign companies and engineers at the turn of the century was tied to advancements in national industry and technological research, particularly supported by the state and embodied in the engineering and entrepreneurial circles around associations such as the Clube de Engenharia (1880, Rio de Janeiro) and the Instituto de Engenharia (1916, São Paulo).[13] The same spirit permeated the creation of the Associação Brasileira de Cimento Portland/ABCP (1936), followed by the Associação Brasileira de Normas Técnicas/ABNT (1940), which intended to unify methods and criteria for industrialized products.

In Rio de Janeiro, technological research in the field of construction was conducted within the Instituto Nacional de Tecnologia/INT (1921), while in São Paulo it began earlier in the Gabinete de Resistência dos Materiais (1893), later known as Laboratório de Ensaios de Materiais/LEM (1926) at the Politécnica. Having become independent in 1934 and renamed Instituto de Pesquisas Tecnológicas/IPT, it carried out technological research at the University of São Paulo and, even as late as the 1960s, was still one of the few institutions where women engineers were able to occupy positions of leadership and engage in the social and economic development of the country, contrary to the restrictions imposed by the sexist ambiance of professional circles and, even more so, of construction sites. Indeed, Frida Anna Maria Hoffmann, the first woman to graduate from the Politécnica of São Paulo in 1928, found a place as chemical engineer at the IPT in 1935.[14]

In the early 1970s, while the country was experiencing the so-called "economic miracle" and large construction sites were rising up all over the place, from housing developments to infrastructures, the lack of qualified labor and the rapid mechanization of concrete production without the necessary technological development, caused a number of serious accidents.[15] These disasters triggered a new generation of studies on con-

10   Marcos Eduardo Neves, *Servenco, sobrenome Steinberg* (Rio de Janeiro: Rotativa.Art, 2011).

11   Danielli Cristina Borelli Cintra *et al.*, "Palácio Gustavo Capanema: estrutura e construção," *CONCRETO & Construções*, no. 100 (October/December 2020): 89–98.

12   Augusto Carlos de Vasconcelos, "História do Concreto Armado," in *Contribuições para a História da Engenharia no Brasil*, ed. Milton Vargas (São Paulo: EPUSP, 1994), 79–147.

13   Milton Vargas, ed., *História da Técnica e da Tecnologia no Brasil* (São Paulo: Editora UNESP, 1994), 225–45.

14   Maria Cândida Reginato Facciotti and Eni de Mesquita Samara, *Mulheres Politécnicas: Histórias e Perfis* (São Paulo: Escola Politécnica da USP, 2004).

15   Paulo Helene, "Concreto: ciência, tecnologia, desenvolvimento e qualidade de vida," *CONCRETO & Construções*, no. 97 (January/February/March 2020): 5.

16   Augusto Carlos de Vasconcelos, "Maria Noronha," *Revista Engenharia*, no. 589 (2008): 41–42.

17   Éride Moura, "Yasuko Tezuko. Na seara masculina," *Construção São Paulo*, no. 2168 (August 28, 1989): 23–26; "Entrevista Maria Alba Cincotto," *CONCRETO & Construções*, no. 96 (October/December 2019): 12–20.

↑ *Revista da Diretoria de Engenharia*, no. 12 (September 1934) of which Carmen Velasco Portinho was editor-in-chief

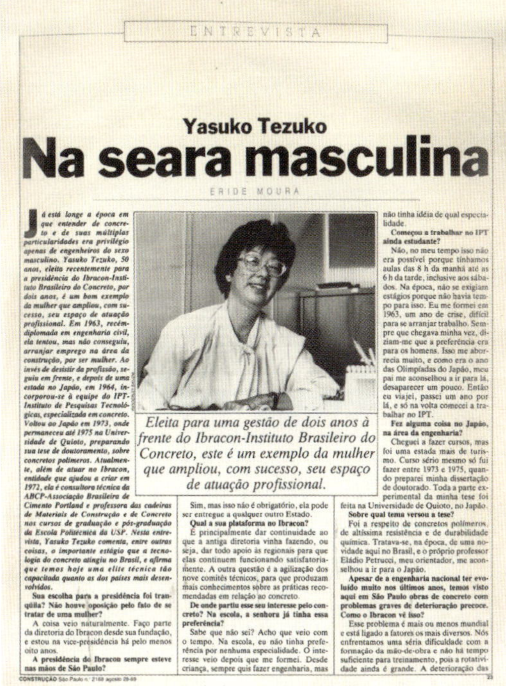

↑ "Yasuko Tezuko. Na seara masculin. Entrevista," *Construção São Paulo*, no. 2168 (August 28, 1989): 23. Biblioteca da Escola Politécnica da Universidade de São Paulo

crete and its construction systems—from pathologies to the analysis of durability and concrete additive performance—that found support in the newly established Instituto Brasileiro do Concreto/IBRACON (1972). There were two women engineers behind these advancements and among IBRACON's founders: Maria Apparecida Noronha (Mackenzie, 1951), and Yasuko Tezuka (Escola Politécnica, 1963), as well as a diligent chemist who worked at the IPT, side by side with engineers, namely Maria Alba Cincotto (Universidade de São Paulo, 1961). All three had training experience at international research institutions and were involved in both technological experimentation and teaching, as well as contributing to the construction industry.

Among those pioneering researchers in the 1960s, Noronha was the only one with real experience in construction sites, having been involved in the sophisticated construction of the Anchieta highway connecting São Paulo to the coast, which was headed by her father, the engineer Francisco Azevedo. In the early 1960s, she began to focus on the technological control of concrete, becoming a recognized figure in the field through her association with the engineer Luiz Alfredo Falcão Bauer, before going on to start her own firm Azevedo Noronha Engenheiros Associados in 1981.[16] In their turn, both Tezuka and Cincotto began their careers at IPT,[17] sharing projects and publications consecrate to pathologies related to concrete and mortars, corrosion of concrete reinforcements, or concrete additives and composite, both inside and outside the institution. Tezuka became head of the Laboratory of Concrete Research and then president of IBRACON from 1989 to 1991, launching its first publication *Concreto* in 1991.

CONCLUSION

While the involvement and achievements of the country's first female engineers in the 1920s and 1930s, particularly in Rio de Janeiro, were fueled by a clearly feminist position and militantism related to the suffragist movement, in the 1960s and 1970s feminist aspirations reemerged from within social movements and resistance to the dictatorship. In this context, despite the persistently authoritarian and male chauvinistic atmosphere of engineering circles, the female professional's drive to contribute to society at large was mostly operated in the materiality of the construction site, far from the ideological engagement of the first pioneers. Nevertheless, both generations bore a fundamentally feminine characteristic that one might suggest was part of the female realm of experience, being particularly apparent in the awareness of engineering as a fundamental collective enterprise within the public and private sphere. As suggested by Simone de Beauvoir, however, "one is not born, but rather becomes a woman," meaning that being part of a common enterprise does not mean a woman's place is in the back office.

SCHOOL IN LEUTSCHENBACH

	ZURICH, SWITZERLAND
	2002–2009
ARCHITECT	CHRISTIAN KEREZ
ENGINEER	JOSEPH SCHWARTZ

The School in Leutschenbach, north of Zurich, is designed as a simple, elegant, single block containing all of the functional spaces, from classrooms to the cafeteria to the gym.

The building, with its completely glass-paned walls, has a distinctive structure consisting of a system of large steel beams in a lattice pattern that creates pronounced overhangs and is supported by six base columns. The ground floor serves mainly as a point of entry and access to the building's other spaces; a central double ramp leads to the upper levels. The classrooms are arranged on three floors, all set within the first structural framework, while the upper floor is the gym, a bright, panoramic space that also serves local sports associations. The result skillfully blends the expressiveness of the steel structure with exposed concrete elements and transparent glass panes. The building is the fruit of a long process of collaboration between Kerez and Schwartz, which entailed the creation of over 100 study models.

School Building, Zurich,
2009. Photo Leonardo
Finotti. Courtesy Leonardo
Finotti

HSBC MAIN BUILDING

HONG KONG

1979–1986

ARCHITECT   FOSTER + PARTNERS

ENGINEER   OVE ARUP AND PARTNERS
                   GERHARD JACOB "JACK" ZUNZ
                   MIKE GLOVER

The evolution of the structural schema of the *Hongkong and Shanghai Banking Corporation* building is an interesting exercise in dialectics between architect and engineer. Norman Foster's inspiration to suspend the buildings floors on three large framework structures became, in the hands of Arup's studio, a chevron system—first triple, then multiple—and ended up developing together the solution they called "hangers." Here, the idea of suspension translated into five two-story-high trusses that cover a span of 33.5 m in the center and 10.7 m cantilevered beyond them at both ends. Suspended on this gigantic frame are the 36, 44 and 29 floors of the three adjacent blocks that make up the 183-meter-high tower. Eight steel masts compose the main vertical structure. Each mast is made up of four 1.5-meter-diameter and 10-centimeter-thick columns. The centrifugal arrangement of the supports—as well as all of the utilities and elevators—allows for a dizzying 10-story atrium, with a public plaza on the ground floor and 62 escalators weaving through the space. Due to the high-traffic area of the project, much of the building was prefabricated, from the structure itself to the restroom areas.

→ HSBC Main Building, Hong Kong, 1986. Photo Ian Lambot. Courtesy Arup

JOHNSON WAX RESEARCH TOWER

	RACINE (WI), USA
	1943–1950
ARCHITECT	FRANK LLOYD WRIGHT
ENGINEER	JAROSLAV JOSEF POLÍVKA

Ten years after the completion of the Johnson Wax administrative office building, with its forest of "dendriform" columns supporting and shaping a roof composed of large, circular reinforced concrete elements, Wright created the company's research tower in Racine. Despite the architect's reluctance to publicly acknowledge Polívka's role, the engineer's contribution was fundamental in bringing the project to fruition.

The new structure, as opposed to the horizontality of the previous building, is a vertical mass; a central nucleus with vertical access elements, bathrooms and utility rooms supports the cantilevered upper floors. The floor slabs of the various levels, which alternate square and circular floor plans, are made of reinforced concrete with a tapered section that recalls the dendriform columns of the office building.

The circular-floor-plan levels, with a diameter slightly smaller than the sides of the square floors, create double-height spaces. The tower has an elegant, singular appearance with its rounded corners and a coplanar outer shell of alternating bands of brick and transparent glass tubing.

↑ Johnson Wax Research
Tower under construction,
Racine, 1950. Courtesy
The Frank Lloyd Wright
Foundation Archives (The
Museum of Modern Art |
Avery Architectural & Fine
Arts Library, Columbia
University, New York)

BURJ KHALIFA
TOWER

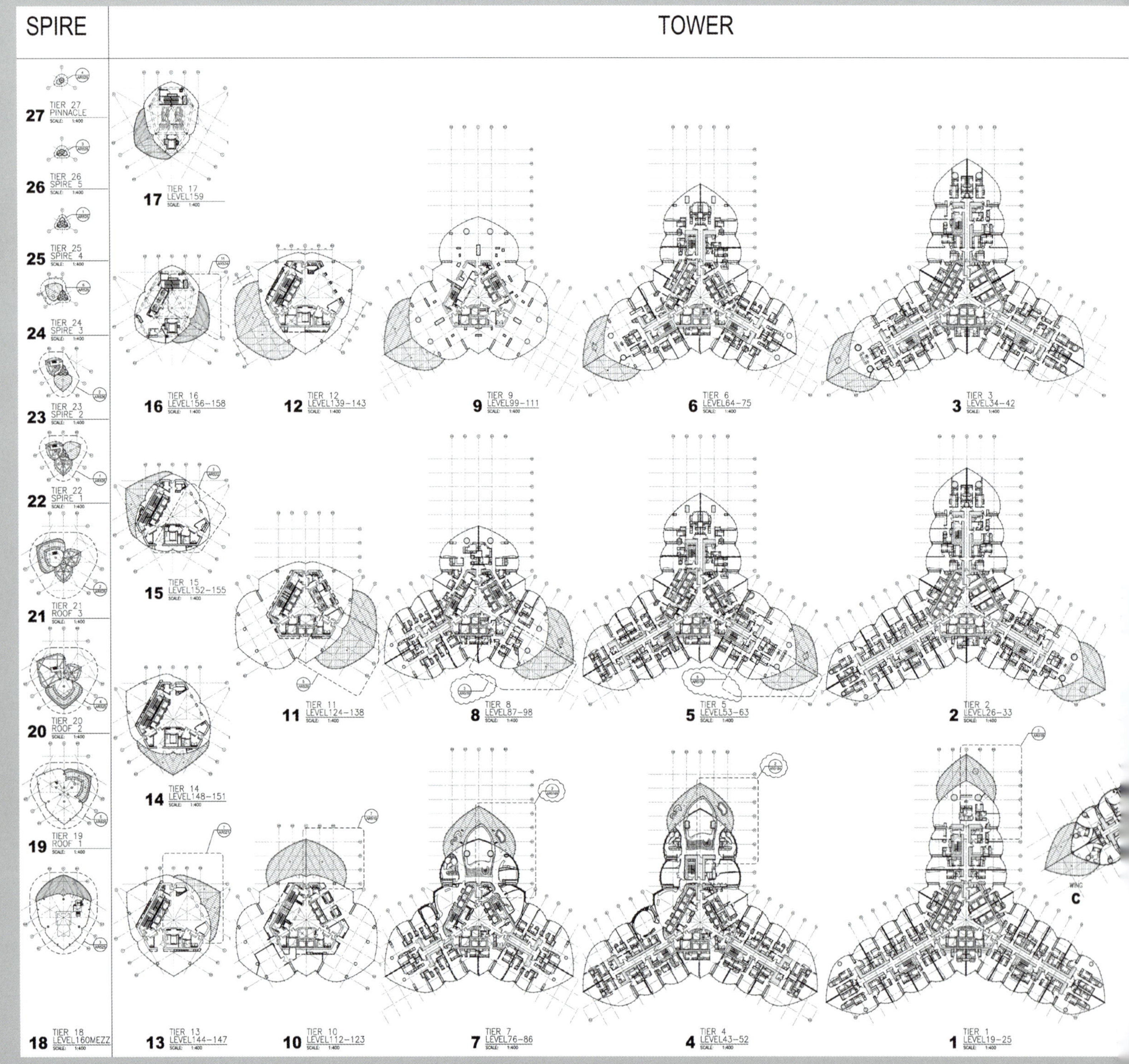

| ARCHITECT | ADRIAN SMITH |
| | SOM |

| ENGINEER | WILLIAM FRAZIER "BILL" BAKER |
| | SOM |

The quest for height has always been a stimulus in the development of structural engineering. The Burj Khalifa took this pursuit to extremes, earning the status of tallest building in the world with its 828 meters.

The structural core of the skyscraper is a hexagonal nucleus of reinforced concrete, inside which the elevators run. To keep this slim vertical element from upending, stepped buttresses were added, hidden within the blocks that make up the building's distinctive triple-lobed footprint. The buttresses themselves are stiffened by transversal walls to resist bending and twisting.

One of the main problems with tall buildings is the effect of wind forces. To avoid the risk of wind vortices making the structure vibrate at its natural frequency and creating a resonance effect, SOM came up with a spiral shape, varying the height of the blocks that make up the building.

To support the Burj Khalifa's weight, a thick reinforced concrete base platform was used, in turn supported by 192 foundation posts.

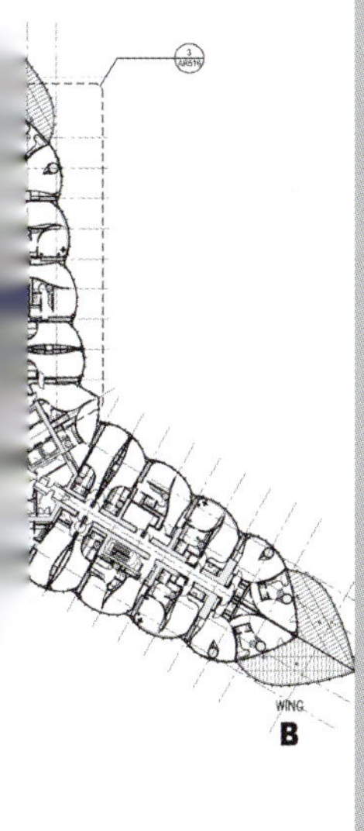

← Burj Khalifa Tower, Plan, Dubai, 2010. Courtesy SOM

875 NORTH MICHIGAN AVENUE SKYSCRAPER

	CHICAGO (IL), USA
	1964–1970
ARCHITECT	BRUCE GRAHAM SOM
ENGINEER	FAZLUR RAHMAN KHAN SOM

SOM responded to a request for a multifunctional complex of offices, commercial businesses and residences with an innovative proposal, thanks to the synergetic collaboration between architect Bruce Graham and engineer Fazlur Rahman Khan. Rather than two separate buildings, the Chicago studio proposed the first mixed-function skyscraper, dedicating the lower floors to commercial businesses and offices, and the upper ones to over 700 apartments.

The revolutionary structure was designed by Rahman Khan, whose experimentation focuses on tubular systems for tall buildings that can take advantage of perimetral pressure balancing, reducing the need for internal supports. The external skeleton of 875 North Michigan Avenue is thus a very large tubular reticular structure, tapered towards the top, that lends great stiffness to the building and distinguishes the façades with colossal diagonal elements in steel, most of which are 20 stories high.

↓ 875 North Michigan Avenue
Skyscraper, Chicago, 1970.
Photo Ezra Stoller. Courtesy
SOM. © Ezra Stoller | Esto

BANK OF CHINA TOWER

	HONG KONG
	1982–1989
ARCHITECT	PEI COBB FREED & PARTNERS
ENGINEER	LERA LESLIE E. ROBERTSON SAWTEEN SEE

The Bank of China headquarters stands out in the Hong Kong skyline with its 368-meter height and iconic prismatic profile. Built in a city densely packed with tall structures and often buffeted by typhoon winds, the tower, designed by Pei in collaboration with the engineers from LERA, responds with a structural solution that meets stability requirements and distinguishes the building's architecture.

Four triangular prisms spring from a 52-meter-per-side cube to reach different heights; the diagonal cuts across their tops create atriums flooded with natural light, with spectacular views of the bay.

A steel framework encloses these four structures, lending rigidity to the building and reducing the need for internal supports. The large diagonal beams and the mirror-glass façade make the tower an immediately recognizable element in Hong Kong's urban landscape.

↑ Bank of China Tower, Hong
Kong, 1989. Photo Paul
Warchol. Courtesy Pei Cobb
Freed & Partners

CCTV HEADQUARTERS

BEIJING, CHINA

2002–2012

ARCHITECT	OMA
	REM KOOLHAAS
ENGINEER	ARUP
	CECIL BALMOND
	RORY MCGOWAN

Rem Koolhaas sets Arup the challenge of a continuous-loop-shaped skyscraper that generates a three-dimensional experience of the vertical dimension and offers a shape-shifting perception depending on the observer's point of view. Its functions—offices, recording and production studios, and a broadcasting center—are metaphorically and physically interconnected in a 234-meter-high, 51-story potentially infinite ring. The complex building is composed of two leaning towers rising from an L-shaped plinth inclined at 6°. On level 36, the two towers are connected by a cantilevered bridge, the *Overhang*, from floors 9 to 13. Structurally, it is a continuous tube with a mesh visible on the façade: a web of steel bars arranged diagonally on the two-story module that densifies, thins out or changes thickness depending on the stress its components are under, as if visually manifesting the loads it bears. The structure is highly indeterminate, in that every new schema alters the distribution of forces in a continuous, iterative process of adapting a model to reality.

ENGINEERING LIGHTNESS

Mohsen Mostafavi

In the spring of 1951, the Festival of Britain, a showcase for achievements in the arts, architecture, technology, and industrial design, opened to great fanfare in London's Southbank. Among the most enduring icons of that event are photographs of a slender structure approximately 90 meters in height erected near Westminster Bridge, along the embankment of the river Thames. The Skylon, the futuristic installation, was raised 15 meters off the ground and held in mid-air by a series of cables linked to a delicate supporting structure.

The name Skylon is attributed to a woman not directly linked to the project and incorporates the words sky, pylon, and then a relatively new material, Nylon. Nylon as a synthetic thermoplastic polymer was developed in the 1930s, but its use became ubiquitous in the 1940s with women's stockings, which were generally referred to as nylons. But the production of nylon was re-directed during the war toward making parachutes and parachute chords.

The architects who designed the Skylon, Philip Powell and Hidalgo Moya, were at first ambivalent about the made-up name, but came to accept its multiple evocations as an apt description of their project. Both the tensegrity structure and its name became emblematic of the post-war desire for a modern and technologically forward-looking Britain.

One of the reasons for the structure's success may have been its capacity to be at once an object of wonder and a symbol of flight. Its form was reminiscent of a shuttle about to be launched into space. The floating, weightless quality of the Skylon's main element, a "cigar-shaped" piece with pointed ends, was made possible by minimizing the need for a major supporting structure. The Skylon's hovering element evoked a sense of awe in visitors akin to that of witnessing the levitating body of a magician's assistant.

The architects collaborated with engineer Felix Samuely to achieve the structure's magical qualities. Born in Vienna in 1902 and educated in Berlin, Samuely resettled in London in 1933, making a name for himself as an innovative engineer and influential teacher.

His extraordinary knowledge of engineering, together with his interest in innovative solutions, must be appreciated in the context of both pre- and post-war Europe, with the combined pressures of time and limited resources. The circumstances meant that things had to be done quickly, using easily available and transportable materials. One striking example is the iconic De La Warr Pavilion (1935) by Serge Chermayeff and Erich Mendelsohn, with a pioneering site-welded steel frame by Samuely. Built in under a year, this sleek "horizontal skyscraper," as Mendelsohn termed it, stands as one of the earliest examples of modernist architecture in Britain.

Yet it is for his contribution to the Skylon and his capacity for creating "lightness" that Samuely is perhaps best remembered. The Skylon exemplified the fortuitous and optimistic encounter between design and engineering at a moment when the careful utilization of resources and the economy of means were also linked to the possibility of a better future, one that looked beyond the recent experiences of Nazism and war. It is both ironic and inspiring that Britain found itself propelled towards its future by so many émigrés, including Felix Samuely.

But the Skylon, one of the emblems of that future, did not last long. The decision was made to dismantle the structure and sell it as scrap metal. Perhaps no one then considered it important to hold on to what would have become part of the nation's tangible heritage. The same thing happened to the Dome of Discovery, the festival's other major structure. Or perhaps the logistics of transforming a temporary structure in need of constant maintenance and calibration into something more functional and permanent was too much for anyone to consider. In any case, all that remains are the photographs of the Festival of Britain and the name Skylon, which has proved more enduring than the actual physical artifact. The latest version of the name is for a series of designs for a hydrogen-fueled spacecraft. A few years after the dismantling of the Skylon, the world of engineering and architecture also lost the opportunity to witness the further development of Felix Samuely's wealth of engineering ideas, including his speculations on lightness: he died of a heart attack in 1959, just days before his 57th birthday. Nevertheless, his legacy—including his collaborations with architects, his many research papers, and his influence as a teacher of structures for architects—lives on.

After Samuely's death, leadership of the FJ Samuely engineering firm was delegated to a young engineer, Frank Newby, who at the age of 32 was one of the rising figures in the field. Newby had originally joined Samuely's practice in 1949, not long after graduating from Cambridge, and had worked on the Skylon. But he left the firm in 1952 on a Marshall Aid scholarship to travel in the United States where he met and collaborated with several important architects and designers including Charles and Ray Eames, Bertrand Goldberg, Eero Saarinen, Konrad Wachsmann, and Richard Buckminster Fuller.

On his return from the United States, Newby rejoined Samuely and became a partner in 1956. A generous and sociable person, he benefited from his time in the USA, where he was exposed not only to new and different approaches in architecture but also to the potential role of an engineer in the collaborative process between design and engineering. And in fact, the rest of his career would exemplify this approach to design. Later in life, Newby acknowledged the immense influence of his American sojourn as well as the influence of his mentor, Felix Samuely, whom he credited with teaching him the three-dimensional character of structures. Not surprisingly, Newby also spoke of learning about the role of joints in design from Konrad Wachsmann, who was then at the Institute of Design in Chicago.

THE BRUSSELS EXPO

Not long after becoming a partner, Newby collaborated with the architect Edward D. Mills on the British Industrial Pavilion at the Brussels Expo '58. Unlike the Festival of Britain, which had focused solely on celebrating the achievements of British artists and designers, the Brussels Expo marked the beginnings of a phase of broader European cooperation.

As with the journey to the United States, the Brussels Expo with its collection of speculative projects left its mark on Newby. Expo '58, like earlier Expos, dealt with forward-looking social and cultural issues; it, too, was of short duration, with an emphasis on ease of assembly/construction and disassembly/demolition. In the post-war period, there was an emphasis on such events to promote innovation and technological advancement. The optimistic belief in the promise of technology also distinguished a few of the European pavilions from their counterparts from other parts of the world, which focused on tradition and the celebration of the past rather than possibilities for the future. The influence of these factors is evident in the images of the French Pavilion with its large open interior and its lightweight membrane structure.

The most iconic pavilion at the Brussels Expo was the outcome of a collaboration between Le Corbusier and the composer, theorist, and engineer Iannis Xenakis. As Le Corbusier was in India in that period, Xenakis has been credited as the main designer of the pavilion. He was clearly the main figure responsible for the execution of the project, funded by the Dutch electronics company Philips as the hub for multi-media events at Expo '58. The structure of the pavilion, made up of a series of reinforced-concrete hyperbolic paraboloids, enabled interplays between architecture and music, literally creating acoustic spaces. Such reciprocities, including possibilities for the spatialization of sound, played an important role in Xenakis's later career as a full-time composer of "concrete musical compositions." Despite Xenakis's success as a composer, one is left imagining what he might have achieved in the world of architecture if he had not left Le Corbusier's atelier or if he had continued his spatial experiments at the intersection of architecture, mathematics, and music. Still, the completion of the Philips Pavilion was also the wellspring of the idea of architecture as a sensorial environment, an architecture that is as much intertwined with the human body and human emotions as it is with technological and engineering innovations.

THE SNOWDON AVIARY

The combination of his collaboration with Felix Samuely, his American experience, and the opportunity to encounter the pavilions at Brussels Expo prepared Frank Newby for the next phase of his career. Newby, like Samuely, was able to work on a broad range of projects, and soon after assuming leadership of the firm he was appointed as the engineer for Eero Saarinen's new American Embassy in London, in 1960. But it was another collaborative project that would more visibly demonstrate his capacities as a structural engineer. The new Aviary for the Zoo in London's Regent's Park, completed in 1964, involved a collaboration between Antony Armstrong-Jones, Cedric Price, and Frank Newby. Armstrong-Jones, who had been given the original commission, presumably in part if not wholly because of his marriage to Princess Margaret, the sister of Queen Elizabeth II, had studied architecture as an undergraduate at Cambridge but had failed his second-year exam; he was joined by Price, who had also been at Cambridge for the first part of his architectural training before moving to the AA to complete his diploma. Despite his lack of professional qualifications, Armstrong-Jones, who became an important photographer and was given the title of Lord Snowdon on account of his marriage to a member of the royal family, counted his contribution to the Aviary, now named after him, as one of his major achievements. But it is the collaboration between Cedric Price and Frank Newby that is often recognized as being responsible for the innovative design.

The zoo itself featured many architecturally significant projects, including the famous and much-loved Penguin Pool, built in 1934. That project was the outcome of a productive partnership between the Georgian-British architect Berthold Lubetkin and his firm, Tecton, together with Ove Arup who as the engineer managed to design one of the most beguiling pieces of the structure. The Penguin Pool, like the Skylon and the Aviary, is the epitome of visual lightness. But unlike the Penguin Pool with its theatrical staging for the "performance" of penguins moving across its thin, interlocking double ramps that submerge into the water, the Aviary is a habitat, an environment that encapsulates and expresses the freedom of flight within the boundaries of the lightweight mesh that defines the three-dimensional form of its structure. Still, no less of a performance was expected from birds in flight than from the penguins. Such is the nature and role of zoos, as places of entertainment for the visitor. The Aviary's design, however, enabled the visitor to move through it and to be at one with the birds within the confines of its enclosed environment. One of the distinguishing features of the Snowdon Aviary, compared to other tensile structures of the time, is the relationship between the main element of the structure and the topography of its sectional "constructed ground." A varied series of triangular aluminum tubular sections, cables, and mesh shape the overall forms of the main structure, which is anchored to the ground. The treatment of the topography, together with elevated walkways, enabled visitors to view birds in their natural habitat on the ground as well as in the air, looking down to the ground without disturbing the birds, and also "hovering" in the air like the birds in flight. The visitor's movement within the environment of the Aviary produced a more dynamic relation than in many of the other buildings at the Zoo, which, partly due to necessity, clearly demarcated the division between the visitors and the animals.

In many ways, the Snowdon Aviary is the most significant tangible manifestation of Cedric Price's belief in the necessity of an active and participatory relationship

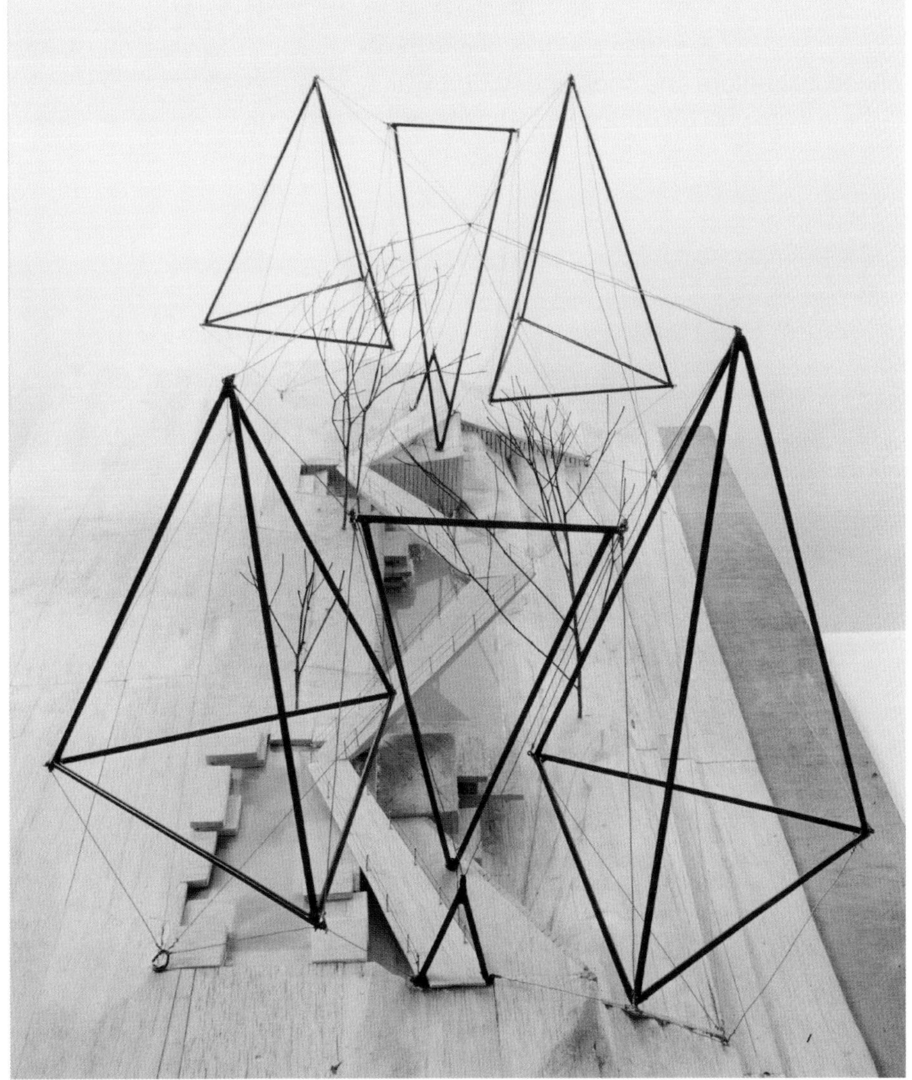

between architecture and its occupants. But even more than this, his interest in and commitment to the liberative dimension of this interaction came into play in the design of the Aviary. The role of technology was equally important. The collaboration and dialogues between Cedric Price and Frank Newby are an exploration of the relationship between technology and the ephemeral and sensorial qualities of the structure.

Currently, the Zoo is working with Foster + Partners to convert the Aviary as part of a larger complex for monkeys. The Penguin Pool, however, was abandoned in 2004 as a home for penguins due to damage caused to the penguins' feet after the restoration of its ramps.
Despite their fate, both the Penguin Pool and the Snowdon Aviary remain two key icons of modern British architecture. The Aviary is still one of the truly significant examples of a lightweight structure and one of the few to survive beyond the short duration of a festival or world's fair. In that context, the pavilion as the manifestation of so many speculative and experimental projects in architecture is almost invariably something temporary. The Aviary is also an outstanding example of collaboration between the three main protagonists of the project, and between design and engineering.

THE RISE OF OVE ARUP

After the Aviary, Frank Newby worked on a diverse array of buildings with a variety of architects. One of his major achievements, with James Stirling and James Gowan, was the Engineering building at the University of Leicester. Though its structure is very different from Newby's earlier work, this building has also achieved an iconic status. But it is an irony that neither Newby nor the practice he led, FJ Samuely & Partners, despite the brilliance of both men, went on to develop a more substantial body of experimental work in structural engineering, especially concerning the idea of engineering lightness.

It is often said that during the period just before and soon after World War II, there were only two engineers whose work

↓   Ove Arup, Kingsgate Bridge, Durham, 1963, Courtesy of Durham University Library. Photo by staff of Fillinghams of Elvet Bridge

had a transformative impact on architecture in the UK. One was Felix Samuely, and the other was Ove Arup. Two foreigners whose contribution to the world of architectural engineering cannot be underestimated. But only Arup's firm continued to thrive after the death of its founder. Why is that? Many people who knew Arup well say he was as much a philosopher as he was an engineer. He was clearly entrepreneurial, but beyond that, he had a very clear, deep-rooted ethos about the world and about the role of architecture and engineering within it. Even though the firm has always employed many brilliant engineers, its emphasis is on the quality of the organization and the brand, not the cult of the individual.

Some thirty years after the completion of the Penguin Pool, Arup personally designed his last piece of work, the Kingsgate Bridge, across the River Wear, in Durham. In its own way this footbridge, which was completed in 1963, is as much concerned with lightness as the Penguin Pool was, but it also explored the relationship between design and implementation. By all accounts, Arup spent a great deal of time—perhaps beyond what would normally be required for a project of this scale—studying a variety of options. He finally decided on a lightweight, reinforced-concrete structure which was built in two halves on either side of the river, with each piece then rotated 90° and connected in the middle by a bronze expansion joint using a gear bearing. The simplicity of this project or, rather, the thought that had gone into making it, makes it seem a simple and light undertaking, but it exemplifies Arup's philosophy, which is why he considered it one of his favorite projects.

One of the ways in which Arup safeguarded both the innovative spirit and the longevity of his organization was by creating separate, semi-autonomous design departments. And it was one of these departments, later known as Structures 3, which developed the engineering expertise for the design and construction of large lightweight structures. The department was originally set up in 1967 with Povl Ahm, another Danish engineer, who had worked on the Sydney Opera House among other projects. The day-to-day leadership of the department was left to its executive director Edmund (Ted) Happold. A year later the team were joined by Peter Rice, the brilliant Irish engineer who, like Povl and Happold, had worked on the Sydney Opera House, and returned to the practice after 18 months working in the USA. The team at Structures 3 not only became a powerhouse of engineering creativity but also gained a reputation for expertise in lightweight, tensile, and membrane structures.

FREI OTTO AND THE ART OF THE LIGHTWEIGHT STRUCTURE

In 1966 Ted Happold, in conjunction with the architect Trevor Dannatt, had entered a competition for the design of a hotel and conference center in Riyadh, Saudi Arabia. Although they did not win, their third-placed entry was selected by King Faisal to be realized in Mecca, along with that of their fellow competitors Rolf Gutbrod and Frei Otto. The competition led to a lifelong collaboration between Happold and Otto who, with his partner, invited Arup to be the engineers for the Mecca project. The most significant part of the collaboration between Happold and Otto in Mecca concerned the design of the auditorium with a suspended cable roof. Here, a series of steel cables and stiffening structural angles support an insulated sandwich roof with corrugated aluminum cladding.

The collaboration between Otto and Happold in Saudi Arabia was an important transitional step on the way to two of Otto's most significant lightweight structures: the 1972 Munich Olympic Stadium designed with the architect Günther Behnisch, and the 1975 Multihalle, Mannheim, with the architect Carlfried Mutschler, and Ove Arup & Partners as the engineers, built for the National Garden Show. These projects helped to establish Frei Otto's reputation as the leading expert in and proponent of lightweight structures.

The Munich project was to be the symbol of a progressive and democratic Germany, but its aspirations were marred by multiple complications and challenges. First, the architects had to set their design apart from the Nazi-era approach used in the 1936

Berlin Olympics. Architecturally, this aim was achieved with Behnisch & Partners' anti-monumental gesture of carving the event facilities into the ground—akin to a landscape—rather than constructing a giant building and covering it with Frei Otto's tensible structure above. Despite numerous objections to the project and its structural feasibility, it ultimately opened in time for the games.

Frei Otto himself was critical of the client's decision to use rigid panels instead of a lighter-weight, more malleable material. But regardless of the problems, the Munich stadium was an immense design and construction undertaking and one that provided a series of valuable research and learning opportunities for its designers, e.g., determining how to ensure that the structure did not produce adverse lighting conditions such as shadows that would hinder the athletes' performance.

But the Multihalle at Mannheim may have given Frei Otto the most satisfaction as the outcome of productive collaborations, not just with Carlfried Mutschler and his colleagues Joachim and Winfried Langner, but also with Ted Happold, Ian Liddell, Michael Dickson, and other engineers from Arup. Even Sir Ove Arup himself traveled to Stuttgart to help with the project. Frei Otto spoke of the inherent risks associated with this experimental project in a conversation with the architect Heinrich Klotz, in 1977. "The assembly of the Mannheim Hall was breathtaking, but I was also a bit scared. This huge wooden carpet on the ground! It rocked terribly when you walked across it. There was a certain point at which we thought it would be impossible for the thing to ever be stiff enough. Only after we made our load test, which showed how incredibly stiff the dome could be, did our courage return. Admittedly, the calculations showed that everything was fine, and the engineers meticulously checked every detail—but the calculation is one thing, the belief in it another."[1]

Ian Liddell, one of the original engineers involved in the design and calculations of Frei Otto's wooden grid shell structure, has recently paid tribute to the importance of this innovative undertaking and placed it within the wider context of the designer's work. According to Liddell, the task of carrying out the statistical calculations for the project was originally entrusted to the Mannheim engineers Bräuer und Späth. But when they realized the limitations of purely mathematical calculations regarding the stability of the shell, Ove Arup & Partners were engaged as the engineers, on Frei Otto's recommendation. Happold and Liddell, as the lead representatives of the firm, stepped into the role in 1973, while the original engineers continued with the ground works.[2]

One of the main challenges of the Mannheim project was the question of the structure's behavior and the difficulty of predicting the outcome with any degree of certainty. The situation was compounded by the limited time factor. In response to this complex situation and without the benefit of the type of digital and software tools available today, according to Liddell, the team made the decision to: (a) carry out investigations into the design loads; (b) conduct desk studies and hand calculations on shell buckling; (c) test models of the structure; and (d) make hand calculations to approximate the member forces.

The calculations and testing of models for the Mannheim project oscillated between sophisticated and abstract mathematical theories, the use of scientific papers and technologies such as wind tunnels, and more basic explorations such as hanging chain models that could simulate the behavior of the full-scale project. It was perhaps the accumulated knowledge of this multi-faceted, trial-and-error approach that alleviated some of Frei Otto's fear about the viability of the structure. The uncertainties and the risks associated with a project such as the Mannheim Multihalle are unacceptable to most clients and design consultants. But the design and the engineering of this type of temporary, lightweight structure can help us understand the potential for both alternative and sustainable modes of building construction.

BURO HAPPOLD, A GLOBAL ENTERPRISE

The success of the collaboration between Frei Otto and Ove Arup & Partners presumably played a part in Ted Happold's decision to set up his own engineering firm in 1976, when he was appointed professor of architecture and engineering at the University of Bath. Happold was able to invite others, including Ian Liddell and Michael Dickson, to join him in the new practice, which became known for its expertise in lightweight, tensile and membrane structures, among other areas, as well as its subsequent collaborations with Frei Otto. Today, Buro Happold, as the firm was named, is a global engineering firm.

The firm's early work included projects in the Middle East, where the concept of a large lightweight roof appears in keeping with the aesthetics of tents and the temporality of a nomadic desert lifestyle, as well as providing a reprieve from the heat of the sun. During its early days, Buro Happold also worked on a series of mechanical umbrella structures for the rock band Pink Floyd on their 1977 tour of the USA. Buro Happold's growth as a practice has been paralleled by an increase in the size and scope of many of their projects. In the process, the idea of lightweight structures, which for Frei Otto was always somehow linked to questions of duration and sustainability, has generally been supplanted by more permanent and durable manifestations of the concept, as in the McArthur Glen Designer Outlet, completed in 2000 by the Richard Rogers Partnership in Ashford, or the Great Court of the British Museum, from the same year, by Foster + Partners.

Frei Otto and Buro Happold's collaborations also included two projects at Hooke Park, with the architect Richard Burton of ABK (Ahrends, Burton, and Koralek), for the furniture designer John Makepeace. Makepeace had originally established a School for Craftsmen in Wood, which later became Parnham College and trained a generation of furniture designers. The buildings at Hooke Park are in the midst of a wood in Dorset and were designed by different architects. For the structure of the main workshop, Otto and others used spruce thinnings from the forest, a locally-sourced building material that was

essentially without any monetary value or structural strength. There is a simplicity and rawness associated with this structure that runs counter to the technological aesthetic of the more complex projects that Buro Happold carried out with other architects.

THE INGENUITY OF PETER RICE

The evolution of the notion of lightness also owes a debt to the Irish engineer Peter Rice who, before his untimely death in 1992, collaborated on numerous key projects with innovative architects. In addition to his role as a member of Structures 3 at Ove Arup & Partners, where he had worked with Ted Happold, Rice played an influential role in the design of the Pompidou Center in Paris, among other projects. His work on the Lord's Mound Stand (1985–87) with Michael Hopkins and Partners, where he engineered the PVC-coated canopy roof structure, demonstrated his capacity for engineering lightweight structures with special aesthetic and spatial qualities. Part of the challenge of designing a stand for watching cricket, as opposed to other sports such as soccer, is the fact that it has historically been played only on a village green and in the summer. The task was thus in a sense to translate this experience into the design, including the lightness of the tents that would be assembled on the cricket grounds. The final scheme manages to combine many of these qualities and enhance them with a sense of levity, celebration, and fun. The design reduced the number of columns to six to minimize disruption to sightlines. The columns are linked by a plate girder which enables lattice trusses to be cantilevered out from them. The columns rise like celebratory masts, with the structures' tension members tied to the ground, a permanent structure despite its fragile and temporary nature.

Rice's important and inspirational posthumously-published book, *An Engineer Imagines,* from 1994, provides a window on his thinking about lightweight structures, a term which he found "broad" and "inappropriate." Instead, the chapter uses

---

1   Quoted in Georg Vrachliotis, *Frei Otto, Carlfried Mutschler. Multihalle* (Leipzig: Spector Books, 2017), 124. See also Heinrich Klotz, ed., *Architektur in der Bundesrepublik. Gespräche mit Günter Behnisch, Wolfgang Döring, Helmut Hentrich, Hans Kammerer, Frei Otto, Oswald M. Ungers* (Frankfurt am Main: Ullstein, 1977).

---

2   Ian Liddell, "Frei Otto and the Development of Gridshells," *Case Studies in Structural Engineering* 4 (2015): 39–49.

the title *Fabric* to designate "a group of surface structures made from fabric or tension or compression nets."[3] Rice also pays homage to Frei Otto for his contribution to the field and recognizes the shift from the use of modelling techniques, such as Otto's experiments with soap film surfaces, to the development of computer methods, including Finite Element Analysis. According to Rice, the development of new techniques had reached a point "where the limits of what can be designed and built are the limitations of materials and the limitations of the designer's inventiveness, not, as has hitherto been the case, the limitations of analysis and specification methods."[4]

THE END OF AN ERA

Ironically, the end of a certain period or phase in the development of lightweight or fabric structures was marked by the design and construction of the Millennium Dome, designed by Mike Davies of the Richard Rogers Partnership, with Buro Happold as the engineers. Twelve masts support a canopy roof made up of PTFE, a form of Teflon-coated fiberglass fabric, with the entire roof structure apparently weighing less than the air contained within it. The Millennium Dome, built as a marker of the twenty-first century, is also reminiscent of the Dome of Discovery, designed by Ralph Tubbs and built, along with the Skylon, for the Festival of Britain in 1951. Both were in turn presumed to be inspired by the Trylon and Perisphere structures of the 1939 New York World's Fair.

The 50-year period that separates the Festival of Britain from the Millennium Dome also covers one of the most remarkable and productive periods in the development of architectural engineering. The firms of FJ Samuely, Arup, and Buro Happold were all set up by talented and charismatic engineers for whom lightness came to play an important role in the evolution of their practices. The entrepreneurial capacities of Ove Arup and Ted Happold led to the formation of two global practices that have made collaboration with other consultants one of the hallmarks of their approach. For these engineers, the idea of lightness appears to have been as much part of an economy of means as it was an engineering feat.

The research and teaching of both Felix Samuely and Frank Newby, the organizational structure of clusters or teams at Ove Arup & Partners, and the connections between academia and practice at Buro Happold all helped these firms to focus on research and experimentation as well as the pragmatic realities of their clients' needs. The formation of Structures 3 at Ove Arup & Partners also coincided with Frei Otto's research efforts at the Institute for Lightweight Structures at the University of Stuttgart. The collaboration between Otto, Happold, Liddell, and others at Mannheim marked a very particular and special moment in the history of architecture and engineering. The aim was of course to make the structure a reality, but it was also sustained by a belief in the idea of constructing large-scale structures that would leave a light touch or imprint on the planet, a precept that has become critical for designers today.

In contemporary design, there is often a distinction made between craft and industrialization, or handmade and mass-production. But exploring the intersections between design and technology, as was the case with Mannheim, often necessitates the capacity to negotiate between such distinctions. In that regard, the work of Frei Otto shares a certain affinity with that of Jean

MOHSEN MOSTAFAVI

Prouvé in its utilization of both the hand and the machine for exploring, or modelling, the possibilities and potentials of their projects. In both their work, the on-site experience of how things are fabricated or made is inseparable from their design imagination.

Similarly, the work of Achim Menges, a contemporary architect and researcher, lies at the intersection of computational design, biomimetics, structural engineering, and fabrication. Paying homage to the contributions of Frei Otto among others, Menges also uses the pavilion as a heuristic device, but one that is primarily reliant on the inter-relations—or at times on the limits of relations—between computation, materials, and construction. Menges now runs the Institute for Computational Design and Construction at the University of Stuttgart, where Otto was once a professor at the sister Institute for Lightweight Structure. Menges was also a young staff member and recent graduate of the AA when he attended the workshops Otto and his daughter Christine conducted at Hooke Park. Since then, the ecological concerns embedded in Frei Otto's work have gained much greater attention, and the importance of the construction industry having a much lighter footprint on the planet has become ever more urgent.

The research carried out by the ICD (Institute of Computational Design) and others is part of a global attempt to find ways to reduce embodied energy as part of the construction process. Wood as well as other lightweight materials such as carbon fiber can now be utilized in less conventional and more innovative ways to produce new forms and new spatial conditions. In time, these investigations will likely also transform the building industry. The concept of collaboration, once limited to architects and engineers, is now being expanded to include a much wider array of disciplines and consultants in order to incorporate social, cultural, and economic aspects of the built environment to complement those of architecture and engineering.[5] In this regard, the notion of lightness, which played a key role in the imagination of architects and engineers, may once again assume a more important place in contemporary design discourse. Only then will the lightness of engineering assume the same analogical qualities promoted by Italo Calvino in his desire for lightness in literature, and the weightlessness of verbal texture.

---

3   Peter Rice, *An Engineer Imagines* (London: Ellipsis, 1994), 95.

---

4   *Ibid.*

---

5   The Deutsche Forschungsgemeinschaft (German Research Foundation) recently announced its support of a new research center at the University of Stuttgart as part of a plan for the formation of a series of Clusters of Excellence. The center will foster the collaboration of multi-disciplinary experts with the aim of rethinking design and construction based on the integrative use of digital technologies and lightweight principles.

HALL OF NATIONS AND HALLS OF INDUSTRIES

	NEW DELHI, INDIA
	1970–1972
ARCHITECT	RAJ REWAL
ENGINEER	MAHENDRA RAJ

The center of the Asia '72 International Trade Fair in Pragati Maidan and a symbol of postcolonial Indian rebirth, the complex was made up of five halls connected by a system of ramps. Large column-free spaces—73×73 m square and 30 m high in the case of the Hall of Nations and 40×40 m and 18 m high for the four Halls of Industries—were created thanks to the world's first space-frame structure in reinforced concrete, chosen for cost-effectiveness, availability of materials and quality of labor. The modules of the structure were square-based pyramids—4.9 m per side and 3.5 m high in the case of the larger hall, and 3.6 m by 2.6 m high for the other halls—which created truncated pyramid blocks with a 54°44'8″ angle of inclination. Mahendra Raj's creative genius was evident in the detail of the rhombic section of the frame members, just 25 cm per side. The form was determined both by intrinsic conditions—the angle of inclination of the modules, intersections with 9 or 12 members, a minimum of 4 steel bars per member—and extrinsic ones-unqualified labor and a lack of advanced technology available. The structure was demolished in 2017.

← Hall of Nations, New Delhi, 1972. Photo Franco Panzini. Courtesy Franco Panzini

GC PROSTHO MUSEUM RESEARCH CENTER

Kengo Kuma masterfully blends spatiality, light and materials, with particular attention to traditional Japanese construction techniques. It is no coincidence that the design for the GC Prostho Museum Research Center revolves around a popular Japanese game based on mechanical interlocking wooden pieces, the *Cidori*. Thanks to Jun Sato's studies on wooden structural systems, Kengo Kuma developed a functional, decorative apparatus that dematerializes the simple cement block of the building and characterizes both its exterior and interior appearance. Wood strips with square cross-sections 6 cm per side were assembled without screws, 50 cm from one another, to create a self-supporting covering the envelops and invades the museum. The project's expressive power is indicative of a type of architecture that focuses its conception on emphasizing handcraftsmanship in the construction of buildings.

→ GC Prostho Museum Research Center, Kasugai, 2010. Photo Daici Ano. Courtesy Kengo Kuma & Associates

ARCHITECT	KENGO KUMA AND ASSOCIATES
ENGINEER	JUN SATO

HÖHENRAUSCH.2 – BRÜCKEN IM HIMMEL (BRIDGES IN THE SKY)

In 2009, to mark Linz's year as European capital of culture, a new structure was inaugurated: a panoramic wooden walkway above the roofs of the Passage shopping center and a multi-story parking lot in the middle of the city. This first construction, designed by Atelier Bow-Wow, was joined in 2011 by two temporary bridge structures designed by the Conzett Bronzini Partner AG studio, which expanded the aerial walkway, passing through the bell tower of the nearby Church of the Ursulines. One bridge was supported by two wooden space-frame structures that shifted weight, respectively, onto the shopping center roof via steel plates, and onto the wall of the bell tower; to lighten the point load on the church, wooden rods were inserted, connecting the structure's support points to the upper edge of the bell tower's window.

The second bridge rested directly on the ground through a truss framework about 25 meters high, made up of a grid-like column with 4 steel pedestals anchored to concrete bases, and a fan-shaped structure the supported the walkway's deck. The deck itself was of plywood stiffened by a solid wood longitudinal beam.

↓ Höhenrausch.2 – Brücken im Himmel (Bridges in the Sky), Linz, 2011. Photo di Otto Saxinger. Courtesy Otto Saxinger

GRAND ROOF, FESTIVAL PLAZA, EXPO '70

OSAKA, JAPAN

1970

ARCHITECTS
KENZO TANGE
URTEC

ENGINEERS
YOSHIKATSU TSUBOI
MAMORU KAWAGUCHI

The first Asian Expo held in 1970 in Osaka was a true festival of futuristic metabolist architecture. The Grand Roof was the spectacular central element—in terms of size and audacity—of the entire event: a megastructure that covered a 108×291.6 m rectangular lot. With its symbolic 30-meter-high spatial reticular structure, it contained all of the exhibition spaces and covered the large plaza in front of it. The edges of its square-based pyramids were 10.8-meter-long steel bars, 50 cm in diameter if horizontal and 35 cm if oblique, of thicknesses that ranged from 7.9 to 30 mm depending on the state of tension. The joints were 80-centimeter steel spheres, and transparent plastic pneumatic cushions covered the roof. Weighing a total of 4,800 tons, the structure was assembled on the ground and raised by means of pneumatic jacks along the six trusswork columns that supported it.

↑ Grand Roof, Festival Plaza,
Expo '70, Osaka, 1970.
Courtesy Bill Cotter of
worldsfairphotos.com

LIGHT AS CLOUD

Seng Kuan

Two historiographical questions loom over the narrative of structural design in postwar Japan. The first concerns the 1970 World Exposition in Osaka (Expo '70 hereafter). Despite the wealth and intensity of experiments with novel structures, materials, and construction methods showcased on this extraordinary occasion, as one surveys the ensuing decade of architectural production in Japan, one scarcely notices any impact of the Expo's cornucopia of daring experiments. So, what was Expo '70's legacy? The second question relates to the enduring allure of spaceframe and lightweight, large-span structures as a disciplinary pursuit in Japan in the postwar period. Implicated here is the specific contention between the concrete and steel industries in the context of Japan's economic ascendence, as well as the influence of Ludwig Mies van der Rohe's architecture in this country, which is otherwise overshadowed by the overwhelming presence of Le Corbusier.

The two crowning achievements of Japan's modern architectural ingenuity are surely the Yoyogi National Gymnasium of 1964, built for the Summer Olympics in Tokyo, and the Festival Plaza of 1970 for Expo '70 that took place six years later. Both complexes were the work of architect Kenzo Tange, in collaboration with engineers Yoshikatsu Tsuboi and his disciple Mamoru Kawaguchi. Much has been written about Yoyogi elsewhere.[1] Suffice it to say that it emerged out of the unique disciplinary symbiosis between architectural design and structural design in Japan, centered at the

University of Tokyo with its strain of architectural rationalism in which both Tange and Tsuboi were inculcated.[2] The structural framework of the larger No. 1 Gymnasium at Yoyogi consists of three parts. At the top is a cable suspension system for the main roof ridge, hanging off two monumental pylons 126 m apart. Prominently revealed at the apex of the pylons is the innovative use of dampers. The gymnasium's lower portion, where the audience stands are located, is a concrete bowl. These two systems—the flexible cable on top and rigid bowl underneath—are connected by a semi-rigid roof canopy. Rather than letting the skeletal frame of this canopy fall to its natural contour, each steel girder is individually bent to achieve the specific curvature Tange desired. This intervention epitomizes Tsuboi's famous adage that "true beauty lies in the vicinity of structural rationality,"[3] a principle that also manifests itself in the oblique positioning of the backstays to the suspension cables, creating a swirling ground plan that guides spatial flow between the plaza outside and the gymnasium's interior.

Built as the focal point of Expo '70, the Festival Plaza is covered by an essentially uniform roof structure (the Grand Roof) measuring 108 m wide by 291.6 m long, an area larger than four soccer fields combined. Situated at the crossing of the two main axes of the Expo grounds and adjacent to the main entrance, this large rectangular space serves as the main organizing device for the broader urban ensemble. The 7.64-m thickness between the spaceframe's two horizontal planes encases various display mechanisms intended to animate the Festival Plaza. This layer is also partially decked to create an exhibition venue, featuring capsule residential prototypes by Tange's protégés Kishō Kurokawa and Sachio Ōtani.

The great achievement of the spaceframe at Expo '70 lay in its superlative scale, in terms of both the spaces it enclosed and the dimensions of cast steel components, fabricated by Yawata Iron & Steel together with Sumitomo Metal. The spaceframe consists of a grid of equilateral square pyramids. This horizontal element is in turn supported by six piers rising 30 m off the ground, together forming two enormous bays, each spanning 108 m by 75.6 m. There are further cantilevers of 37.8 m on either edge of the longitudinal axis and 16.2 m on the transverse axis.

The desire for uniformity was the foremost challenge in the spaceframe's design. Its chords are all identical in length, at 10.8 m, and come in just two thicknesses, with the horizontals being girthier at 500 mm in diameter and the diagonals more slender at 350 mm. These chords are connected by spherical joints measuring 800–1,000 mm in diameter, also made of cast steel. All these components amounted to a self-weight of 4,100 tons for the spaceframe. Supported by only six piers with wide spans in between them, the roof's horizontal plane has considerable variations in load. The need for a large circular aperture in the center, allowing Tarō Okamoto's *Tower of the Sun* to pierce through, further complicated structural calculations. In comparison, the struts at Montreal's Biosphere, built for the 1967 Expo, were far shorter and more slender.[4] The geodesic dome's upper and lower halves also have entirely different characteristics: the upper part being a vault with struts that are gradually hollowed, and the lower part a bowl with solid struts.

A lesser-known follow-up to this remarkable lineage of large-span structures in Japan—involving the same coterie of personalities as Yoyogi and Expo '70's Festival Plaza—was West Japan General Exhibition Center in Kitakyūshū, Fukuoka prefecture, designed by Arata Isozaki in collaboration with Kawaguchi, both now fully independent from their

1   Seng Kuan, "Tange's Yoyogi, World's Yoyogi," *a+u*, no. 589 (October 2019): 5–12.

2   Kenzo Tange was a student at Tokyo Imperial University (renamed University of Tokyo in 1948) in 1935–38, returning to graduate school there in 1942, and teaching there until 1973. Yoshikatsu Tsuboi began studying at the same school in 1929 and served as a full-time faculty member there from 1942 to 1968.

3   Mike Schliach, "Yoyogi Gymnasiums, Mamoru Kawaguchi and Modern Double-Curved Lightweight Structures," *a+u*, no. 589 (October 2019): 76–81.

4   The struts at the Biosphere range from 1.7 m long with a diameter of 7.3 cm to just about 3 m long with a diameter of 10.2 cm. See esp. Réjean Legault, "The Death and Life and Buckminster Fuller's US Pavilion at Expo 67," in *Montreal's Geodesic Dream: Jeffrey Lindsay and the Fuller Research Foundation Canadian Division*, ed. Cammie McAtee (Halifax: Dalhousie Architectural Press, 2017), 97–115. I would like to thank McAtee and Legault for sharing further archival material on the Biosphere with me.

↓ Arata Isozaki, Mamoru Kawaguchi, West Japan
General Exhibition Center, Fukuoka, 1977. Photo
Shinkenchiku-sha

5   Taneo Oki, Akira Tarashima, Kōji
     Kamiya, Masamitsu Nagashima, Tadashi
     Yoshikawa, and Keiichirō Mogi, "Koa
     shisutemu—kukun no mugenteisei,"
     Shinkenchiku 30, no. 1 (January 1955):
     58–61.

6   "Wakkusuman zeminaaru," *Shinkenchiku*
     31, no. 2 (February 1956): 57–68.
     Wachsmann's US Air Force Hangar
     project is included in Sigfried
     Giedion, *A Decade of Contemporary
     Architecture*, 2nd ed. (New York:
     Wittenborn, 1954), 262. The same
     volume also showcases Egon Eiermann's
     textile mill building (1949–51) in
     Blumberg, Germany (244–45). The scheme
     for the Haramachi plant bears close
     resemblance to Eiermann's version, but
     Eiermann's roof truss does not taper
     off toward the edges.

respective mentors Tange and Tsuboi. This most significant continuation to the forward-looking experimentations at Expo '70 was not realized until seven years later, in 1977. The vast main hall is covered with a cable-stayed roof system spread over eight bays, each 21.8 m wide with a 50-meter-deep span. Each of the eight modular roof plates is held in place by monumental steel masts of 70 cm in diameter on either side, that sit on top of concrete plinths via a delicate hinge joint that is proudly on display—in the same manner as the dampers at Yoyogi. The beauty of West Japan General Exhibition Center lies in the articulation of steel masts and cables. Each mast is connected to eight evenly distributed points on a modular roof plate, at the crossing of the joists and beams. These eight cables are in turn tied into four knots at the top of the mast, as a modified harp, countered by four parallel cables on the anchorage side.

The application of spaceframe technology in architectural design emerged in the early 1950s, led by the likes of Stéphane du Château, Richard Buckminster Fuller, and Konrad Wachsmann, and quickly appealed to Tange and others in Japan as an alternative to shell structures in its potential to offer large, flexible, and structurally efficient spaces. Tange and Tsuboi began their partnership with a pair of concrete shell structures —Hiroshima Children's Library and Ehime Prefectural Citizens' Hall, both completed in 1953—but shell structures ultimately fell short of the vast "social-scale" spaces Tange strove for in his pursuit of a new architecture in building Japan's postwar democratic order. His laboratory at the University of Tokyo embarked on nonhierarchical, universal spaces, under the pretext of core systems, looking at shell structures together with novel structural systems and juxtaposing Eero Saarinen's Kresge Auditorium (1955) with Mies's scheme for Mannheim National Theater (1952–53, unbuilt).[5] Steel promised far longer spans. Tange's first foray into steel-frame structures was Tosho Printing Company's Haramachi plant, in Shizuoka prefecture, completed in 1955, where a truss system allowed a maximum span of 40 m. This far exceeded the 10-meter depth achieved by the inverted shell of Hiroshima Children's Library. The modified diamond truss system at Haramachi is thickest at the center, resting on two rows of piers, and tapers off toward the edges, maximizing the surface area of floor-to-ceiling glazing on edges free from any load-bearing members.

In developing the Haramachi project, Tange's chief lieutenant Takashi Asada closely studied modern manufacturing processes and systems theory. In fall 1955, just after the completion of the Haramachi plant, Asada further arranged to have Konrad Wachsmann visit Japan and offer a two-week seminar, with several like-minded, elite laboratories at various universities each sending two delegates.[6] Wachsmann's visit marked a watershed moment in the development of steel lightweight structures in Japan. Tange's laboratory was represented by Arata Isozaki and Keiichirō Mogi, members of the research group on core systems mentioned above. Yoshikatsu Tsuboi's lab sent Kawaguchi. This first meeting between Isozaki and Kawaguchi set in motion a collaborative relationship—no less fruitful and

↓   Kenzo Tange, Yoshikatsu Tsuboi, Hiroshima Children's Library, Hiroshima, 1953.
Photo Chūji Hirayama. Courtesy Tange Associates

→   Kenzo Tange, Fugaku Yokoyama, Tosho Printing Company Haramachi Factory, Shizuoka, 1955.
Photo Chūji Hirayama. Courtesy Tange Associates

significant than that of Tange/Tsuboi—that would flourish for almost six decades, yielding the Festival Plaza at Expo '70 and West Japan General Exhibition Center along the way. The theme chosen for the 1955 seminar was "classroom units," based on Wachsmann's continuing work on prefabrication and the spaceframe concept. Two identical, rectangular spaceframes constituted the floor and ceiling, and over the course of nine sessions participants were asked to challenge the formal potential of what amounted to total flexibility in design by adding various generic architectural components to the inhabitable space sandwiched in between the two slab frames.[7]

In a return to the epigraph and Tange's desire for a cloud-like effect in the Festival Plaza, it is worth remarking that in Tange's early works, during the two decades leading up to Expo '70, one can observe his ongoing quest to reduce the weight of structures. This effort is of course a corollary to the rationalization of structures and maximizing of spans, but the aesthetic implication here is worth highlighting, as we consider some of his other major works from the same period, such as Kurashiki City Hall (1960) and Yamanashi Press and Broadcasting Center (1966), which are in the Brutalist language of *béton brut* associated with Le Corbusier. Tange's earliest works such as Hiroshima Children's Library and Shimizu City Hall (1954) exude the sense of lightness found in the contemporary works of Mies van der Rohe and Alison and Peter Smithson's Hunstanton School (1954). While much of the critical attention on Japanese postwar architecture has privileged the Corbusian legacy, it is easy to overlook the Miesian connection and the gradual ascendence of steel-frame structures in the same period.

Japan's steel industry has been extraordinarily effective in promoting its products for civil engineering and architectural use. The former Yawata Iron & Steel Company, a core constituent of present-day Nippon Steel after several rounds of corporate mergers, launched the sophisticated architectural journal *Karamu* in 1962 to showcase innovations in steel-based construction. In the late 1960s, the period leading up to Expo '70, the journal introduced the Japanese audience to Conrad Roland's study of long-span structures, developed from his 1967 book on Frei Otto, and du Château's Tridimensional Pyramitec system, featuring his work at the Foire Expo in Nancy.[8] Directly anticipating Isozaki and Kawaguchi's West Japan General Exhibition Center was an article by the young American architect Peter Pran, summarizing his master's thesis from Illinois Institute of Technology (IIT) titled "An Exhibition Hall with a Suspended Roof Structure." Referring to the recently completed Verrazzano-Narrows Bridge in New York, Pran's scheme called for a new modular system of suspension cable units as framing for interior spaces of unprecedented scale.

Peter Pran was one of many students at IIT in the early 1960s to have benefited from the mentoring of Myron Goldsmith and Fazlur Khan,[9] with the former carrying on Mies's pedagogical program at IIT after working for Pier Luigi Nervi and the latter being a great structural engineer at Skidmore, Owings and Merrill. Pran worked at Mies's office in the early 1960s and participated in the Neue Nationalgalerie and Chicago Federal Center projects. Sharing the same experience was Meiji Watanabe, who similarly studied with Goldsmith and Khan at IIT, graduating in 1962 and then going to work for Mies. Watanabe's master's thesis at IIT was an elaboration on Goldsmith's celebrated Steel Exhibition proposal for the 1964 World's Fair (1960), developed into an exhibition hall project for trains.[10] His return to Japan in 1965 coincided with the construction of Japan's first true skyscraper,

7   Interest in lightweight structures intensified through the 1960s, provoked by the *Dome over Manhattan* proposal (1960) by Richard Buckminster Fuller and Shoji Sadao. This project, together with Tange's *A Plan for Tokyo 1960*, published a few months later, illuminated a radically new order of magnitude in thinking about the urban environment made possible by technology. The realization of the Biosphere in the American Pavilion at the Montreal Expo in 1967 provided further instigation.

8   Stéphane du Château, "Sanjigen kōzō: piramitekku," *Karamu*, no. 21 (1967): 89–91.

9   Christine Dufresne, *Myron Goldsmith: Poet of Structure* (Montreal: Canadian Center for Architecture, 1991). Catalog of an exhibition of the same title, presented at the Canadian Center for Architecture, March 13–June 21, 1991.

10   Meiji Watanabe, *Train Exhibition Hall* (master's thesis, Illinois Institute of Technology, 1962).

11   "Wa shi tei," *Kenchiku Bunka*, no. 230 (December 1965): 51–55.

12   Iida Yoshikuni, ed., *Kokusai tekkō chōkoku sinpojiumu* (n.p., 1970). The sculpture symposium was part of a series that began in 1959 through the leadership of Austrian sculptor Karl Prantl at a quarry outside Vienna. Two years later, in 1961, the leading Austrian steel producer Böhler sponsored the first symposium dedicated to steel sculptures.

13   These masts held in place a vast roof structure covering 2,618 square meter in area. In the same manner as the Festival Plaza's Grand Roof, there was thickness to this layer. The four main gallery spaces hang from the roof frame, suspended in midair, leaving the ground level completely clear.

the Kasumigaseki Building (1968), just as the country abolished its height limit of 31 m. Appropriately, he was put in charge of the building's curtainwall detailing. It is also notable that Watanabe's own house (1965), a Miesian glass box elevated from the ground by four pairs of I-beams, was sponsored by Yawata Iron & Steel to showcase this new architectural aesthetic.[11]

Japan's steel industry ventured far beyond the sponsorship of architectural journals and show houses, seeking every opportunity to promote steel as a cultural icon of contemporaneity. One of the most fascinating episodes of Expo '70 was a symposium on steel sculptures, cosponsored by the Japan Iron & Steel Federation and the newspaper *Mainichi Shimbun*.[12] Among the works created was a tensegrity structure of steel tubes and cables by Kenneth Snelson, an American artist with deep understanding of tension and compression. Jean Tinguely and George Rickey were among the other artists invited from overseas, and Yoshikuni Iida, Kazuo Yuhara, Michio Ihara, and Osamu Wakabayashi were the four Japanese participants. The thirteen works created were placed at key locations along the main east-west corridor of the Expo grounds.

With regard to tensegrity structures, it is worth remembering that the team behind the UK Pavilion at Expo '70, namely Powell and Moya together with engineer Charles Weiss, was also responsible for the Skylon, a soaring icon of postwar recovery built for the Festival of Britain in 1951. While the later pavilion in Osaka did not share the Skylon's magical lightness, its use of efficient structures to lift architecture into the air—liberating the ground plane on the scale of public space—resonated with the main Festival Plaza. The UK Pavilion's four pairs of steel masts, each standing at 32 m, formed a silhouette reminiscent of an ocean liner and were among the most prominent structures on the Expo skyline.[13]

Expo '70 was a cornucopia of novel technologies, structures, and materials. Pneumatic structures, such as the Fuji Pavilion, for which Kawaguchi also served as engineer, left a profound impression. Renzo Piano designed the Pavilion of Industry, a tent-like structure with fiberglass panels, as part of the Italian contingent. The biggest triumph undoubtedly went to steel and the new architectural language this material entailed. In addition to the pavilions and sculptural works already noted, the other major works in steel included the Expo Tower by Kiyonori Kikutake with engineer Gengo Matsui, the Sumitomo Fairytale Pavilion by Sachio Ōtani with Toshihiko Kimura, the Toshiba Pavilion by Kishō Kurokawa with Tsuboi and Yasuo Suzuki, the Takara Beautilion by Kishō Kurokawa with Shigeru Aoki, and the Pepsi Pavilion by Takenaka Construction. Japan became the undisputed leader in the technical design and fabrication of steel structures, even if architectural fashion shifted toward new directions.

As we approach a conclusion to this story, it bears reiterating the full passage by Kenzo Tange from which the epigraph was extracted. While aspiring for a cloud-like structure for Expo '70's Grand Roof, he was disappointed by the eventual outcome: "In the final analysis, the idea did

↓   Meiji Watanabe, *Train Exhibition Hall*, thesis project, 1962

not work out. I actually wanted to erect a frame that would be more neutral and self-effacing, that people might not notice or even miss it if were gone. I wanted as flexible and simple a frame as possible; if it could have been done, I would have liked an invisible one. But after building the roof, I learned that a spaceframe is surprisingly solid and not nearly as flexible as I had hoped it would be."[14] Reaching its climax at Expo '70, Tange's interest in novel structural techniques in collaboration with engineers like Tsuboi and Kawaguchi waned in the ensuing decade, as he turned his attention to even larger, urban-scale commissions in Japan and abroad.

The locus of architectural creativity in Japan in the years following Expo '70 shifted to the generation of Arata Isozaki and Kazuo Shinohara, as evidenced in new directions in terms of style, scale, and discursivity. In 1971, the Architectural Institute of Japan awarded its annual prize to Shinohara's recently completed houses in his so-called Second Style. The generation to come, comprised of Tadao Andō and Toyo Ito, was already peeking over the horizon. This genealogical progression was mirrored in the engineering community. Toshihiko Kimura emerged as the emblematic figure of the 1970s, through his agile solutions to a wide variety of spatial situations and materials, rather than singular devotion to certain grand strategies. Masato Araya and Mutsuro Sasaki received their training in Kimura's atelier during this pivotal period. It is tempting then, following the foregoing narrative, to propose Toyo Ito as the eventual heir to the spirit of Expo '70, in terms of the desire for lightness that eluded Tange. Ito's works in the mid-1980s, starting with his own house Silver Hut, opened up new paths in the sensorial pursuit of ephemerality through the nimble use of light steel and aluminum frames and mesh. The 1995 exhibition *Light Construction*, organized by Terence Riley at the Museum of Modern Art in New York, anointed Ito and his protégée Kazuyo Sejima as torchbearers of the new movement, precipitating the next phase of tremendous vitality in Japanese architecture.

14   Kenzo Tange and Noboru Kawazoe, "Some Thoughts about Expo '70: Dialogue between Kenzo Tange and Noboru Kawazoe," *The Japan Architect* (May/June 1970; reprint Spring 2019 as no. 113): 15–20.

↓   Kenneth Snelson, Tensegrity Structure during
the installation, Expo '70, Osaka, 1970.
Photo Osamu Murai

AMERICAN PAVILION, EXPO '67

MONTREAL, CANADA

1967

ARCHITECTS   CAMBRIDGE SEVEN ASSOCIATES
SHOJI SADAO

ENGINEER   RICHARD BUCKMINSTER FULLER

The American Pavilion at Expo '67 on Montreal's Île Sainte-Hélène is the most iconic of Richard Buckminster Fuller's geodesic domes. Traversed by the monorail and with a 37-meter escalator—the longest ever built at the time—, this class-1 (icosahedral) double-layered cupola is 61 m tall and has a maximum diameter of 76 m. The exterior surface of the dome is made up of equilateral triangles about 3 m per side, while the interior is of hexagons less than 2 m per side, for a total of 24,000 steel bars. To obtain the homogeneous appearance of the façade, variations in local resistance to stress are absorbed by the internal thickness of hollow profiles rather than by their diameter, which is either 88.9 mm or 73 mm. The curved fiberglass shell was integrated with a complex system of sunscreens and ventilation panels that simulated an animal's biological temperature and humidity self-regulation process. A 1976 fire burned the shell but left the steel structure intact.

PALAZZETTO DELLO SPORT

ROME, ITALY

1956–1960

ARCHITECT   ANNIBALE VITELLOZZI

ENGINEER   PIER LUIGI NERVI

The engineer and builder Pier Luigi Nervi was a great innovator in the use of reinforced concrete, managing to exploit its structural capacities and aesthetic potential, and simultaneously optimizing material utilization and the constructive process.

The Palazzetto dello Sport at The Olympic Village, created in collaboration with Annibale Vitellozzi, is an emblematic example of what was called the "Nervi system." The main innovation was the material, ferrocement, invented and patented by Nervi in 1943; this concrete mix over dense but lightweight metallic mesh allowed for the creation of thin yet durable elements. Ferrocement was used to make the 1,620 rhomboidal blocks, just 2.5 cm thick, that make up the shell, and were used as formworks for casting the 4-centimeter-thick reinforced slab and serving as its ribs: 36 inclined Y-shaped trestles support the 60-meter-diameter ribbed cupola. The other great innovation was the prefabrication of elements directly at the worksite, which sped up the construction process while reducing costs.

↑ Palazzetto dello Sport, Rome,
1960. Courtesy Collezione
MAXXI Architettura,
Pier Luigi Nervi Archive

EDEN
PROJECT

	BODELVA, UNITED KINGDOM
	1995–2001
ARCHITECT	GRIMSHAW ARCHITECTS
ENGINEERS	ARUP ANTHONY HUNT

Among the initiatives financed by the UK to mark the new millennium was the Eden Project, the ambitious plan to create a large greenhouse in Cornwall to host a tropical biome and a Mediterranean biome.

The site chosen for the new construction, a quarry that was being decommissioned, had a complex topography to adapt to, a situation exacerbated by the final phase of excavation in progress, which continuously altered its conformation.

To work around this problem and move forward with the design for the project, Grimshaw, inspired by the flexibility and adaptability of soap bubbles, proposed a series of domes generated by the intersection of spheres with the ground. These domes, drawing on the heritage of geodesic structures, are based on steel structures with two layers of hexagons. The inner layer uses standard-model space frames developed by the MERO company, which also proposed a specially-designed type of node for the exterior hexagons. The domes are connected by large steel framework triangular-section arches.

To contain costs and keep the structure's weight to a minimum, the designers created a system of inflatable cushion-cells made of ETFE, a thermoplastic polymer used in inflatable structures.

PATENTING ARRANGEMENT

José Aragüez

Structural engineering involves an operational use of aspects pertaining to science and a scientific frame of mind to devise and craft form. In other words, engineering revolves around the scientization of form. The central role of math, geometry, and physics; a focused intensity devoted to the artifact itself, and less so to context in the wider sense; an interpretation of nature as a source of patterns and configurational laws, rather than as one of mimicry; a profuse enactment of logical, procedural thinking; a lesser emphasis on the experiential dimension in comparison to architecture—the most characteristic engineering inclinations are and have traditionally been connected with its scientific character. Indeed, a rational, scientific strain in engineering skills, which was becoming increasingly pronounced, was central to the split between architecture and engineering at the end of the eighteenth century.

One field that paints a meaningful picture of the evolution of this scientization of form in engineering is that of patents. Painfully under-researched in the histories of both engineering and architecture,[1] the bodies of patent production released over the last two centuries thoroughly reflect the multiple phases of progress that have followed one another. Extremely broad in reach, patent laws vary from continent to continent and from country to country, but a central criterion of patentability is shared. It requires novelty relative to so-called "prior art," that is, previously publicly available information concerning the subject matter to be patented. The European

1   In terms of architectural patents, two of the few recent references in English are Mark Garcia, "Architectural Patents and Open-Source Architectures: The Globalization of Spatial Design Innovations (or Learning from 'E99')," *Architectural Design* 86, no. 5 (September 2016): 92–99, and Martina Decker, "Novelty and Ownership: Intellectual Property in Architecture and Design," *Technology | Architecture + Design* 1, no. 1 (2017): 41–47. Regarding a host of different subjects around civil and structural engineering patents, such as their purposes, scope, laws, international developments, and trends, see Stephen L. Keefe, "Civil Engineering and Patent Law Blog," https://www.keefeip.com/civil-engineering-and-patent-law. Accessed June 16, 2021. For a brief overview of the civil engineering patent system and history in the USA as well as a few patent examples, see Christopher A. Rothe, "Using Patents To Advance The Civil Engineering Profession," *Civil Engineering Magazine* 76, no. 6 (June 2006): 66–73. More generally, for a lucid and precise introductory account of the patent system in the USA, see Craig A. Nard, "History and Architecture of the Patent System," in *The Law of Patents* (New York: Aspen Publishers, 2008), 1–48.

2   See "Patentability Requirements," https://www.epo.org/law-practice/legal-texts/html/guidelines/e/g_i_1.htm. Accessed July 1, 2021.

3   See under "Novelty And Non-Obviousness, Conditions For Obtaining A Patent," https://www.uspto.gov/patents/basics/general-information-patents. Accessed June 29, 2021.

4   This primary armature or ensemble, I have come to call "spatial infrastructure." For more on the epistemology around this newly coined term, see the forthcoming book by José Aragüez, *Spatial Infrastructure: Essays on Architectural Thinking as a Form of Knowledge* (Barcelona: Actar, 2022). Although sometimes spatial infrastructure and load-bearing framework are one and the same (e.g., at Mansilla + Tuñón's MUSAC – Museo de Arte Contemporáneo de Castilla y León, Spain), they do not always necessarily coincide. At FOA's Yokohama Terminal, for example, the material construct embodying the building's primary spatial organization is a continuous, nondirectional surface—encompassing bifurcating paths, flat open areas, and smooth transitions between levels—which is not itself the primary load-bearing structure. Rather, this surface is held in place by a discrete, bi-directional assemblage of transversal ribs and longitudinal girders.

Patent Office specifically calls for an "inventive step" and for the invention's susceptibility to "industrial application."[2] The United States Patent and Trademark Office demands "nonobviousness," that is, that the invention not be obvious to a person of regular skills in the field where the invention is claimed.[3] Certain kinds of patents are granted on the basis of the utility of the invention; others, on the aesthetic appearance and ornamental features thereof. The legal constellation around the prospect of securing a patent is complex, especially when considered internationally. But at its core lies originality: the subject matter to be patented must constitute a demonstrable addition to the repository of everything else conceived beforehand in the lineage of developments in question.

ENGINEERING PATENTS AND SPATIAL ORGANIZATION

In addition to chronological innovation maps, an analytical study of patents discloses the niches of invention on which a given discipline has most consistently placed emphasis as much as those remaining somewhat or completely unexplored. In the case of engineering, an examination of patents from the nineteenth century to the present reveals a number of central categories. The most significant of these encompasses components and methods used in structural design. From the early advances in reinforced concrete patented by Joseph Monier and François Hennebique over the last few decades of the nineteenth century, to Ildefonso Sánchez del Río's 1954 single curved, reinforced brick vault; from the patents involving prestressed concrete obtained by Eugène Freyssinet in the late 1920s, to Frei Otto's 1961 tent roof; from Pier Luigi Nervi's 1949 isostatic floor, to the Bubble System AG that Heinz Isler and his collaborators sought to register in 1976—patents here include beams, slabs, columns, walls, and other structural members along with construction systems, details, processes, and techniques. A second category consists of inventions pertaining to materials science, for example, Joseph Aspdin's Portland Cement, patented in 1824, and Eduardo Torroja's adiathermic concrete, in 1928. Machinery can be identified as a third genre of patents, spanning anything from concrete mixers to cabins for hydraulic shovels. Lastly, the category under which modeling, and calculation systems are found; from numerous patents developed around finite element methods, to computational analysis and BIM.

There is one salient trend that these categories evince: the structural engineering patents germane to the materialization of buildings have primarily engaged the aspect of form concerning new constructional possibilities. There is another aspect of form that appears to have been largely neglected, namely that concerning spatial organization and a number of related aspects such as configuration, arrangement, and disposition. These define the boundary conditions for a series of human activities to be housed within a bounded region of space at the building scale. More precisely, form involves organization in a two-fold sense. On the one hand, it comprises the three-dimensional material set of elements that makes up a building's primary internal armature or ensemble, prior to the introduction of secondary partitions.[4] Form, therefore, *embodies* the very organization of those elements. On the other hand, that three-dimensional ensemble generates a first series of sub-volumes of programmable space ordered in a manner linked to—but not coincidental with—its material elements. Form *begets* a specific organization of space.

A study of patents begins to suggest a tendency whereby structural engineering has contributed much innovation in terms of constructional possibilities, while it has failed to substantially expand beyond a reduced number of spatial modalities. Indeed, these have mainly included the single, shed-like space; some version of the large-span roof (pleated surfaces, shells, etc.); variations of the old basilica (i.e., configurations in parallel naves); and more generally, open layouts punctuated by columns. Even the engineering thinking behind the work of notable figures on the edge between architecture and engineering, like Nervi, Eladio Dieste, and Santiago Calatrava, is essentially restricted to the sculptural gesture or external envelope, rather than aiming at the internal arrangement of space.

While the vast majority of structural engineering patents have engaged one aspect of form, there are exceptions, albeit rare and with a marked limitation. Take August Komendant's 1980 patent for a "modular, multi-floor building." It lays out a system of rectangular semi-boxes—no floor and no ceiling, just four walls—which are concrete-cast as rigid units. These semi-boxes are meant to be placed in between concrete slabs and further bound together by post-tensioned tendons running through walls and slabs. There is certainly spatial organization involved here, that of the semi-boxes engendering a series of spaces both inside them and in between. However, it is not the patent's focus. It is, rather, only a consequence of an invention otherwise motivated by criteria centered around construction methods and load-bearing capabilities, as the objects of the invention make it clear: "suitable for locations which are subjected to severe dynamic forces," "can be erected quickly and inexpensively," "molds can be used more efficiently," "structural units can be handled with relatively low-capacity construction equipment," etc.[5] No wonder there are no floor plans on the patent document. The range of sectional and layout variability seems quite limited as tendons and walls are dependent upon each other and alignment in section is required for the tendons to maintain vertical continuity. In other words, the semi-boxes ought to be stacked on top of one another in between the floor slabs, which are prescribed as horizontal. Le Corbusier's Maison Dom-Ino propounded a spatial organization where a pile of horizontal slabs is held apart by vertical supports. Essentially, the dispositional logic implicit in Komendant's patent is not so different, and perhaps more restraining. From this standpoint, his 1980 invention takes us back to 1914.

In the minority of structural engineering patents where spatial organization is manifestly present, it is predominantly so as a by-product of other concerns. Architects, on the other hand, have shown an inclination to patent inventions where spatial organization does appear as a primary subject matter. Their scope is, however, rather narrow too. Consider the following series of representative patents by architects: a typical iron skyscraper where a novelty is introduced as to how the stairs are arranged in plan within the vertical core area, with most of the efforts otherwise devoted to construction and fireproofing issues;[6] a multi-story building in which the floor slabs alternately rotate around a central axis containing a vertical core, with all floor slabs otherwise horizontal and equidistant from one another;[7] a non-elevator low-rise residential building, with conventionally stacked units, that offers a ground floor laid out so that it is easily disabled- or handicapped-accessible;[8] a "loft-city" concept by which double height, horizontal floors are repetitively piled up to form a building of indeterminate

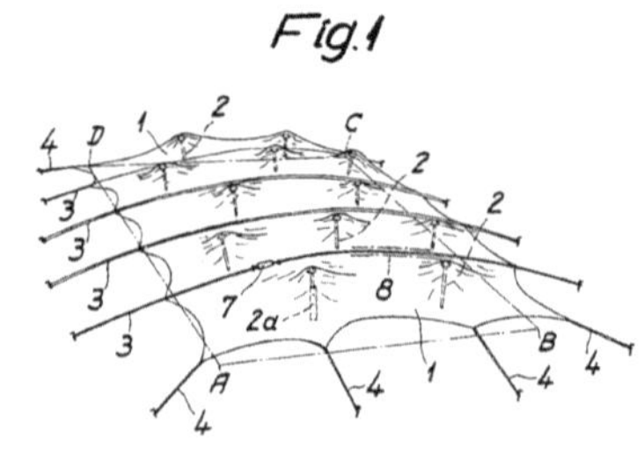

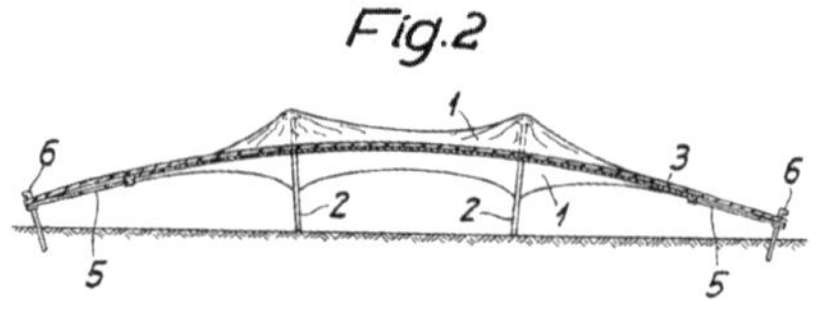

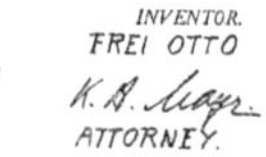

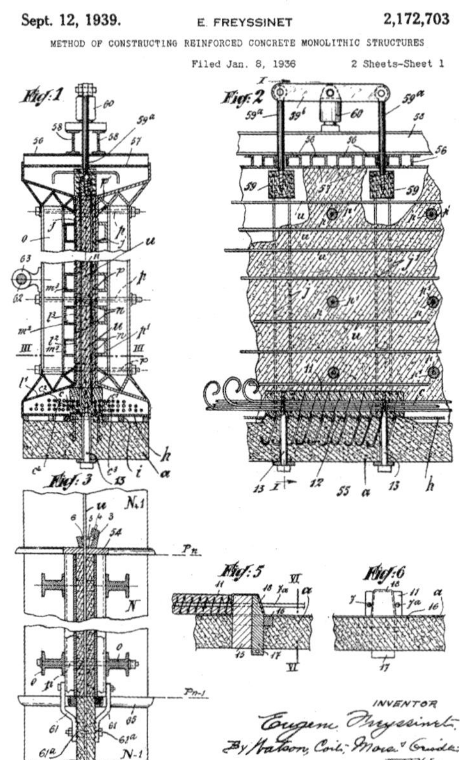

height and program, one where freedom of horizontal and vertical partition is suggested within each level;[9] a housing building devised around a central core and equidistant structural floor slabs where variability exists at the level of secondary horizontal and vertical partitions within the duplexes that repetitively fill up the envelope;[10] a scheme comprising a multi-story housing building on top of a podium holding a garage which, articulated around stacked horizontal floors equidistant from one another, makes a number of modest contributions in terms of parking spaces and circulation in addition to details concerning apartment access and service rooms;[11] a system of vertically stacked dwelling or commercial units for both low- and high-rise construction which, relying on regularly distributed load-bearing walls and conventional layouts, allows for different volumetric configurations within the boundaries set by parallel horizontal floors as well as more or less hackneyed split-level and double-height conditions.[12] The pattern emerging in these and many other similar patents is one where no innovation occurs at the level of the building's essential spatial organization—its primary three-dimensional material ensemble—yet only regarding particular layout details, vertical and horizontal partitions, accessibility, circulation, and modularity. Not unlike the tendency detected in structural engineering patents, no radically novel alternatives concerning models of spatial organization at the building scale are found among patents by architects. Restricted by a proclivity to prioritizing basic functional considerations, those have remained within the confines of a few spatial modalities, often gravitating around the Dom-Ino scheme and its derivatives.

ARTICULATING A SUBDOMAIN OF THE ARCHITECTURE-ENGINEERING HYBRID

A synthesis of these diagnoses makes it plain that to address the aspect of form generally overlooked in the culture of engineering, efforts ought to focus on spatial organization and do so on the grounds of engineering's scientific thinking. Through the harnessing of systems, the implementation of more and more sophisticated analytical models, and an emphasis on rule-based judgments rooted in logic and mathematics, an epistemology around the establishment of scientific grounds on which to base design practice and research channeled an understanding of the new technologies emerging in the post-war decades—such as those involving information, computers, and artificial intelligence—no longer with a view to problem-solving alone, but also with respect to their synthetic, projective capabilities. As a consequence of this shift, breaking down formal processes into their smallest sets of constituents gained tremendous precision, which in turn allowed such processes to incorporate a much greater degree of complexity in terms of the relationships between those constituents. Mobilizing the inheritance of this epistemology with today's tools has an enormous potential for the conception of new models of spatial organization at the building scale.

To work in that direction, there is one tradition bred by the intersection of science and architecture that is particularly relevant: that of *the architecture-engineering hybrid*.[13] During the period subsequent to

← Eugène Freyssinet, *Method of Constructing Reinforced Concrete Monolithic Structures* (US Patent Nº 2,172,703), patent registered on September 12, 1939. Courtesy United States Patent and Trademark Office

← Frei Otto, *Tent-Roof* (US Patent Nº 2,988,096), patent registered on June 13, 1961. Courtesy United States Patent and Trademark Office

5   See under "Objects of the Invention," US Patent no. 4,195,453 (reg. on Apr. 1, 1980).

6   US Patent no. 383,170 (reg. on May 22, 1888).

7   US Patent no. 3,226,889 (reg. on Jan. 4, 1966).

8   US Patent no. 6,079,171 (reg. on June 27, 2000).

9   US Patent no. 2005/0086874 (reg. on Apr. 28, 2005).

10 European Patent no. 1 273 741 B1 (reg. on Sep. 26, 2007).

11 US Patent no. 7,497,055 (reg. on Mar. 3, 2009).

12 US Patent no. 2017/0362814 A1 (reg. on Dec. 21, 2017).

13 The term "architecture-engineering hybrid" relates to Antoine Picon's "hybrid architect engineer." See Antoine Picon, *Hybrid(e). Marc Mimram architecte ingénieur* (Gollion: Infolio, 2007). While Picon referred to the figure of one particular hybrid architect-engineer, here a different term is used to more generally allude to a design domain at the intersection of the two disciplines and to suggest implications at an epistemological level.

Jean-Nicolas-Louis Durand's teachings and all through the nineteenth century, much of what Giedion famously termed "new" architecture (that triggered by the industrial revolution) came about as a result of significant cross-pollinations between the two fields. Paxton's Crystal Palace of 1851 and Barlow's St. Pancras Station of 1868, both in London; Dutert's Galerie des Machines in Paris of 1889; Tony Garnier's La Mouche in Lyon of 1914; Freyssinet's hangar in Orly of 1923; or the modernist factories designed by engineers such as Owen Williams, Giacomo Matté-Trucco, and Marco Zanuso can be cited here as representative examples of that "new" architecture.[14] Yet the advances brought about by the coming together of architecture and engineering, in these and similar instances, translated primarily into a fascination with either large spans or the emerging constructional possibilities enabled first by iron and glass and later by concrete. One would be hard pressed to find radical alternatives to received models of intricate spatial organizations for hosting human activities in those decades of "new" architecture in the Giedion sense.

It is rather over the second half of the twentieth century that a relatively small subdomain within the tradition of the architecture-engineering hybrid can be identified which shows an as-yet largely untapped, immense potential to offer those alternatives. This subdomain of design and research can be defined along two axes that clearly distinguish its *modus operandi* within that entire tradition. First, it exploits some of the core engineering inclinations laid out above—such as the central role of math and geometry, a marked physical empiricism, the importance of procedural thinking, the interpretation of the organizational laws of nature in terms of design, and a focused intensity devoted to the artifact itself—on the basis of their attunement to yielding architectural outcomes, with their distinctive intricacy and relational properties.[15] Second, it capitalizes on the extraordinary power of those inclinations to facilitate the conception of the kinds of patterns, rules, and codifiable gestures that spawn the unmistakable singularity of models of spatial organization in architecture featuring true newness.

Upon closely examining the tradition around the architecture-engineering hybrid, many engineers emerge who ventured into architecture. Yet very few can be claimed to pertain to the subdomain of design and research outlined above. On one side are engineers whose production in architecture limited itself to two fundamentally engineering themes: the shed and versions of the large-span roof. Isler and Félix Candela, for example, would fall into this category. There are others whose design approach may be considered as both architectural and engineering, but not as *hybrid*. They certainly operated in both architecture and engineering, but they faced architectural scenarios with the conventional design approach of an architect, and engineering scenarios with the approach of an engineer. As a result, their architectural work did not differ substantially from that which could have been conceived by an architect. This category includes figures like Marc Mimram, whose residential projects on the Barbès and Jaurès boulevards, for instance, can only be judged as rather commonplace buildings. A third group comprises names like Nervi, Dieste, and Calatrava. Their architecture features clear traces of an engineering attitude towards design. But, as mentioned above, these traces do not appear to have any significant impact on the internal arrangement of space; only at the level of sculptural gesture or external envelope. Unlike that of Isler and Candela, the production of the hybrid subdomain delineated here transcends the typically engineering typologies; unlike Mimram's, its outcomes are indissolubly linked to

14 Giedion dated the birth of a "new" kind of industrial architecture to around the year 1830. See Sigfried Giedion, *Building in France. Building in Iron. Building in Ferroconcrete*, Texts & Documents (Santa Monica, CA: The Getty Center for the History of Art and the Humanities, 1995), 86.

15 The complexity of functions and activities to be housed in a building (say, a museum or a school, relative to a bridge or a dam) gives rise to the characteristic intricacy and relational properties of architectural form in contradistinction to those of engineering form. With the exception of a building's load-bearing structure—an engineering form to be sure, but one featuring a distinctive internal three-dimensionality determined by architecture's inhabitability—engineering forms such as roads, shells, and roof structures lack the same degree of intricacy in their unfolding, even when they do so three-dimensionally. Frei Otto's membranes and Heinz Isler's sheds come to mind as relevant examples: their organizational intricacy is practically negligible even when compared to that embodied in a simple single-family house. Fundamental differences in degree and kind of organizational intricacy distinguish architectural form from engineering form.

16 In many ways, this phenomenon represents a logical evolution of the shift toward an acute scientization of design that has been unfolding across developed countries since World War II.

the engineering-inflected design attributes through which they were begotten; unlike Nervi, Dieste, and Calatrava, the design thinking at its core tackles the internal spatial intricacy characteristic of architectural form, beyond questions concerning the envelope.

Protagonists in this subdomain are not necessarily architect-engineers in any customary sense. Rather, it is the ensemble of their work which, embodying a three-dimensionality characteristic of the nature, purview, and scale of architecture, is here interpreted as establishing an important subdomain in the tradition of the architecture-engineering hybrid. One such protagonist worth mentioning is the Israeli geometer, architect, and engineer Michaël Burt. His body of work, chiefly grounded in structural and theoretical morphology, proves to be one of the earliest and most thoroughgoing investigations into the discovery and visualization of models for the subdivision of space based on patterns of configurational continuity. The American physicist and computer scientist Alan Schoen can be added as someone also operating around morphology. He developed a large number of two-dimensional tiling patterns and infinite, triply periodic minimal surfaces. Engineer and theorist Cecil Balmond is a further example. He is an early and one of the few translators of aspects of nonlinearity and algorithmic reasoning into design moves of significant architectural consequence, contributing applications of design frameworks thus initiated to the conception of entire buildings (i.e., beyond small pavilions, façades, and pieces of furniture). Taken together, the production and design thinking constituting this subdomain point to fundamentally new ways of organizing space at the building scale and come to relate to a critical twenty-first-century phenomenon: an ever-closer rapport between architecture and engineering, and the ever-growing presence of scientifically minded designers in architecture that comes with it.[16]

One central characteristic of the hybrid approach of figures like Burt and Balmond is a *two-fold structural awareness*. In synthesizing elements pertaining to the logic of a building's physical support and the organizational traits of form, such two-fold structural awareness catalyzes a productive link between the feasibility of a three-dimensional physical frame and its aptness to housing a set of human activities. By "productive link" two things are meant. First, wherever there is one principal logic governing both of those aspects of an architectural configuration, an efficiency of design thinking results that would be absent if two separate logics were required—efficiency that is usually favored from an engineering standpoint. Second, turning properties and laws typically associated with the engineering control of a three-dimensional physical frame into a generative spatial code in certain specific ways can push the bounds of possibility of architectural configurations. Procedures to that effect may involve a veiled coextension of force and spatial organization (in contrast to either the total neglect of force, or the typical determinism of form-finding processes) or exploiting the pliable systematicity inherent to differentiated patterns of form-generation.

↓ Dieste y Montañez, Citricos Caputto Fruit Packing Plant, view of the roof from the inside, Salto, 1971–1972. Photo Julián Palacio

NICHE OF OPPORTUNITY

Should inventions arisen out of the hybrid subdomain put forward here be registered, they would come to fill a historical gap in the legacy of engineering patents by engaging the aspect of form involving spatial organization. Notably, some of Burt's and Schoen's abstract geometric models describing spatial arrangements realistically capable of housing a set of human activities could be interpreted as bases for buildings. They would have to be worked out both structurally and architecturally in some detail, with a view to patenting them on grounds of their overall functional performance as well as their internal (re-)configurability, flexibility, and spatial possibilities. Some of Balmond's design methods articulated simultaneously around, on the one hand, numerically or geometrically controlled sequences of order, unfolding patterns, and rule sets, and on the other an understanding of structural performance, could be patented in relation to the specific class of spatial arrangements they generate. As could his variations on the Vierendeel beam along with its compositional capabilities to originate a building holding a series of alternating inhabitable interiors and big voids.

As references for registering inventions of that sort, there are a few exceptions to the tendencies identified above in engineering and architectural patents which, though lacking in organizational variability as presented, are nonetheless quite informative. For example, a 1970 patent proposes a high-rise building made up of individual houses that are arrayed on a checkerboard pattern around a cylinder void;[17] a scheme registered in 2006 combines a set of three-dimensionally staggered apartments into one coherent volume.[18] Another relevant reference is OMA's "Patent Office," a series of patent abstracts laying out concepts rooted in spatial manipulations and subversions under the rubric of "Universal Modernization Patent"—abstracts which obviously would have to be rigorously developed to measure up to patentability standards.[19]

Far from being an end in itself, seeking to address the aspect of form that has been the least probed in engineering's historical process of scientization is a project justified by scientific thinking's unique capacity to facilitate the conception of new models of spatial organization at the building scale. And engaging scientific thinking in a manner different from that reflected in engineering's patent history happens to be intrinsic to that project.

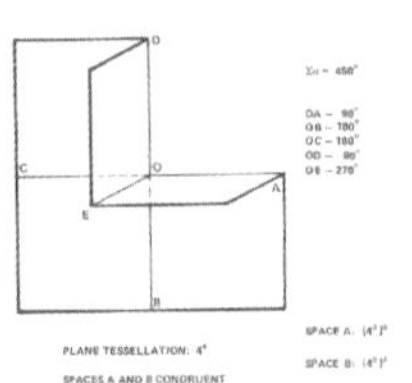

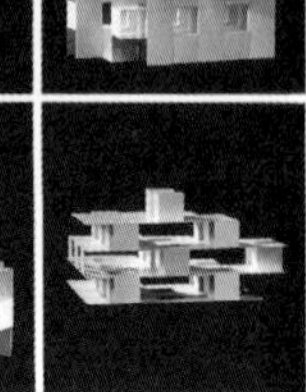
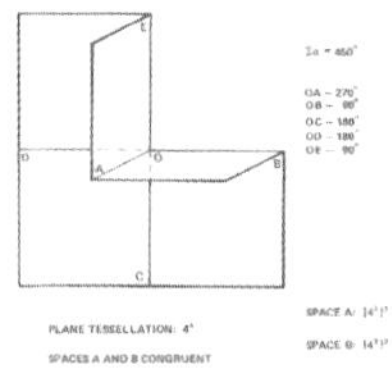

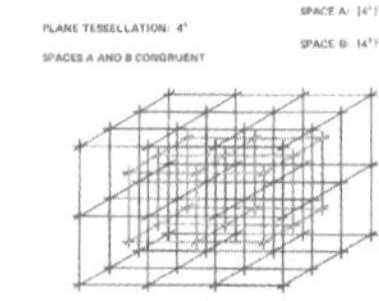

↑　*Multilayered Polyhedra*, in Michaël Burt, Menachem Kleinmann, Avraham Wachman, *Infinite Polyhedra* (Haifa: Technion – Israel Institute of Technology, Faculty of Architecture and Town Planning, 2005, 1st edition 1974), 15, 50

→　Josef Küpper, *House of Houses*, model, 1964. The concept was patented in 1970 as *Detached Building Units on Plural Support Platforms*

17　US Patent no. 3,535,835 (reg. on Oct. 27, 1970).

18　European Patent no. 1 455 033 B2 (reg. on Jan. 4, 2006).

19　Rem Koolhaas and AMO/OMA, "Patent Office," in *Content*, eds. Rem Koolhaas and Brendan McGetrick (Cologne: Taschen, 2004), 73–83, 510–13.

THE PAVILION PARADOX: CONTAINER OR CONTENT?

Luca Di Lorenzo Latini

In ancient times, this simple
assertion was enough to shake
the foundations of Greek truth:
"I lie." "I speak," on the
other hand, puts the whole of
modern fiction to the test.[1]

MICHEL FOUCAULT

The object of this essay is a particular type of architecture, the exposition pavilion. A quintessentially aphoristic type of design in which an architect or an engineer concisely expresses a single formal concept and/or structural rule, the pavilion plays on the paradox inherent to its function, displaying both the hosted content and the container that hosts it. The aim is to highlight, by connecting salient phases in modern and contemporary history, how the intrinsic qualities of this marginal type of architectural specialty—namely freedom of composition and temporariness—are indispensable for the creation of innovative, heterogeneous experiments in the field of engineering: real built tests of alternative structural ideas.

ARCHITECTURE

The history of modern architecture is strewn with iconic moments, some of which have been embodied by exposition pavilions.[2] Where functional limitations and strict situational spatial and temporal imperatives fall away, the expressive impulse achieves its purest and most direct form. The Esprit Nouveau and Soviet Union Pavilions, respectively designed by Le Corbusier and Konstantin S. Mel′nikov for the Exposition internationale

1   Michel Foucault, *Aesthetics, Method, and Epistemology (Essential Works of Foucault, 1954–1984, vol. 2)*, ed. James D. Faubion (New York: The New Press, 1999).

2   A first discussion of the matter in Marco Mulazzani, "Spazio dell'arte/ arte dello spazio. Padiglioni espositivi del XX secolo," in *Arti & Architettura 1900/1968*, ed. Germano Celant (Milan: Skira, 2004), 11–15.

3   For a more in-depth analysis,
     Massimiliano Savorra, *Capolavori
     brevi. Luciano Baldessari, la Breda
     e la Fiera di Milano* (Milan: Electa,
     2008).

des arts décoratifs et industriels modernes in Paris (1925), and the German Pavilion designed by Ludwig Mies van der Rohe for the International Exposition in Barcelona (1929), were autonomous objects that displayed themselves, over and above the ephemeral content within them. The long genealogical line to which they pertained covers over a century of experimentation on architectural language and ontological declarations, up to the manifesto designs of the twenty-first century such as the Dutch Pavilion by MVRDV at the Hannover Expo (2000), the Blur Building by Diller Scofidio on the lake in Neuchâtel for Expo.02 (2002), and the Danish Pavilion by BIG and Arup at the Shanghai Expo (2010).

In its current forms and uses, the exposition pavilion is a product of the early twentieth century, a bourgeois translation of the *Gesamtkunstwerk* cultivated by the Viennese Secession and transplanted into the new industrialized world by German Expressionism, with the aim of melding architecture, advertising graphics and industrial products. While the nineteenth century was the century of expansive halls and galleries, the twentieth century brought these small, temporary objects that hovered in a new zone somewhere between capitalist competition and national pride. There was a shift from the enormous containers produced by nineteenth-century engineering, in which the measure of space was absent, and boundaries were evanescent—like Joseph Paxton's Crystal Palace in London (1851), Ferdinand Dutert and Victor Contamin's Galerie des Machines in Paris (1889), and Vladimir Šuchov's innovative structures at the All-Russia Exhibition in Nižnij Novgorod (1896)—to the ultimate level of condensation that made the pavilion a pure communications device. Fortunato Depero's "typographic architecture" is the clearest example of the extreme outcome of this process. In the book pavilion he was commissioned to design by the Bestetti e Tumminelli and Fratelli Treves publishing houses at the 3rd Biennale delle arti decorative in Monza (1927), the communicative apparatus—three-dimensional letters and words—swallowed up the space, structure and program all at once.

Works by Peter Behrens and Bruno Taut can be taken as very early archetypes of this pervasive and congenital paradox. Behrens designed the Delmenhorster Linoleum-fabrik "Ankermarke" for the Dritte Deutsche Kunstgewerbeausstellung in Dresden (1906) and the AEG Pavilion at the Deutsche Schiffbau-Ausstellung in Berlin (1908), as well as designing the companies' coordinated images based on the stylistic elements of the pavilions. Taut was the creator of the Iron Industry Pavilion at the Internationale Baufach-Ausstellung in Leipzig (1913) and the Glass Pavilion at the Deutsche Werkbund-Ausstellung in Cologne (1914), which played on an interesting metonymy: they communicated ideas of iron and glass by being expressions of the respective materials.

This overlapping of syntax and semantics—the amplified embodiment of the famed "duck" from *Learning from Las Vegas*—overcomes the apparent paradoxical dualism between container and content to embrace antinomy as a generator of meaning. If the container becomes content, then architecture's bond with function will begin to tear. The vertex of the Vitruvian triad, *utilitas*, is weakened to the point of making architecture into inhabitable sculpture—pure *venustas*—or a useless machine—pure *firmitas*—,as was demonstrably taken to extremes in two pavilions designed by Luciano Baldessari and Marcello Grisotti at the Fiera Internazionale of Milan: the Breda Pavilion (1952) and the Sidercomit Pavilion (1954).[3] In the first, the structure, a metallic trellis framework covered with plastered me-

↓ Hans Leuzinger, Robert Maillart, GUNIT-Zementhalle in construction, Swiss National Exhibition, Zurich, 1939. Courtesy ETH-Bibliothek Zürich, Bildarchiv

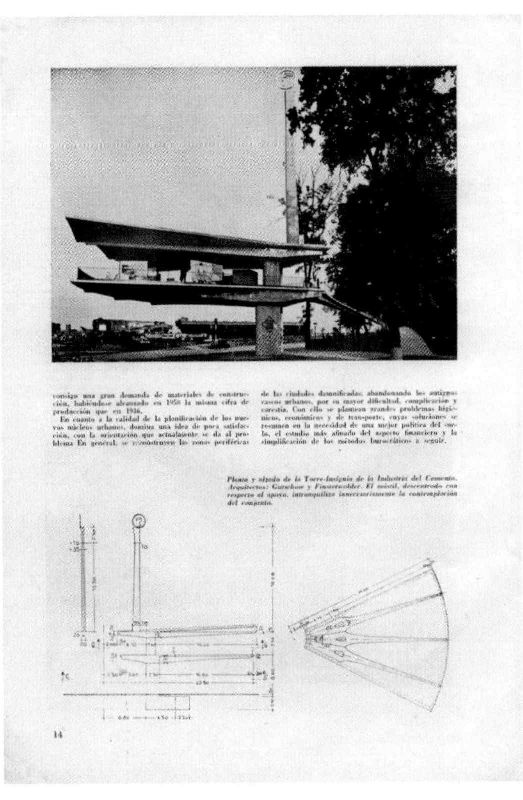

consigo una gran demanda de materiales de construcción, habiéndose alcanzado en 1950 la misma cifra de producción que en 1936.

En cuanto a la calidad de la planificación de los nuevos núcleos urbanos, domina una idea de poca satisfacción, con la orientación que actualmente se da al problema. En general, se reconstruyen las zonas periféricas de las ciudades damnificadas, abandonando los antiguos cascos urbanos, por su mayor dificultad, complicación y carestía. Con ello se plantean grandes problemas higiénicos, económicos y de transporte, cuyas soluciones se resumen en la necesidad de una mejor política del suelo, el estudio más afinado del aspecto financiero y la simplificación de los métodos burocráticos a seguir.

Planta y alzado de la Torre-Insignia de la Industria del Cemento. Arquitectos: Gutschow y Finsterwalder. El mástil, descentrado con respecto al apoyo, intranquiliza innecesariamente la contemplación del conjunto.

14

↑ Niels Gutschow, Ulrich Finsterwalder, Cement Industry Pavilion, Constructa Bauausstellung, Hannover, 1951, in *Revista Nacional de Arquitectura*, no. 123 (1952): 14

---

4   Agnoldomenico Pica, "Architettura pubblicitaria per la Sidercomit alla Fiera di Milano," *Architettura Cantiere*, no. 7 (1955): 7.

5   Agnoldomenico Pica, "Organismi pubblicitari," *Spazio*, no. 7 (1952–53): 58–60.

6   Carl Jegher and Mirko Roš, "Ergebnisse der Belastungsversuche an der Zementhalle der LA 1939," *Schweizerische Bauzeitung*, 120 (1942): 293–295.

7   Drawings and period photographs in: Ramón Andrada, Arturo Guerrero and Casimiro Iribarren, "CONSTRUCTA: La primera Exposición de la Construcción celebrada en Alemania después de la guerra. HANNOVER, 1951," *Revista Nacional de Arquitectura*, no. 123 (1952): 9–28.

tallic netting—Stauss lattice—was utterly at the service of plastic lyricism: a 25-centimeter-thick white belt which, in a harmony of parabolas, hyperbolas and conchoids, rose to reach 18 m in height and created an 8-m cantilever. In the second, mechanical-structural metaphor became form. A precarious architecture of unsteady equilibriums and disturbing imbalances extended into the void thanks to a complex interplay of counterweights among three elements: the metallic wings that unfolded into a roof; the projection room incorporated into the spacing of two truss beams with 30 m of light; and the protruding roof of the entrance, folded into an upside-down wing. As Agnoldomenico Pica noted, these ephemeral constructions were justified solely by their "exquisitely publicity-oriented—that is, essentially oratory—function,"[4] "since it is clear that here, a discourse based on the usual canons of usefulness and economy of construction would be completely false."[5]

ENGINEERING

The metonymic process that architects can trigger is all the more visible in pavilions developed by engineers to highlight a material, a technology or a construction technique. A predilection for univocal, unequivocal structural concepts can generate demonstrational projects like Robert Maillart's Zementhalle for the Schweizerische Landesausstellung on the shores of Lake Zurich (1939). Designed in collaboration with the architect Hans Leuzinger, the pavilion was a direct expression of a technical/financial problem: how to use the least material possible to cover a large space with no intermediate supports. The response was a thin cement shell, just 6 cm thick, in the shape of parabolic catenary tracing the funicular polygon within it. With a frontal height of 15.25 m, the pavilion was statically a barrel vault with its sides resting on two L-shaped cantilevered slab bases. This corbelled-vault system was raised 3.55 m off the ground by two pairs of tapered columns that established the position of the central, 3-meter-wide bridge and two everted ribs—maximum section 24×94 cm—that acted as transverse stiffeners. While in front the shell rose to a height of 11.7 m from the ground level and had a maximum span of 16.1 m, in the back, the size of the "mouth" was reduced to 9.1×11.1 m due to an accentuated splay. At the end of its period of utilization, the pavilion was load-tested by professor Mirko Roš of the Eidgenössische Technische Hochschule in Zurich (1940),[6] who took it to the point of complete collapse, with the aim of understanding the effective behavior of the shell—*spritz-beton* or gunite over a grid of 8-mm iron mesh—by collecting empirical data on its deformations.

Unlike Maillart, who geometrically explored the formal possibilities best suited to the properties of cement, anticipating the work of Félix Candela and Heinz Isler, Ulrich Finsterwalder, with his Cement Indistry Pavilion at Constructa Bauausstellung in Hannover (1951),[7] staged a test of brute force based on reinforced concrete's resistance to bending. The space of the pavilion—circa 250 sq. m and 3.5 m in height—was raised 6 m off the ground and compressed between two cantilevered slabs in the form of annulus sectors with a 2-m inner radius and 24-m outer radius. Two series of three tapered beams, respectively 126 and 90 cm thick at the junction and about 20 cm at the free end, held up the slabs—the lower horizontal one, and the upper one of curved petals—respectively covering an overhang of 14.8 and 16 m on the front and 4.1 and 4.6 m on the back side. The six beams

extended like spokes from three trapezoidal, reinforced concrete columns, 210 cm wide on the ground floor level and 140 cm on the top floor, eccentrically placed relative to the pavilion on a foundation footing that extended towards the center, thus balancing the masses in play. Completing the work were a slim, tapered 16-meter-high vertical element balanced atop the rear cantilever of the corrugated roof, and a spiral access stair with central beam. The overall effect was of a structure that opened out in a fan shape, defying gravity: perfect propaganda for the material's capacities.

While Maillart and Finsterwalder's pavilions demonstrated the versatility of concrete through unexpected and spectacular feats, the Aluminum Centenary Pavilion by Jean Prouvé and Michel Hugonet in Paris (1954)[8] aimed for a cynical, fractal reiteration of aluminum to publicize its lightness, ductility and cost-containment aspects. Prouvé shaped aluminum—a ubiquitous and polymorphic material that had the capacity to be structure, covering and fitting—in such a way as to obtain prefabricated elements that were easy to assemble, disassemble and recycle. The pavilion, assembled in just 21 days at Port du Gros Caillou on the banks of the Seine, was based on the repetition of a trilithic system with 15-meter-clearance external wind braces, and created a covered space 152 meters long, surrounded by alternating glass and aluminum panels. The 114 parallel beams were divided into three distinct elements and made with 4-millimeter-thick aluminum sheets bent to create a U-section, which also served as a clever rain gutter. Placed at a constant center distance of 134 cm, they alternated with 1.6-millimeter-thick aluminum roof panels connected via diecast aluminum joints. Partially reconstructed in 2000 at the Parc des Expositions di Villepinte in the department of Seine-Saint-Denis, it can be considered the precursor—in terms of both the use of the material and its historical vicissitudes[9]—of Toyo Ito and Masato Araya's Aluminum Pavilion in Bruges (2002). The innovative beehive structure, created with 125-millimeter-wide, 3-millimeter-thick strips and reinforced by large oval stiffener sheets,[10] was removed in 2013 after years of polemics surrounding the tautological impossibility of finding a specific long-term function for the "useless, temporary" architectural object.

EXPOSITION

The three large post-World War II expositions—the Exposition Universelle et Internationale de Bruxelles 1958, the Exposition Universelle et Internationale Montréal 1967 and the Japanese World and International Exposition Osaka 1970—were unparalleled moments in terms of the quantity and quality of experimentation carried out, in which architectural inventiveness and new structural models came together in the pursuit of the "wonder effect."[11]

In Brussels in 1958, two general categories of structures were delineated: reinforced concrete shells that worked by compression, and tensile structures that used cables or other taut elements. The first category included the Civil Engineering Pavilion designed by J. Van Doorselaere and A. Paduart with sculptor Jacques Moeschal. The second category comprised, in addition to the American Pavilion, two of the most important works by René Sarger, a student of Bernard Lafaille: the French Pavilion

8   For a more in-depth analysis, Axel Vénacque, *Jean Prouvé. Le pavillon du centenaire de l'aluminium: un monument déplacé* (Paris: Nouvelles Éditions Place, 2001).

9   Prouvé's pavilion was dismantled in 1956 and stored by André Lannoy, reconstructed in a different way in Lille at the Palais de la Foire and saved again in 1993 thanks to the efforts of the Ministère de la Culture et de la Communication. It was reconstructed again in 2000, but only three-fifths of the original length and exclusively with glass façades. Ironically, Ito and Araya's pavilions was also dismantled and conserved, awaiting possible future relocation.

10 For a more in-depth analysis, Dana Buntrock and Masato Araya, *Toyo Ito's Second Age of Aluminum: Toyo Ito and Masato Araya's Experiments in the Structural Use Of Aluminum*, ACSA/AIK int. conf., Seoul 2014. Available at acsa-arch.org.

11 For a complete discussion, Isaac López César, *World Expos. A History of Structures* (Barcelona: By Architect Publications S.L., 2017).

12 For a more in-depth analysis, Marc Treib, *Space Calculated in Seconds. The Philips Pavilion. Le Corbusier. Edgard Varèse* (Princeton, NJ: Princeton University Press, 1996).

13 Patent no. US2682235A, entitled *Fuller Geodesic Dome*, dated June 29, 1954, geometrically defines a polyhedron designed projecting the vertices of an icosahedron or a dodecahedron onto a spherical dome. In 1922, Walther Bauersfeld had created the first geodetic dome with reinforcement in concrete for the Zeiss planetarium in Jena. The 16-meter-diameter structure had a German patent no. 415,395 entitled *Method for the construction of cupolas and other domed surfaces in reinforced concrete*, limited to defining the construction method without indicating the geometric form.

14 For more on the role of models, Georg Vrachliotis, ed., *Frei Otto: Thinking by Modeling* (Leipzig: Spector Books, 2016).

and the Marie Thumas pavilion-restaurant. The former, designed by Guillaume Gillet and Jean Prouvé, was covered by two hyperbolic paraboloids formed of a network of cables suspended between edge beams, a concept inspired—like the Dorton Arena by Matthew Nowicki and Fred Severud (1953)—by Lafaille's competition entry design for the Centre des Industries Mécaniques (1951). The restaurant, a collaboration with Baucher, Blondel & Filippone, owed its original undulating form to a structural system made up of concave-curved stay cables suspended between eight inclined, converging spindly columns and convex-curved stabilizing cables anchored to the foundations.

Straddling the two categories was the Philips Pavilion by Le Corbusier and Iannis Xenakis, equivalent to a shell structure, but at the same time wrapped in a network of steel post-tension cables.[12] The result was a surprising object that blended the archetypes of the tent and the cave in a complex volume, geometrically constructed from the intersection of 12 hyperbolic paraboloids. These abstract segments, in physical reality, were the reinforced concrete ribs—40 cm in diameter—of the main frame, within which concavities were created using small prefabricated 5-centimeter-thick cement slabs and 7-mm steel cables positioned every 50 cm. Edgar Varèse's sound composition, Philippe Agostini's direction and Jean Petit's visions contributed to defining this Gesamtkunstwerk (total work of art) of the modern technological world, the raw material of which was an evanescent concentration of lights, colors, sounds and images in motion. The 480 seconds of the *Poème électronique* became part of an indivisible whole, melding with the organic, fluid space of the pavilion itself.

Expo '67 in Montreal produced two of the most important symbols of twentieth-century engineering: the American Pavilion—today the Biosphere—and the Pavilion of the German Federal Republic. On Île Sainte-Hélène, in collaboration with Shoji Sadao, Richard Buckminster Fuller designed the most iconic of his geodesic domes, a type of structure he had patented in 1954.[13] 24,000 steel bars made up a double-layered spherical dome 61 m high and 76 m in diameter. The 3.05-meter-per-side equilateral triangles on the external surface were visually overlain with the 1.88-meter-per-side hexagons of the inner layer. The curved fiberglass shell incorporated a computerized sun-screening and ventilation system. In 1976 the acrylic panels burned in a spectacular fire, but the steel structure was left intact.

Frei Otto, Rolf Gutbrod and Fritz Leonhardt's German Pavilion was a turning point in the history of tensile structures, due to its absolute freedom of form based exclusively on natural processes of self-definition. Unlike the geometric rigidity of Otto's earlier designs, such as the Music Pavilion in Kassel (1955), the irregular form of the Montréal Pavilion was the result of empirical experimentation on a series of scale models, which sprung from visionary experiments with soapy liquid, leading to 17-meter-high prototypes produced at the Institute for Lightweight Structures in Stuttgart.[14] The structure's behavior was directly determined by tangible physical laws inferred *a posteriori*, and not by abstract mathematical formulas conceived *a priori*. In fact, Otto obtained the smallest possible surface to cover an area of 8,000 sq. m through the automatic adaptation of a high-surface-tension liquid to equi-tensional

↓ Le Corbusier, Iannis Xenakis, Philips Pavilion in construction, Expo '58, Brussels, 1958. Courtesy Royal Philips, Philips Company Archives

surfaces, while Leonhardt deduced the stress state of the web of cables by topographically measuring bubbles with optical instruments. The result was a continuous anticlastic surface erected in eight weeks, generated by the deformation of a web of steel cables—50×50 cm and 12-mm diameter mesh, 54-mm edge cables—and held up by eight struts between 14 and 38 m high. The mesh, stabilized by pre-stressed rods and with rotating clamps in the nodes, had its inner curve covered by a translucent polyester membrane and PVC sheets. The teardrop-shaped "oculus" windows around the masts served as skylights and also allowed the shifting of loads between different mesh areas. In the wake of the "natural autoshape" concept, Otto collaborated with Shigeru Ban to design the Japanese Pavilion at the Hannover Expo (2000), mixing the strained gridshell system from the Multihalle in Mannheim (1975), which he had designed with Ted Happold based on upside-down models that adapted naturally to the funicular curvature, with Ban and Gengo Matsui working on cardboard structures.

In 1970, Osaka hosted the first Asian Expo: a grand festival of architecture permeated with utopian and metabolistic ideas. Here, the boundary between architecture and engineering was completely blurred in a sort of structural expressionism, represented by examples like the Takara Beautilion by Kisho Kurokawa, the Australian Pavilion by James Maccormick and the Brazilian Pavilion by Paulo Mendes da Rocha. At the center of it all was the Grand Roof by Kenzo Tange, designed with Yoshikatsu Tsuboi and Mamoru Kawaguchi. The exhibition space was lifted to 30 meters high inside a reticular open framework structure that covered a rectangular surface area of 31,500 sq. m, assembled on the ground and hoisted by means of pneumatic jacks along the six columns that held up the roof.

But the most innovative contribution of Expo '70 was in the area of pneumatic structures, anticipated by the seminal transportable *United States Atomic Energy Commission* exposition pavilion by Victor Lundy, Fred Severud and Birdair Structures (1960). In the American Pavilion, David Geiger and Horst Berger put their patent for low-profile pneumatic roofs into practice. The flame-retardant, waterproof fiberglass and vinyl surface was slightly curved through pressurization and reinforced by diagonal cables. Inserted into a super-elliptical ring of partially-buried reinforced concrete, it rose just 6.5 meters from the ground and covered 83.5×142 m of free space. With Yutaka Murata, Kawaguchi designed two inflatable pavilions: the Floating Theatre, and the Fuji Pavilion, the largest pneumatic structure of the era. Sixteen pressurized tubular arches 4 m in diameter, 72 m long and connected with 50-centimeter strips made up a circle 50 m in diameter. Geometrically, the pavilion's organic shape was the result of an inversely proportional relationship between span and height, in which the length of the tube was constant: while the two middle arches formed perfect half-circumferences, the ends rose progressively as the distance between the bases diminished. The tube was made of two layers of PVA glued together with a neoprene adhesive, with an exterior coating in Hypalon and an inte-

← Frei Otto, German Federal Republic Pavilion in construction, Expo '67, Montreal, 1967. Courtesy saai | Archiv für Architektur und Ingenieurbau am Karlsruher Institut für Technologie (KIT)

↓ Yutaka Murata, Fuji Pavilion, Expo '70, Osaka, 1970. Courtesy Kawaguchi&Engineers

15 For a complete discussion, Marco Mulazzani, *I padiglioni della Biennale di Venezia* (Milan: Electa, 2004).

16 Arup worked on every pavilion from the beginning of the series until 2012, but in the cases specified he was also a designer.

17 Vandini Mehta, Rohit Raj Mehndiratta, Ariel Huber, *The Structure. Works of Mahendra Raj* (Zurich: Park Books, 2016): 40.

rior coating in PVC. Kawaguchi and Murata further explored the theme of air-supported structures in two pavilions for the World Orchid Conference in Tokyo (1987).

Two transparent, overlapping air-supported structures were also to make up the design for the Nordic Countries Pavilion by Sverre Fehn, who had been the creator of the Norwegian Pavilion for the Brussels Expo and the Nordic Countries Pavilion in the Gardens of the Venice Biennial (1962), a lucid expression of the structural logic in reinforced concrete, surrounded by other masterpieces like the Dutch Pavilion by Gerrit Rietveld (1954), the Venezuelan Pavilion by Carlo Scarpa and Alvar Aalto's Finnish Pavilion (1956), as well as the Canadian Pavilion by BBPR (1957) and James Stirling's Electa Pavilion (1991).[15]

FABRICATION

In the year 2000, the Serpentine Gallery in London wanted to create a temporary pavilion to host its 30th anniversary gala. The project, by Zaha Hadid, became the first in a successful series of star-architect-designed pavilions in the gallery's garden each summer. It was the litmus test of a new relationship between architects and engineers, with star-architects on one side and a few large engineering firms on the other. Pavilions by Daniel Libeskind (2001), Toyo Ito (2002) and Rem Koolhaas (2006) were all created with Arup/Cecil Balmond,[16] as were those by Álvaro Siza and Eduardo Souto de Moura (2005), reviving a previous collaboration between Siza and Arup on the Portuguese Pavilion at the Lisbon Expo (1998).

In 2016, Bjarke Ingels' pavilion brought a new issue to the forefront: the discrete element, assembled in complex patterns, structurally expressed thanks to the support of AKT II—Adams Kara Taylor—, who had been the creators of the British Pavilion at the Shanghai Expo designed by Thomas Heatherwick (2010). BIG and AKT II's invention was an indicator of a preponderant approach in the field of contemporary structural engineering: the revival of the exposition pavilion as an object for experimentation on both constructive processes and alterative materials. The most fruitful seeds could be found at universities, in research groups that straddled the educational and professional spheres, guided by the will to achieve an ever-closer correlation between computational form-finding and non-standard production. Examples include the ETH Zürich Block Research Group led by Philippe Block and Tom Van Mele, and the pairing of ICD and ITKE, led respectively by Achim Menges and Jan Knippers at the University of Stuttgart. These collectives highlight an alternative mode of form production that differs from the traditional relationship between the architect and the engineer, so well summarized in an anecdote recounted by Mahendra Raj: "Charles [Correa] came to me and placed a crumpled paper on my desk. He said, 'Raj, this is a pavilion for Hindustan Lever for the Industrial Fair in Delhi [1961]. Do you think we can build it?'."[17]

FUJI PAVILION, EXPO '70

	OSAKA, JAPAN
	1970
ARCHITECT	YUTAKA MURATA
ENGINEER	MAMORU KAWAGUCHI

The collaboration between Mamoru Kawaguchi and Yutaka Murata revolved around the exploration of a particular type of structural solution that used pressurized air as a raw material: pneumatic structures. Both the Floating Theatre and the Fuji Pavilion for the Osaka Expo held in 1970, as well as the two pavilions for the 1987 World Orchid Conference in Tokyo, were inflatable pavilions.

The circular layout of the Fuji Pavilion was 50 m in diameter, making it the largest air-supported structure ever built at the time. It consisted of 16 pressurized tubular arches 4 m in diameter, in a complex series of layers: exterior covering in Hypalon resistant to UV radiation, high temperatures and chemical agents; a first layer of PVA; neoprene adhesive; a second layer of PVA; an internal layer in PVC. The constant 72-meter length of the arches, combined with the planimetric rigidity of the circle, generated the structure's organic form.

↑ Fuji Pavilion, Expo '70
Osaka, 1970.
Courtesy Bill Cotter of
worldsfairphotos.com

BRUGES PAVILION

	BRUGES, BELGIUM
	2002
ARCHITECT	TOYO ITO
ENGINEER	MASATO ARAYA

Originally intended to last only a year, the Aluminum Bruges Pavilion was dismantled, not without controversy, on November 5, 2013, eleven years after its construction. The structure used no pilasters or beams; rather the entire surface of the walls and roof statically collaborated to support it thanks to its beehive shape. Aluminum strips, 125 mm wide and 3 mm thick, were bent at 60° angles and soldered together in an alternating, mirroring pattern. The large, 3-millimeter-thick aluminum ovals were not purely decorative, but were the fundamental stiffeners of the structure, which thus absorbed the bending moment without deformations. To predict the pavilion's structural performance, Masato Araya used physical models, including full-scale ones. The result was a tunnel 16 m long, 6.75 m wide and 3.75 m high, covered in 12-millimeter-thick polycarbonate panels and built in just over a month.

← Bruges Pavilion, Brussels, 2002. Photo Stefaan Ysenbrandt. Courtesy Toyo Ito & Associates Architects. © Stefaan Ysenbrandt

STEVE JOBS THEATER

	CUPERTINO (CA), USA
	2009–2017
ARCHITECT	FOSTER + PARTNERS
ENGINEERS	BRIAN ECKERSLEY JAMES O'CALLAGHAN

Located in the Apple Park campus in Cupertino, the Steve Jobs Theater is almost completely underground, with the exception of the entrance pavilion, an example of grand experimentation and structural innovations hidden beneath an appearance of aesthetic simplicity. A large, 60-meter-diameter circular roof in carbon fiber with 44 radial panels seems to float weightlessly above a wall of glass. In fact, the lenticular disc is supported by a 41-meter-diameter cylinder formed by panels composed of 4 layers of 12-millimeter-thick structural glass.

In light of the seismic risks in California, the glass structure is connected via structural silicone to a steel channel designed to deform before the glass breaks. Two stone-clad staircases and an innovative glass elevator that rotates on helicoidal guide rails take visitors to the lower level where the auditorium is located, along with various utility rooms.

↓ Steve Jobs Theater, Cupertino, 2017. Photo Nigel Young. Courtesy Nigel Young, Foster + Partners

PLASTICITIES: ARCHITECTS AND THE PROMISE OF MATERIAL GENIUS

Lucia Allais

The modern romance between architecture and engineering has been recounted mostly as a story of structures and structural engineers. Yet in the last few decades a new species of architectural engineers has captured imaginations by taking materials, not structure, as their focus. They produce patent applications and robot-printed prototypes. Their most spectacular projects are short-term structures such as exhibition pavilions, built quickly but exuberantly. Whether it is a move from "hard" to "soft" matter, from "passive" to "active" substances, from "static" to "dynamic" systems, from bland to "responsive" environments, or from synthetic to "bio-generated" tissue, the impact of new materials on the future of architecture is announced in these small projects with incredible amounts of historical hubris. And the design personalities that have emerged from this trend all attribute at least partial credit to materials science and engineering (MSE), a discipline that is about a half-century old and has "the ability to design materials in a bottom-up manner to match almost any performance requirement."[1] Through appeals to this scientific ethos, new materials are introduced as bringing into architectural culture new intellectual freedoms—a "plasticity" of matter and thought, as the architect Jenny Sabin has put it.[2]

This all sounds very new, although in actual fact new materials have long been heralded by modern architects as harbingers of scientific genius. In 1929, the designer Charlotte Perriand was inspired to write a manifesto announcing that metal would soon replace wood in furniture and

1   Martin Bechthold and James C. Weaver, "Materials Science and Architecture," *Nature Reviews Materials* 2, no. 12 (December 2017): 1, doi.org/10.1038/natrevmats.2017.82. See also D. Michelle Addington and Daniel L. Schodek, *Smart Materials and New Technologies: For the Architecture and Design Professions* (Oxford, MA: Architectural Press, 2005), 3.

2   Andrew P. Lucia, Jenny E. Sabin, and Peter L. Jones, "Memory, Difference, and Information: Generative Architectures Latent to Material and Perceptual Plasticity," in *Knowledge Visualization Currents: From Text to Art to Culture*, eds. Francis T. Marchese and Ebad Banissi (London: Springer, 2013), 178.

3 Charlotte Perriand, "Wood or Metal?," *The Studio* 97, no. 433 (April 1929): 278–79.

4 Paul Weidlinger and John Peter, *Aluminum in Modern Architecture* I (New York: Reinhold Publishing Corporation, 1956), 244.

5 See Daniel Kula and Élodie Ternaux, *Materiology: The Creative Guide to Materials and Technologies* (Amsterdam: Frame Publishers; Basel: Birkhäuser, 2014), 5.

6 Cited in Hadas A. Steiner, *Beyond Archigram: The Structure of Circulation* (New York: Routledge, 2009), 172.

7 See, for example, Hannah Schreckenbach, "Mud as a building material in developing countries – Primitive or appropriate?," *GATE*, no. 1 (March 1985).

8 François Dagonet, "Preface," in *The Material of Invention*, ed. Ezio Manzini (Milan: Arcadia Edizioni, 1986), 15.

9 Paola Antonelli, *Mutant Materials in Contemporary Design* (New York: The Museum of Modern Art; Distributed by Abrams, 1995), 9. Catalog of an exhibition of the same title, presented at the MoMA, New York, May 25–August 27, 1995.

10 The Museum of Modern Art, "Built by Silkworms: Neri Oxman's 'Silk Pavilion II'." Artist Stories, 2020: *https://youtu.be/MUVv4wtyMPE*. Accessed June 23, 2022.

housing. "IT IS A REVOLUTION," she proclaimed. Wood may have been a "natural material," but it behaved unpredictably and aged too soon; steel was more easily standardized and shaped. Through its properties, steel also gave architects access to a profound epochal knowing. "The FUTURE will favor materials which best solve the problems propounded by the new man [sic]," she predicted, "the type of individual who keeps pace with scientific thought, who understands his age and lives it."[3] After steel came aluminum. In 1953, American manufacturers published a volume promising that aluminum would lighten the physical *and mental* load of architects and engineers, helping "throw off the shackles of our thinking."[4] After aluminum came plastic, then bitumen, then silicone, and so on. Over the next half-century, science-curious architects developed a habit of declaring that every novel substance delivered by industrial research would help them to think differently.[5]

In the 1960s, as plastics were being introduced into the building trades, vaunted qualities apparently started pertaining to the internal composition of people's minds. Building in plastic promised "an extension of personality," as Archigram put it in 1962.[6] From then on, engineered materials were promoted as active agents of rationality. Even mud and other low-tech building materials were re-introduced to architects as fresh sources of human ingenuity, to be studied in dedicated institutes.[7] In the 1980s, MSE departments proliferated in universities and governments, intensifying and diversifying the new materials available on the market. This was introduced to designers as an event in the history of thought: "Material is being 'intellectualized'," declared François Dagognet in his preface to Ezio Manzini's now-classic 1986 manual, *The Material of Invention*.[8] By the time Paola Antonelli announced the arrival of what she called "mutant materials" in a landmark exhibition at the Museum of Modern Art of New York in 1995, she described the materials themselves as doing the learning. "Materials are being transformed from adjuncts in passive roles to active interpreters of the goals of engineers and designers," she wrote.[9] In 2020, Antonelli reprised her advocacy of this idea by inviting Neri Oxman, an architect who heads a materials laboratory rather than a design studio, to build a structure in the museum. In a filmed interview, Oxman and Antonelli appeared in the space, marveling at the seductively soft woven mesh that was being assembled all around them by a network of human and nonhuman collaborators, including architects, engineers, and an army of insects.[10] A trained ear could still hear the hubris beneath the wonder, however. Rather than ameliorating nature as Perriand had done, Oxman appeared to be overseeing a transformation in the other direction: a wholesale replacement of the material substrate of the human-made environment, mesh by mesh, by natural agents themselves.

In other words, the field of materials science and engineering has offered avant-garde architects a kind of utopia, driven by the replacement of one material with another, and by the promise of ever-greater plasticity. Plasticity in this scenario refers not to the property of one material, but to a meta-property of engineering: a capacity to absorb change; a kind of making that changes the maker; a "genius" achieved not so much through preplanned calculation, but by channeling material generation in real-time.

But how does the new architectural materialism actually intersect with materials science engineering and what does it share with the "material turn" in contemporary philosophy? Despite their rhetoric of cutting-edge innovation, these designers are tacitly moved by a more ancient belief that there is a direct path from material to form. This "hylomorphism" has Aristotelian roots and is also found in the attitude to technology of early twentieth-century modern architects, who treated industrial production as a kind of second nature.

KNOWING IS PRODUCING

There is more to architects' engagement with MSE than the usual "exchange of metaphors."[11] What makes materials science so attractive is that it defines itself as a marriage of abstract speculation and applied functionality. "A basic feature of materials science," writes Bernadette Bensaude-Vincent, is that "knowing and producing are never separated."[12] Furthermore, because MSE was a field of engineering before it became a laboratory-based science, its networks continue to operate fluidly between commercial enterprise and basic research, comparable to the way in which architecture exists simultaneously as a field of academic research and a profit-making profession today. Engineered materials thus seem to fit easily in the architect's toolkit, as shortcuts from concept to implementation. Given this emphasis on productivity, it is all the more ironic that the fundamental scientific principle of materials science is not about creation and invention, but about conservation and constancy across change—the principle, usually attributed to Antoine Lavoisier, that "nothing is lost, nothing is gained; all is transformed."[13]

Strictly speaking, the science of materials is chemistry, an experimental field that was formalized at the end of the eighteenth century in the Parisian laboratory of Lavoisier and his wife, Marie-Anne Paulze Lavoisier. Equipped with a set of scales, a vacuum chamber, and an elaborate note-taking apparatus, they weighed every substance that went into and then came out of a set of reactions, discovering that air's role in combustion was not "mechanical" but "chemical." The Lavoisiers overturned centuries of pre-chemical knowledge, according to which the world was made up of substances—fire, water, and so on—each associated with a certain principle of transformation. Thus "fire" had been associated with the element "phlogiston," and the Lavoisiers' feat was ostensibly to have produced "dephlogisticated air." What they had really done, however, was to decompose air into oxygen and hydrogen. Not only was air not an element at all, but the principle regulating its change was the same universal principle common to all matter: conservation of mass. Crucially for the later history of materials, any substance discovered this way could be named, described, placed in a grid, and compared to others. Lavoisier's own interests reached far and wide; he researched air but also gypsum, and published a paper comparing different methods for lighting the streets of Paris.

This new set of operations for naming, classifying, and characterizing properties still constitutes the *modus operandi* of materials science today. As Isabelle Stengers has put it, "The idea that chemical properties are 'relational' ran counter to the whole chemical tradition since Aristotle."[14] To be clear, modern chemistry did validate one aspect of Aristotle's theory of materiality: that what differentiates "matter" (something found in nature), from a "material" (something for human use), is precisely its identification as such. But modern chemistry opened the door for rethinking the composition of vastly different parts of the natural and human-made world, together.

↑　Neri Oxman, Silk Pavilion II, MoMA, New York, 2020. Screenshot from *Built by Silkworms | Neri Oxman's "Silk Pavilion II" | ARTIST STORIES*, The Museum of Modern Art, New York, 2020

→　*Laboratoire et table des raports [sic]*, plates, in Denis Diderot, *Encyclopédie*, 1765–1776, vol. III (plates), unpaginated

11　Antoine Picon and Alessandra Ponte, eds., *Architecture and the Sciences: Exchanging Metaphors* (New York: Princeton Architectural Press, 2003).

12　Bernadette Bensaude-Vincent, "The Construction of a Discipline: Materials Science in the United States," *Historical Studies in the Physical and Biological Sciences* 3, no. 2 (January 2001): 223.

13　Bernadette Bensaude-Vincent, "Lavoisier: A Scientific Revolution," in *A History of Scientific Thought: Elements of a History of Science*, ed. Michel Serres (Oxford, UK; Cambridge, MA: Blackwell, 1995), 455–82. See also Bernadette Bensaude-Vincent, "The Concept of Materials in Historical Perspective," *N.T.M.* 19 (2011): 107–123.

14　Isabelle Stengers, "Ambiguous Affinity: The Newtonian Dream of Chemistry in the Eighteenth Century," in *A History of Scientific Thought*, ed. Serres, 378.

Laboratoire et table des Raports

Elements of Enlightenment chemistry still motivate architects' talk about materials today—most remarkably, an inherited sense of wonder. Indeed, even as Lavoisier distanced himself from physics and subjected the notion of substance to rationalization and control, historians remind us that "chemistry continued to be a science of passion and belief, rather than cool-headed deduction."[15] Other aspects of architects' thinking are owed to later developments of the mid-twentieth century, when discovering a new material became a matter of combining the properties of other, existing materials.

Today MSE is devoted exclusively to producing "properties." Again, a broad mandate for the re-description of "nature" is latent in this program. Simply put, the world looks different if one navigates it searching for properties and behaviors, in order to then create materials which can be carriers of these behaviors. Articles popularizing MSE use architectural design to depict this incredible power: they speak of engineers as builders, of their laboratories as factories, and of their method as that of "listening to nature."[16] However, MSE brings a significant change to the values that architectural designers derive from building science. With structural engineering, optimization tacitly serves as a design ethic—for example, using less material for greater performance. Flexibility is also often a metaphor: how a structural member reacts to bending becomes a cypher for the engineer's attitude. But a science that searches for properties offers designers a way of being, rather than a way of acting. And since MSE claims it is possible to design behavior on demand, the designer is able to claim a kind of detachment, a freedom *from* value in design.

This stance of detachment is reinforced by another part of materials science these designers inherit from the midcentury: its reliance on visualization. MSE was unified out of separate branches of research in new fields, such as crystallography and electronic microscopy, which rendered "structure" observable across different materials. In the 1960s, this image of chemical structure was seized upon by art and architectural educators such as György Kepes, who were hard at work creating a scientific aesthetics. The visual literacy this literature helped create is central to the legitimacy of today's architect-scientists and their output.

A chemist interested in lighting the city; Bauhaus teachers helping to unify a new science; architects publishing in science journals—it is tempting to read a historical crescendo and an increasing bond in these moments of intense interdisciplinary seduction. But they are in fact rare episodes of convergence. Between them lie two centuries of industrialization, during which the invention and codification of materials as "architectural" was firmly under the control not of scientists, or architects, but of industrial capitalists. Their claims to knowing and producing were also intertwined in the name of economic imperatives. Often violent and usually imperial, these processes worked by extracting substances from one place on the earth, then transforming and translocating them, via machines and factories, into material supplies for building in and on wholly different places on the planet. To be sure, naming and classifying remained essential, but only through the prodigious growth of regulatory bureaucracies. As historians have evocatively shown, one of the most important tools in the modernization of materials was a kind of paperwork: the specification.[17] By the beginning of the twentieth century, an architectural material was redefined as something that could be specified by a dedicated person, still known today as a "spec writer." Thus, plastic was invented in the 1860s but did

15 *Ibid.*

16 Leigh Buchanan, "Building a better chemical factory," *MIT News* (September–October 2021): 13.

17 Katie Lloyd Thomas, "Specifications: writing materials in architecture and philosophy," *ARQ* 8, nos. 3/4 (December 2004); Michael Osman, "Specifying," in *Design Technics: Archaeologies of Architectural Practice*, eds. Zeynep Ç. Alexander and John J. May (Minneapolis: University of Minnesota Press, 2019), 129–62.

18 Antoine Picon, *The Materiality of Architecture* (Minneapolis: University of Minnesota Press, 2021); Mari Lending and Mari Hvattum, eds., *Modelling Time. The Permanent Collection* 1925–2014 (Oslo: Torpedo Press, 2014); Akos Moravanski, *Metamorphism: Material Change in Architecture* (Basel: Birkhauser, 2017); Adrian Forty, *Concrete and Culture: A Material History* (London: Reaktion Books, June 2012).

19 Aristotle, *Physics* (Cambridge, MA: Harvard University Press, 1934), 199a.

↓ *Disciplinary Mix in Materials Science and Engineering*, in VV.AA., *Materials and Man's Needs, Materials Science and Engineering*, COSMAT report (National Academy of Sciences, 1974), 26

not become specifiable as such for a whole century. Similarly, theorists of materiality agree that modern buildings are expected to perform their materiality in a highly semantic way.[18] This opportunity for meaning is clearly made possible by the yawning gap between the production and reception of materials.

HYLOMORPHISMS

If there is not a single, direct correlation between material novelty in architecture and innovation in MSE (or its precursor, industrial science), what, then, motivates this renewed fascination? One answer is hylomorphism—a desire to find a direct path from material to form. This desire can be heard in the language of contemporary designers who claim to have discovered in materials a new immediacy between their sensations of the world and the output of their practice. They seek to cut out the middleman of structure, and of other predictive notions such as proportion, delineation, and geometry. They negate these mediations, staking a claim on empirical sensation. They point to the properties of materials as something concrete, verifiable, outside themselves, to explain their design outcomes. A material necessity leads to their designs, they explain, not their own intentions. This notion of material necessity is a legacy of Aristotle too; hylomorphism was his word for the relationship between form (*morphe*) and matter (*hyle*), articulated in his *Physics* in the context of a theory of causality. And while much of what Aristotle said in *Physics* has been surpassed by current scientific thinking, his conception of causality influenced his ideas about art, which hold continuing sway in any theory of aesthetic realism. Aristotle argued that artists imitated forms found in nature. Unlike Plato, who described forms as abstract ideas that exist only in the mind, Aristotle proposed that forms are only ever manifested in worldly things—including those made by humans. One example Aristotle gave was architectural: "If a home were one of the things provided by nature, it would be the same as is now produced by man."[19] When designers today explain that some aspect of a project was brought into being by its material makeup, they articulate a doubly Aristotelian view: of the necessity of their forms, and implicitly of the artistry of nature.

26

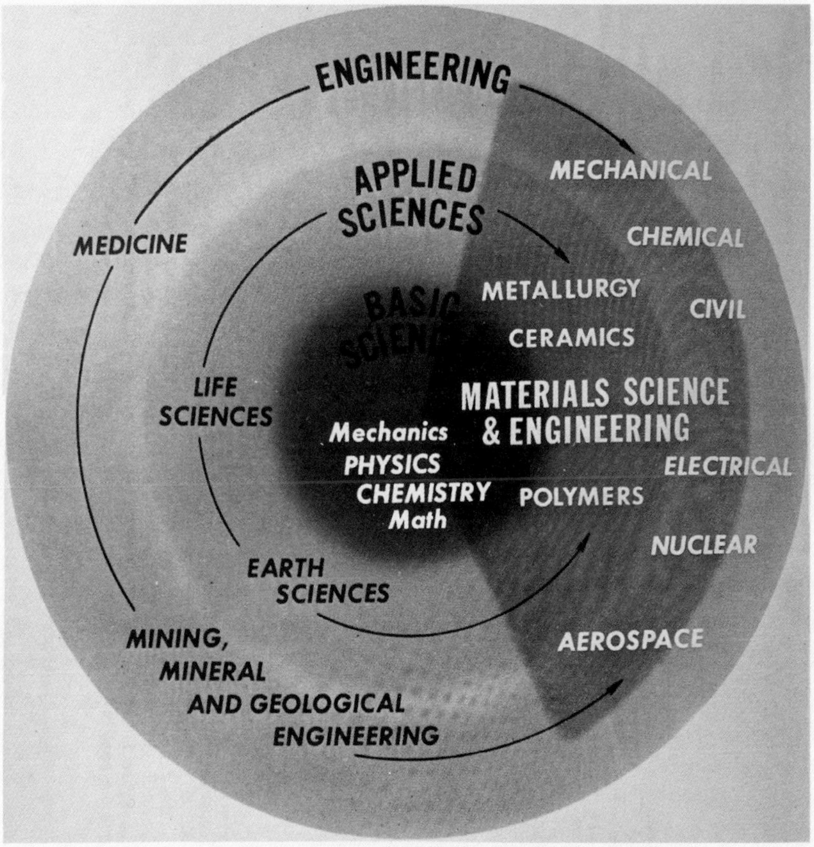

FIGURE 7. Disciplinary Mix in Materials Science and Engineering Subjects within the shaded sector above are considered to be in the field of materials science and engineering. Subjects partly or wholly outside the sector are involved in the field to varying degrees. COSMAT estimates, for example, that among the 150,000 chemists in the country, there are the equivalent of 50,000 chemists working full time in materials. (Illustration adapted from Mineral Science and Technology: Non-metallic Materials, National Academy of Sciences, Washington, D. C. 1969, page 12.)

But is there really a "nature" that coheres like some kind of great artist today? Is this attitude to isolating material phenomena and focusing intently on them not itself a reconstructive exercise, aimed remediating the same nature that was made heterogeneous by technical and scientific exploitation? Architectural modernism offers a helpful precedent. Le Corbusier, for instance, sounded startlingly Aristotelian when he wrote in 1921 that "if blind nature, which produces eggs, were also to make bottles, they would certainly be like those made by the machine born of man's intelligence."[20] His reason for referring to industrial products like bottles and housing as universally intelligent types was strategic: he sought to avert the pressures of Beaux-Arts typological planning. By accepting industry as a kind of second nature, he and others could claim there was no point in continuing to engage the classical tradition (with its elaborate Vitruvian myths about how columns resemble trees, for example). Significantly, this meant that modernists performed a kind of sleight of hand, treating a human-produced "material" as found "matter."

One place to witness modernist designers conflating "material" and "matter" is the history of exhibition design. Lilly Reich, a pioneer of modernist display, owed her breakthrough success in part to her matter-of-fact treatment of industrial materials in exhibitions, and especially to the way in which she departed from a style that had been standard for imperial and international exhibitions since the 1850s. As Matilda McQuaid has put it, Reich "altered the prevailing custom of presenting raw materials and techniques as a mere adjunct to the finished product, by choosing materials and processes as the essence of her installation. And rather than exhibit a material in its natural state, she chose the manufactured raw material as the desired form."[21] Thus her exhibitions helped to change prevailing mentalities, convincing the public that industrial things could be considered "raw" matter. Rather than being something found in the ground (such as an ore), a material was something produced by machines (such as linoleum). With its evenly spaced, equally sized square swatches, Reich's exhibition style can be considered the prototype of the materials library, that orderly collection of samples—of paint, carpet, vinyl, wood, etc.—that inhabits a corner of architecture offices today.

The fact that these conventions of materials science have permeated architectural culture reveals an ongoing consensus about the role of the architect: that the architect designs not *ex nihilo*, but works with "nature," processed into a new kind of raw material and available in a ready-made, always-expandable repertoire. What has changed since Reich and Le Corbusier is that material scientists are working towards the expansion of the repertoire *as a goal in itself*, and that designers see in this a fantasy of infinite variability—or, as they would say, a "plasticity."

PLASTICITIES

What do architects gain when they describe nature as plastic and borrow that plasticity for design? First and foremost, they obtain a way to deal with technological pressures, especially those of computation. The so-called material turn in architecture is sometimes described as a dialectical response to the onslaught of virtual experiences at the turn of the

20   Amédée Ozenfant and Charles-Edouard Jeanneret, "Le Purisme," *L'Esprit Nouveau*, no. 4 (January 1921): 369–86.

21   Matilda McQuaid, *Lilly Reich: Designer and Architect* (New York: Abrams, 1996), 21. Catalog of an exhibition of the same title, presented at the MoMA, New York, February 7–May 7, 1996.

↓ Ludwig Mies van der Rohe, Lilly Reich, *Die Wohnung*, view of the Deutsche Linoleum Werke AG, Weissenhofsiedlung Werkbund Exposition, Stuttgart, 1927. The Museum of Modern Art, New York, Mies van der Rohe Archive. Courtesy Scala Archives

millennium.[22] But the scientific redefinition of materials was already permeating design discourse in the 1980s. It is not virtuoso "virtuality," but on the contrary the inevitable everydayness of the computer and its transformation into a quotidian technology, that helped launch a "materials" subfield of architectural research.

For example, in 1986 Manzini saw the range of materials available as an "indicator of the level of technology."[23] He argued that the history of mankind could be told through the history of tools, because every new material "era" since prehistory had forced a novelty of technique. So when it came to describing the chemistry of plastics, he made an elaborate analogy with the behavior of a plate of spaghetti covered in varying states of meat sauce, clearly to appeal to the daily reality of his Italian readership.[24] Four decades later, after the personal computer became a daily tool—as pervasive as pasta—such analogies became less necessary. Jenny Sabin, one of the most cogent among contemporary laboratory-based architects, makes ceramic projects which are sophisticated, evocative, and precisely calibrated. They also look a lot like she is working with, or to improve, spaghetti. But she has no use for this analogy, because her practice is focused on the tools of robotic fabrication. Materials are useful for teaching her tools sensitivity, not the other way around.

Secondly, plasticity allows designers to stake a claim on "sense and intuition" so they can partake in a new computer-based empiricism.[25] Achim Menges combines computational principles, the latest MSE visualizations, and readings of new materialist philosophy, to call for "non-linear" design processes. In this he relies on philosopher Manuel DeLanda's critique of a "linear" model of scientific causality and his proposal for an "S-shaped" curvature for thought.[26] Of course, in DeLanda's work this curve does not describe an architectural shape, nor a rate of change for a dynamic shape, but rather a scalar modification of this rate of change. The S is a geometry three times removed from any material thing that would be manipulated by an architect. Yet Menges juxtaposes it with enough references to chemical and mechanical processes—a bending piece of metal, the boiling points of substances—that the reader is encouraged to think that, the more complex a physical shape, the less linear the thinking that has gone into it. The trouble is that a designer's use of a learning algorithm does not guarantee the complexity of his or her shapes. The history of art and architecture is replete with complex shapes designed through linear processes, and examples of complex thought-processes that have given rise to simple straight lines or naked monolithic volumes.

Most compellingly, the concept of plasticity describes how designers habituate to their new tools. This is how the term is used in neuroscience. In neuroplasticity, the continued and repeated use of certain parts of the brain modify its material makeup, and therefore the potential of the body controlled by that brain. Philosopher Catherine Malabou has devoted much of her work to revising the principles of continental philosophy in light of neuroplasticity. Her eloquent critique of flexibility—"Flexibility is plasticity minus the genius"—could equally describe new-materialist architects' critique of traditional structural engineering.[27] But Malabou has also warned that plasticity does not necessarily mean freedom, or power. Indeed, it potentially strengthens existing channels of biopolitical control. In design discourses, on the other hand, plasticity tends to be seen as a kind of weapon of the weak—the power of Neri Oxman's silkworms, for example. This deliberate gloss over the question of power is highly problematic. Many digital-materi-

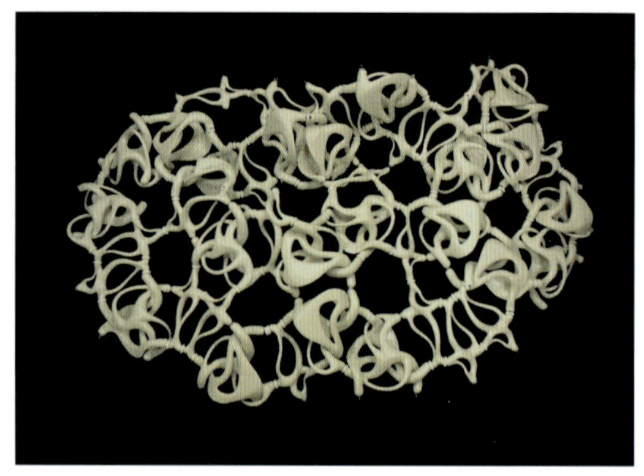

↑ Jenny Sabin Studio, *PolyMorph prototype swath*, FRAC Centre, Orléans, 2013. Courtesy Jenny Sabin

22 See for instance Toshiko Mori, "Introduction," in *Immaterial/ Ultramaterial: Architecture, Design, and Materials*, ed. Toshiko Mori, Millennium Matters 2 (Cambridge, MA: Harvard Design School in association with George Braziller, 2002), XIII.

23 Manzini, *The Material of Invention*, 96.

24 *Ibid.*

25 Achim Menges, *Material Synthesis: Fusing the Physical and the Computational*, special number of *Architectural Design* edited by Achim Menges, 85, no. 5 (September–October 2015): 16.

26 Manuel DeLanda, "The New Materiality," *Material Synthesis*, 17–21.

27 Catherine Malabou, *What should we do with our brain?*, trans. Sebastien Rand (New York: Fordham University Press, 2008), 12.

alist architects who are trying to retool themselves are haunted by the very strong legacy of structural rationalism, which returns through the back door. Neri Oxman's Pavilion at the Museum of Modern Art, for example, relies on an "underlying structure" to guide the silkworms' production—a structure whose shaping and design goes unmentioned. When Oxman and Antonelli marvel at the silkworms' labor in their filmed interview, they look right past this structure and consider only the apparent ingenuity of the insects. This is an aesthetic performance of the highest pedigree, reprising the Enlightenment notion that artists can learn from the beauty of nature by studying its rules.[28] The role of insects, in Oxman's project, is to model a natural genius in a way that can be marveled at. The role of the designer is to intervene without an apparent purpose. In the process, a sleight of hand occurs: the manufactured begins to seem raw again.

Undoubtedly, designers who engage with MSE are genuinely trying to adapt their actions, and even their brains, to new material dynamics. But if plasticity earns them new freedoms, it also confines them to linear, falsely specialized paths. This narrowing is hard to detect, though it is hidden in plain sight. Materials science has seduced designers with its extraordinarily ambitious definition of nature. In return, architects have helped popularize research in materials science, confirming the comforting thought that nature still exists out there, untouched by humans, and ready to teach us design lessons.

28 Immanuel Kant called genius "the talent (natural gift) which gives the rule to art." Art was the act of creating things which seemed necessary, but whose cause could not be identified. Immanuel Kant, "§ 46. Beautiful Art Is Art of Genius," in *Critique of the Power of Judgment* [1790], ed. Paul Guyer, trans. Paul Guyer and Eric Matthews, *The Cambridge Edition of the Works of Immanuel Kant* (New York: Cambridge University Press, 2000), 186–87.

MAILLART'S CONCRETE

Sarah Nichols

The thin plane of reinforced concrete folded slowly to the ground, "like a curtain."[1] Observers on that day in 1940 included Robert Maillart, the structural engineer for the project, and Mirko Roš, the director of the Swiss Federal Laboratories for Materials Science and Technology (EMPA), whose team had just tested the structure with weights and explosives. The temporary structure had been an advertisement for cement at the 1939 Swiss National Exhibition in Zurich, designed with the architect Hans Leuzinger. In the wake of Maillart's death shortly thereafter, the project was lauded as, purportedly, his only opportunity for pure artistic expression in an urban center. Over the next decade, a narrative coalesced around Maillart: a lone genius shunned by the establishment who radicalized structural form in the obsessive pursuit of material economy, who toiled in relative obscurity and thereby could be "discovered" by a popular audience,[2] whose formal inventiveness had a clarity of vision that could, ostensibly, only come from an artistic sensibility. Through the efforts of Sigfried Giedion, Max Bill, and David Billington, among others, Maillart's work in remote parts of rural Switzerland has become familiar to generations of architects and engineers around the globe. Yet along with this dissemination from the hinterlands to MoMA, came distortions about how these thin, reinforced-concrete structures came into being. The story increasingly became about Maillart himself, omitting the network and context of the work. Yet as this happened, the narrative diverged from the way that Maillart and his peers considered work in concrete, which was rarely about the work of an individual but rather as contributions to a broader material culture.

1   Mirko Roš, Empa report no. 99, "Versuche und Erfahrungen an ausgeführte Eisenbeton-Bauwerke in der Schweiz. Zweite Ergängzung" (Zurich: EMPA, 1940), 28.

2   George R. Collins, "The Discovery of Maillart as Artist," in *The Maillart Papers from the Second National Conference on Civil Engineering: History, Heritage and the Humanities*, eds. David P. Billington, Robert Mark and John F. Abel (Princeton, NJ: Departement of Civil Engineering, Princeton University, 1973).

3   Architecture, Civil Engineering, Mechanical Engineering, Chemistry, and Forestry. In addition to the five original departments at the Polytechnikum, there was also a Philosophy faculty (without students) that was intended to assist the departments.

4   David Gugerli, Patrick Kupper, and Daniel Speich, *Transforming the Future: ETH Zurich and the Construction of Modern Switzerland 1855-2005* (Zurich: Chronos, 2010).

5   At the time of Maillart's studies, there were no courses dedicated to structural design in reinforced concrete, but he began working with the material almost immediately upon graduation. After graduating, Maillart worked for a few years at, successively, Pümpin & Herzog, the Civil Engineering Department (Tiefbauamt) of the City of Zurich and Froté & Westerman, before opening Maillart & Cie in 1902. In 1912, he opened another office in Russia and was stranded in Riga at the outbreak of World War I in 1914. In the aftermath, he lost his wife to illness and closed his office. He reopened Maillart & Cie in Geneva in 1919, and from 1929 until his death in 1940 also had offices in Zurich and Bern.

6   The very first project Maillart worked on was the Veyron bridge in Pampigny in 1896, a short span and an unremarkable concrete structure. A handful of projects were completed after the Zementhalle, but none achieved the same level of recognition.

7   Sigfried Giedion, *Space, Time, and Architecture: The Growth of a New Tradition*, 4th ed., enl. (Cambridge, MA: Harvard University Press, 1963), 463. It is of course also worth noting that "his" country (Maillart's) was the same as Giedion's, who also felt that he himself was underappreciated there.

8   Conservative building authorities have similarly been accused of thwarting Maillart in completing a "pure" bridge within an urban context. The structure of his 1899 Stauffacher Bridge in Zurich was hidden beneath neoclassical stone cladding by City Architect Gustav Gull and, as we have seen, the Lorraine Bridge in Bern is also generally considered to be a compromised design.

9   In the case of exposed concrete, aesthetics and risk intersected, as at the beginning of the twentieth century many believed that reinforced concrete required a protective coating or cladding.

10   Lukas Ingold's forthcoming dissertation provisionally titled *Form as the Unknown. Explorations in Structural Design by Sergio Musmeci* examines Musmeci's retreat into radical, unbuilt—and sometimes, practically speaking, unbuildable—proposals.

The view of Maillart as a solitary figure stands in contrast to the discursive notion of the profession seen in Maillart's own writing, as well as to the self-perception of civil engineers in Switzerland and neighboring countries at the time. Civil engineers, as the name suggests, indeed saw their work in service to the state even when they were in private practice. This sentiment was not just at the root of the discipline but still pervaded the educational system and carried through into the structures of practice. Maillart graduated from the Engineering School of the Polytechnikum in Zurich (now ETH) in 1894. The Polytechnikum's civil engineering department was one of five original departments, each related to a crucial aspect of development, such as binding the nation together with infrastructure or developing turbines to generate electrical power.[3] In effect, the Polytechnikum was established to build the state that created it.[4] The Association of Civil Engineering Students visualized this relationship in a drawing from the 1910s depicting the body of an engineer bridging a river, helping the frail, feminine form of the populace across the water. Despite this allegoric figuration, civil engineering more commonly presented itself as a bureaucratized system. In one example from the 1939 National Exhibition, the Swiss Society of Engineers and Architects (SIA) described the work of the architect and that of the engineer. While the architect was shown as a figure guiding every step of the construction process, the engineer was not even present, their work subsumed within a larger field of organization. What was instead represented was the competition process through which commissions for public buildings and bridges in Switzerland are, famously, determined. In other words, architecture was explained as the work of the architect, and engineering through a managerial apparatus.

Concrete was the thread that ran throughout Maillart's rather tumultuous career.[5] His first and final projects of note were forty years apart, and both in Zurich—the 1899 Stauffacher bridge and the 1939 Cement Hall.[6] But in between, most of his work was done farther afield: shed roofs in Spain, flat slabs and mushroom columns in St. Petersburg and Altdorf, cement silos in Cairo, and a number of bridges in rural areas of Switzerland. Maillart's built work was complemented by clear, thoughtful writing. He published approximately 25 articles in the *Schweizerische Bauzeitung* between 1901 and 1938. In essays, personal correspondence, and, briefly, as a lecturer at ETH, Maillart articulated a broader theoretical framework regarding economy and durability and contributed a significant series of articles and reports on how bending is calculated, challenging textbooks and university lessons, arguing that they should be corrected.

Much has been written about the supposed obstacles Maillart faced building in Switzerland. Giedion opined that "During his lifetime his [Maillart's] country did not recognize his significance. He was often hampered and his intentions misunderstood, so that he did not give all that he might have given."[7] There is an inherent conflict between an engineer largely uninterested in "proving" his experimental designs through calculation and risk-averse building authorities whose mandate required conservativism, not in terms of aesthetics (though this was also often the case[8]) but in their assessment of risk in terms of cost, safety, and durability.[9] Yet despite this, Maillart is known through his robust corpus of built work—of the sixty-four projects shown in Max Bill's book, for example, just six are unbuilt. This is quite a contrast in comparison to an engineer like Sergio Musmeci, who became renowned through few built projects and numerous unbuilt proposals.[10] Certainly, the fact that Maillart is known for his built work is related to his interest in the practical over the theoretical. Of the few experimental projects he initiated—as opposed to competitions and commissions—the majority were built as full-scale test structures rather than remaining on paper.[11]

Norms created a partial framework outside of the assessments of public authorities, private clients, or a competition committee. Switzerland was the first country to issue provisional norms for reinforced concrete in 1903, which were revised and made official in 1909 through the work of the Commission on Reinforced Concrete. Maillart was Secretary of the Commission and was involved in revisions of the norms until the 1930s. He thus had a measure of agency in shaping the strictures that would be applied to his work and that of his colleagues. The debates that surrounded these norms spilled out into broader professional meetings and into the pages of the technical press. Maillart was aggressive in these discussions, arguing that engineers should have as much "freedom" as possible. To him, norms often brought "more disadvantages than benefits in that they dull the judgement of the engineer."[12] With numerous ways of calculating reinforced concrete and a number of variables such as the strength of locally-available aggregate, Maillart further argued that restrictive norms would lead to over-dimensioning that would be wasteful both in terms of cost and material. Maillart framed concern about norms in terms of the purported need to ensure that reinforced concrete construction would continue to gain popularity and acceptance—polemically reduced to a choice between allowing or hindering concrete construction.[13] Beyond specific disputes about calculation methods and the validity of maximum allowable stresses, these debates were also about the role of the engineer. Arguing for "freedom" also meant arguing that reinforced concrete should be reserved for a limited number of "experienced and knowledgeable hands." The same attitude applied to construction site labor, as reflected in both norms and professional discussions.[14] Roš put it bluntly: "the untrained working class must stay away from the [reinforced concrete] construction site."[15] This was, of course, not an inevitability: norms could also have been used to make the field more accessible.[16]

In fact, the stringency of Swiss norms was largely immaterial to a practice such as Maillart's due to a loophole written into the original provisional norms that made its way into future official versions. Towards the end of the document, Article 19 stated: "Taking into consideration how new this type of construction is, deviations from the above norms are permissible if they are justified by comprehensive tests and the assessment of competent personages."[17] Maillart's work, developed with little regard to proving his designs through calculation, was exemplary of the type of exception envisioned by such a provision. Rather than operating outside the system, Maillart actually participated in writing the norms, and even his deviation from the norm was quite literally written into the norm itself.

In line with an engineering ethos dedicated to performance and efficiency, Maillart was, as is well-known, a vocal proponent of absolute material economy. For Maillart, the "monolithic character" of reinforced concrete "without joints or bearings" was integral to a general pursuit of material economy.[18] His reasoning was that there would be cost savings from reducing the amount of material, and that lighter buildings would have less internal stresses and were less likely to shift the earth below them, thus improving durability. As his work began to gain recognition in aesthetic terms, he was sometimes asked to speak about aesthetics, and did so somewhat begrudgingly, stressing that aesthetics were not his focus.[19] Yet his position seemed to change in the late 1930s in relation to his disapproval of the National Socialist regime in Germany.[20] Emphasizing the pragmatism of his formal approach

↑ Karl Kobelt, postcard for the Academic Engineer Association, 1910. ETH Library Zürich, Image Archive

11 He tested not just his flat slab system but also a slopeless flat roof intended to hold water for insulation. An elegant proposal for a dam made of thin shells of decreasing height stabilized by water between them was never constructed.

12 Robert Maillart, "Die Brücke in Villeneuve-sur-Lot, nebst Betrachtungen zum Gewölbebau," *Schweizerische Bauzeitung* 85, no. 12 (March 21, 1925): 151–54.

13 Robert Maillart, "Zum Entwurf der neuen schweizerischen Vorschriften für Eisenbetonbauten," answer to the article of Prof. Paris at page 119, *Schweizerische Bauzeitung* 99, no. 10 (March 5, 1932): 115.

14 Article 15 of the 1903 provisional norms stressed that contractors and foremen needed to be both responsible and experienced with reinforced concrete. François Schüle, *Provisorische Normen für Projektierung, Ausführung und Kontrolle von Bauten in armiertem Beton* (Zurich: schweizerischer ingenieur- und architektenverein, 1903).

15   Roš, Empa report no. 99, 14.

16   Amy Slaton's work on the introduction
     of reinforced concrete construction in
     the United States describes a parallel
     battle to define engineering as a
     profession not just through codifying
     procedure but also through markers of
     class and the tacit delineation of the
     social hierarchy of the construction
     site. Amy E. Slaton, *Reinforced
     Concrete and the Modernization
     of American Building, 1900-1930*
     (Baltimore, MD: Johns Hopkins
     University Press, 2001), 72.

17   Schüle, *Provisorische Normen für
     Projektierung, Ausführung und
     Kontrolle von Bauten in armiertem
     Beton.*

18   Theophil Wyss, *Hochbauten in armiertem
     Beton. Vorträge von Rob. Maillart*,
     1912, Hs 664:13, ETH University
     Archives. Unpaginated.

19   "The sense of beauty alone is not the
     only thing that awakens the desire
     to keep sight of the function of
     the whole before that of individual
     pieces. An overall assessment also
     brings economic benefits." Robert
     Maillart, "Aktuelle Fragen des
     Eisenbetonbaues. Nach einem Vortrag
     am Diskussionstag des S.V.M.T. am 12.
     Nov. 1937," *Schweizerische Bauzeitung*
     111, no. 1 (January 1, 1938), 1.

20   A distaste also expressed in family
     letters outside the context of
     aesthetics.

21   Robert Maillart, "Lichtbilder-Vortrag
     Basel," lecture notes, 1938, Hs 1084,
     ETH University Archives.

22   While Maillart seems to have enjoyed
     the recognition he received from
     modernist architects, he also
     turned down offers to attend CIAM
     conferences, and noted elsewhere
     that while any style could lead to
     beautiful or ugly structures, "In
     many places, utilitarian lines and
     modern decoration have created the
     ugliest buildings." Maillart, "Die
     Brücke in Villeneuve-sur-Lot, nebst
     Betrachtungen zum Gewölbebau."

23   According to Carl Jegher's son
     and successor Werner, the four met
     frequently at the Restaurant du Nord
     on Zurich's Bahnhofplatz. Werner
     Jegher, "Mirko Roš" (Obituary),
     Schweizerische Bauzeitung 80, no. 45
     (November 8, 1962), 759–64.

thus became a way of articulating Swiss technical cultural independence from Germany. More generally, Maillart's comments on aesthetics argue *against* the imposition of constraints on form by predetermined aesthetic codes—monumental or otherwise—rather than in favor of a specific new aesthetic. Maillart took issue with the Classical ideal of the continuous arch as something that hindered material efficiency in reinforced concrete. Yet at the same time, he repeatedly declared his aesthetic agnosticism, noting that: "We were taught that the engineer does not have to think about beauty. I have both lived and acted according to that [principle]. [...] Now strangely quite a lot of foreign and also some domestic architects have explained to me that these simple functional structures were more beautiful than those whereby I had tried to achieve something particularly beautiful. I leave this an open question. My conviction is that my proposals represent a technical advancement."[21] The statement points not only to a detachment from aesthetic discourse, but also to Maillart's distance from modern architecture and modernist architects.[22]

The thin monolithic type of construction Maillart pursued was made possible by a network of engineers, manufacturers, public building authorities, site supervisors, and construction workers, all of whom contributed to achieving these bare-minimum structures. In such a small country, relationships in the building trade—as in other industries—tended to cross over from the professional to the personal. The men who comprised Maillart's weekly lunch circle in Zurich were also key protagonists in the realization and dissemination of his work and were a group with considerable influence in building culture at the time.[23] Roš was the long-serving director of EMPA and a charismatic proponent of reinforced concrete construction whose views often echoed Maillart's. Under his direction, EMPA conducted load tests of many of Maillart's structures. Carl Jegher was the publisher of the *Schweizerische Bauzeitung*, the journal of the Swiss Engineers and Architects' Association (SIA), widely read within Switzerland. After asking Maillart to report on a lecture by the Hennebique license holder Samuel de Mollins in 1901, Jegher frequently published Maillart's work and writing for decades thereafter. Florian Prader of Prader & Cie was one of two contractors with whom he worked frequently; he had a similar relationship with the other as well, Eugene Losinger of Losinger & Cie, who was part of his lunch circle in Bern.[24] Both contractors built numerous major projects in reinforced concrete, of which their work with Maillart was only a small portion.

This view of Maillart as an insider differs from the received history of Maillart as an outsider and as an individual genius. Certainly, the conservative civil engineering department at ETH viewed Maillart's approach with suspicion. Yet, in many other significant ways, he was part of the establishment. The process of realizing these structures was both predicated upon relationships in construction-related professions and industries and served to strengthen those very networks. Through frequent collaboration, ties were maintained and trust was built up. Professional bonds were also often strengthened through familial links, with, for example, sons being sent to gain work experience in colleagues' offices, both in Switzerland and abroad. While this relational network produced many admired structures, it was also replete with nepotism. Against the backdrop of a building culture that went to great lengths to be democratic—via public education and public competitions—was a small circle of insiders who could achieve such work through personal ties that skewed the outcome of public vetting processes.

Maillart's appreciators in the fields of architecture and art history have often written about his work as dynamic forms but static, finished objects. Yet the forms of these structures resulted from thinking about the entire process of construction, considerations to which he dedicated as much attention during his lectures at ETH as he did to form.[25] Among these topics, the issue of cost has become part of the popular understanding of Maillart's work, as so many of his office's commissions resulted from underbidding competitors. Maillart also repeatedly emphasized the importance of cost in his writing. Over the course of his career, Maillart's emphasis on cost shifted from a way of supporting the diffusion of reinforced concrete—an aim in line with the desires of manufacturers and reinforced concrete patent-holders, i.e., those who stood to benefit financially from such a claim—to emphasizing cost more broadly as a key criterion for evaluating design, an emphasis that can only be understand in light of the shifting political circumstances of the late 1930s.[26] These later remarks begin to suggest thrift as an ethics of building the state as directly and modestly as possible.

Process is still today an unavoidable concern for concrete construction. It is a material whose quality is determined not just by its composition but by how it is handled on site. To build structures such as Maillart's, close interactions throughout the process from drawing to building were crucial. Material restraint required trust that a structure would be built with both precision and accuracy. Maillart's structures were reliant upon contractors' methods and practices and a realistic assessment of the difference between what was theoretically possible and what was feasible on the construction site. Moreover, Maillart's disdain for excess structural material pertained not just to the finished form, but also to the process of construction as formwork and falsework, which could also lead to considerable material wastage. The centering for Maillart's bridges was approached with as much consideration as the completed structure, designed to use as little material as possible and to make the process of constructing the centering and, later, the bridge atop it as smooth as possible.[27]

Some projects that Maillart seems to have taken pride in that were later ignored are better understood in term of process, particularly the Lorraine Bridge in Bern. Designed in collaboration with the architects Klauser & Streit, it has the appearance of a massive stone arch bridge.[28] Yet the concrete masonry belies the relative lightness of the reinforced concrete grid structure within. While the project has been largely overlooked,[29] it is the one that he wrote most extensively about. A four-part article on the design and construction of the bridge that appeared in the *Schweizerische Bauzeitung* describes how the light centering designed by Maillart & Cie saved wood, enabled by masonry that was self-supporting as each row was completed.[30] He never repeated such a detailed account for any of his other projects.[31] Maillart seems to have viewed the project not as a progressive form—he understood and seemed to accept Bern's view that the bridge should appear massive—but as an intelligent process.

Maillart understood the pursuit of lightness as predicated on a reliable material supply chain. Reducing uncertainty about the material could lead to the exactitude needed to reduce redundancy, allowing lower safety factors based on "trust" in the material.[32] In order to achieve this, cement and aggregates had to perform as anticipated by testing and experience, something that went from challenging to manageable over the course of Maillart's career. Maillart argued that material testing would lead to "cheaper, and therefore more durable buildings, or in other words: quality work."[33] Yet, considering their cost, strong, durable materials, he added, could only be used in moderation, creating a circular argument for materially thin structures. He

---

24 When in Bern, Maillart would dine with the municipal engineer Armin Reber, contractor Eugene Losinger, and two other engineers. Ernst Stettler "Reflections on Maillart" in *The Maillart Papers*, eds. David P. Billington, Robert Mark and John F. Abel, 129. Hs1085 Über RM, ETH University Archives, Princeton Papers, 1973.

25 Wyss, *Hochbauten in armiertem Beton.*

26 In 1936, having been asked to comment on a recent bridge in Germany, he noted sharply that "evaluation of a structure without knowledge of the costs is impossible, as the execution of even the most important commissions only deserves notice when it has been achieved with the least means." Robert Maillart, "Einige neuere Eisenbetonbrücken," *Schweizerische Bauzeitung* 107, no. 15 (April 11, 1936): 157–63.

27 Centering was usually designed either in-house, but contemporaries pursued similar aims. Risch (Richard) Coray, who designed and built the centering for the Salginatobel Bridge, also designed light, clever centering for a whole generation of daring bridge structures, including those for the Rhätische Railway.

28 The original, unsuccessful competition proposal was submitted with Joss & Klauser in 1911. By the time the project was built, the architecture firm had changed partners and become Klauser & Streit.

29 It is typically treated only summarily. The Lorraine bridge is not included in Max Bill's book and is skimmed over only as a biographical detail in Billington's writings.

30 Robert Maillart, "Die Lorraine-Brücke über die Aare in Bern," *Schweizerische Bauzeitung* 97, nos. 1, 2, 3, 5 (January 3, 10, 17, 31, 1931).

31 Including the Salginatobel Bridge that opened the same year.

32 Robert Maillart, "Masse oder Qualität im Betonbau?," *Schweizerische Bauzeitung* 98, no. 12 (September 19, 1931): 149–50.

33 *Ibid.*

↓ Robert Maillart with Klauser & Streit, Lorraine Bridge under construction, Bern, 1929. Courtesy ETH-Bibliothek, Hochschularchiv

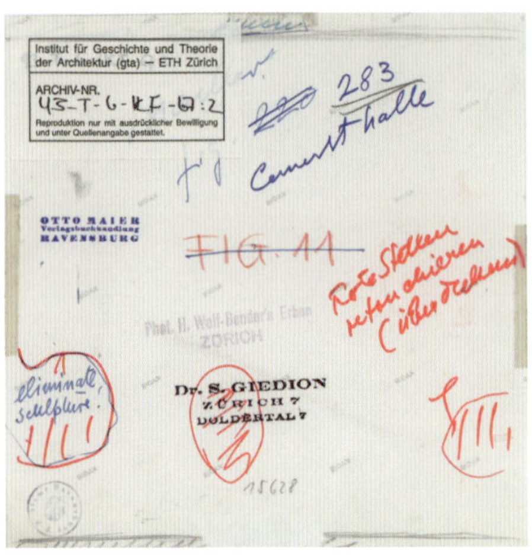

↓ Photo by Wolf Bender later airbrushed at the direction of Sigfried Giedion, Zementhalle, 1939. Courtesy gta Archives, ETH Zürich, Sigfried Giedion

← Sigfried Giedion, Zementhalle, markups on the back of the image, undated. Courtesy gta Archives, ETH Zürich, Sigfried Giedion

↑ Robert Maillart standing below the shell of the Zementhalle during its demolition, Zurich, 1940. Courtesy ETH-Bibliothek, Hochschularchiv

34 Robert Maillart, "Die Brücke in Villeneuve-sur-Lot, nebst Betrachtungen zum Gewölbebau," *Schweizerische Bauzeitung* 85, no. 12 (March 21, 1925): 151–54.

35 Maillart completed work for a Swiss cement subsidiary outside Cairo in 1929, served on committees with many of the cement cartel's members, and was asked to speak at meetings of the VSZKGF several times.

36 Breaking the conventional contract for pavilions at the national exhibition that handed completed pavilions over to exhibiting industries, E.G. Portland agreed to finance any cost overruns on the Zementhalle and contributed substantial additional funding towards its realization. Protocol FGK, *"Zement-, Kalk-, Und Gipsindustrie,"* Bundesarchiv J2.144#1000/1231#6/1107*, July 30, 1938.

also argued that daring engineering structures would serve Swiss industry, noting that: "Switzerland cannot live without its exports; the exportation of our excellent cement, in contrast to that of other products, has enjoyed a considerable upswing, and to make this last, it is surely not without importance to further demonstrate what can be accomplished with these products. Also, a large number of engineers trained here are waiting to be 'exported,' and the value of the Swiss engineer depends not only on what he has learned in the institutes but also on the level of engineering technology that has been reached in Switzerland."[34]

The suggestion supported, of course, not only his own interests, but also those of the cement industry, with which he was well-acquainted.[35] The most visible remnant evidence of this relationship was the Zementhalle, built as the pavilion for E.G. Portland, the Swiss cement cartel.[36] During the National Exhibition, both the process and the products of the cartel's cement were on display beneath the shell. Yet, when the building appeared in art and architecture publications, it was considered a general endorsement for concrete as a modern material. When Giedion published the Zementhalle, the images were airbrushed at his direction to remove any indication that the pavilion had acted as a specific advertisement, with products and logos removed from the images, along with all traces of the specific alliances that had helped to realize the shell. Despite this attempted erasure, these connections continued to exist even after Maillart's death, with much of Billington's work on the engineer, for example, being funded by the Swiss Society of Cement, Lime, and Gypsum Manufacturers (VSZKGF).

Contextualizing Maillart's approach within the contemporary culture of reinforced concrete construction and through his own writings has a certain effect of reining in the myth. But rather than diminishing the significance of this built and written body of work, re-contextualizing it makes it both richer and more complicated. Beyond the legacy of well-known structures, Maillart made a broader and more systemic contribution to reinforced concrete. His work had a reflexive relationship with the contemporary construction culture in Switzerland at the time—both relying on it and furthering its reach. This legacy is complex, as it entails not just technical achievements but also the establishment of an elite system that allowed freedom only for those within a narrow circle, yet it produced structures that articulate a clear set of ethics regarding economy, durability, and pragmatism. Yet while the construction of these works was a domestic matter, these ideas relied on the productive international discourse on reinforced concrete at the beginning of the twentieth century and have in turn continued to influence discussion about this confounding material.

CHURCH OF CHRIST THE WORKER AND OUR LADY OF LOURDES

ESTACIÓN ATLÁNTIDA, URUGUAY

1958–1960

ENGINEER · ELADIO DIESTE

Declared a UNESCO World Heritage Site in 2021, the church of Estación Atlántida, designed by the engineer Eladio Dieste, is an admirable exemplar of architectural quality and structural expressiveness owing to the skillful use of construction materials. Brick is utilized as both a load-bearing structural element and a decorative architectural detail. The reinforced masonry outer walls spring from a straight-line floor plan and curve as they rise, ending in an undulating profile at the point where they connect to the roof, which is itself a sinuous, curving slab in reinforced concrete and brick. The catenary curves optimize the distribution of loads and reduce the use of materials to a minimum. Apertures are inserted in less-stressed points to bring natural light into the building's interior.

The façade, divided horizontally into two sections, is separated by the structure of the side walls, a division marked by an alabaster insert.

↓ Church of Christ the Worker
and our Lady of Lourdes,
Estación Atlántida, 1960.
Photo Leonardo Finotti

NORDPARK RAILWAY STATIONS

INNSBRUCK, AUSTRIA

2004–2007

ARCHITECT ZAHA HADID ARCHITECTS

ENGINEER BOLLINGER+GROHMANN
KLAUS BOLLINGER
MANFRED GROHMANN

The Hadid studio's competition-winning design for the four stations of Innsbruck's hybrid cable railway was inspired by natural glacial ice conformations, with flowing, white forms that "float" over reinforced concrete bases. The roof structures, which soar sinuously resting on just a few supports, were designed by the Bollinger+Grohmann studio; parallel thin steel sheets shape their skeletons, creating an ideal base for the exterior covering. The double-curved shell is of opaque white glass panels with a glossy finish that lend the stations an ethereal atmosphere.

The project was an opportunity to architecturally experiment with curved glass, a material used in the automobile and nautical industries, as well as production techniques like CNC machining (with computerized numeric control) that allowed the utmost precision in the creation of each element.

← Hungerburgstation, Innsbruck, 2007. Photo Werner Huthmacher

MULTIHALLE

MANNHEIM, GERMANY

1974–1975

ARCHITECTS	FREI OTTO CARLFRIED MUTSCHLER JOACHIM LANGNER
ENGINEERS	FREI OTTO OVE ARUP & PARTNERS EDMUND "TED" HAPPOLD IAN LIDDELL

The focal point of the Bundesgartenschau in Herzogenriedpark, the Multihalle is a large, covered, column-free space that blends in with the surrounding park thanks to the organic geometries of its double-curved roof. The structure used by Frei Otto and calculated by Ted Happold at the Arup studio is a self-supporting wooden lattice shell—the "gridshell" introduced in 1897 by Vladimir Shukhov in Vyksa—that covers the main hall, the ancillary spaces, corridors and restrooms without the use of right angles or intermediate supports. It occupies an area of 160×115 m, reaching a height of 20 m with maximum spans of 60 m and 85 m, and is still today the largest wooden gridshell in the world. Inspired by spider webs and soap bubbles, Otto came to conceive the final form through an empirical process, working on counterweighted studio models in wire mesh which, when flipped over, created a surface subjected only to compression. A pair of 50-millimeter-thick wooden beams form the 50×50 cm grid of the shell; they were assembled on the ground first in a flat position, then raised using scaffolding towers and trolley jacks to form the designed configuration.

↓ Multihalle, Mannheim, 1975. Courtesy saai | Archiv für Architektur und Ingenieurbau am Karlsruher Institut für Technologie (KIT)

OLYMPIASTADION, OLYMPIAHALLE AND SCHWIMMHALLE

The Olympiapark for the 1972 Olympics covers an area of 3 sq. km, creating an artificial landscape of 74,800 sq. m made up of lightweight, suspended tensile structures forming hyperbolic geometries that work solely based on tensional stress. The membrane of square panels in polymethylmethacrylate (PMMA), 2.9 m per side and 4 mm thick—which were replaced after twenty-five years—shelters the bleachers of the Olympiastadion (34,550 sq. m, 77,000 seats), the Olympiahalle (21,750 sq. m, 14,000 seats), the Schwimmhalle (11,900 sq. m, 9,000 seats, today reduced to 1,500) and two public spaces. The continuous, double-curved roof surface is created by means of paired 25-millimeter-diameter steel strands arranged to form a mesh grid of squares 762 mm per side, laterally stabilized by a bracing cable and held up by 70- to 80-meter-high steel cable-stayed pylons—8 for the stadium, 4 for the arena and 1 for the pool. Frei Otto, who was brought in on the project by Günter Behnisch after the success of the 1967 German Pavilion in Montreal, was able to meet the design challenge thanks in part to practical experiments with scale models.

	MUNICH, GERMAN
	1967–1972
ARCHITECT	GÜNTER BEHNISCH
ENGINEERS	FREI OTTO
	FRITZ LEONHARDT AND WOLF ANDRÄ
	JOHN ARGYRIS
	JÖRG SCHLAICH

↓ Olympia-Schwimmhalle, Munich, model, 1972. Courtesy saai | Archiv für Architektur und Ingenieurbau am Karlsruher Institut für Technologie (KIT)

MODEL PROLEGOMENA

Guy Nordenson

[…] in other words, if only more theory were added, these theoretical disciplines would harmonize quite well with practice.

> IMMANUEL KANT,
> 1793[1]

Have you ever seen a stuffed genius?

> YI SANG,
> 1936[2]

Models in architecture and engineering operate both in abstract, often computational, modes, and as physical objects. They can represent or present. Most often we think of a "model *of*" some other thing that is or will be. The physical model gives three-dimensional form at reduced scale and in less detail, while computational models are scale-less and often fully detailed. In contrast, architectural or engineering drawings show ideas and objects indirectly. Historically, the more abstract qualities of the drawing have been considered more effective for imagination, both in solitude and in collaboration. Both models and drawings are often recognized as works of art.

When MoMA's Arthur Drexler and Neil Levine staged the revisionist exhibition *The Architecture of the École des Beaux-Arts* in 1975–76[3], Drexler argued its case in an essay titled "Engineer's Architecture: Truth and Its Consequences." He declared that engineering "was the purification of architecture necessary for the final solution—the solution to the problem of existence in historical time. 'Objectivity' *(die Neue Sachlichkeit)* begins by sorting out conflicting demands, but its aim is to end the conflict by producing the definitive building. Should that happen, not style merely but the historical process must come to an end." As Felicity Scott observed in 2004, "Drexler saw the victory of a rationalist modernism

---

1   Immanuel Kant, "On the Common Saying: This May be Correct in Theory, But it is No Use in Practice," *Practical Philosophy*, trans. and ed. Mary Gregor (Cambridge: Cambridge University Press, 1996; originally published 1793), 291–92.

2   Yi Sang, *The Wings* (original title: "Nalgae," *Jo-Gwang*, 1936), trans. Ahn Jung-hyo and James B. Lee (Seoul: Jimoondang Publishing Company, 2001).

3   Arthur Drexler, "Engineer's Architecture: Truth and Its Consequences," in *The Architecture of the Ecole des Beaux-Arts* (New York: The Museum of Modern Art, 1977), 14.

as an apocalyptic elimination of difference, literally (through rhetorical exaggeration) as a fascist homogenization"[4]. This is curious or ironic at best, given both the MoMA's connection to modernism and machine aesthetic and Philip Johnson's presence haunting the exhibition. In response to the MoMA show, the New York–based Institute for Architecture and Urban Studies and Peter Eisenman, Johnson's protégé, staged a 1976–77 exhibition entitled *Idea as Model*. Eisenman wrote: "it seems that models, like architectural drawings, could well have an artistic or conceptual existence of their own, one which was relatively independent of the project that they represented."[5]

This return of the Beaux-Arts *parti* sketch and neo-classical idealism held out drawings and models as works of art that could stand alongside painting and sculpture. Despite the apparent dialectic staged by Drexler and Eisenman, both exhibitions proposed an "autonomous" path more amenable to the emerging neo- (read non-) liberal consensus, disengaged from the "blue jean architecture" bemoaned by Drexler and from any consideration, despite the contemporaneous oil crisis, of environmental impact. It is in this context that I think it is useful to explore some types of models that were emerging at that time and have emerged since then.

MIRROR WORLDS

In the present climate crisis, the most consequential models are global climate models. These "GCMs" are computer-based mathematical representations of the physical processes and interaction of the combined global atmosphere, land surface, ocean, and sea ice. GCMs are used to investigate both the weather under current climate conditions, and the probable climate, weather and other future effects of accumulating greenhouse gases. For its assessment of future climate scenarios, the Intergovernmental Panel on Climate Change relies on suites of these GCMs organized through the World Climate Research Program's Coupled Model Intercomparison Project. In his account of the emergence of these models, *A Vast Machine: Computer Models, Climate Data, and the Politics of Global Warming*, Paul N Edwards[6] refers to John von Neumann's campaign for "high-speed calculation *to replace certain experimental procedures* in some selected parts of mathematical physics," including weather forecasting. As Edwards makes clear, there are no classical experimental options when it comes to testing Earth's climate, no "control" exept in the simulation. Weather models of necessity precede and organize measurement because discrete data points can only be "made sense" of once incorporated into models. The climate models are then verified by hindcasting past weather. Their accuracy evolves as they are calibrated in parallel with changing climate.

David Gelertner[7] anticipated this in his 1991 book *Mirror Worlds* as the "true-to-life mirror image[s] trapped inside a computer—where you can see and grasp [them] whole." Like William Gibson's 1982 idea of cyberspace,[8] the concept of computational space was prescient, including the implied seductiveness of the image-world and the miniaturization of the "true-to-life." The fact that in the case of climate change the future must be studied through the GCM 'crystal ball' only enhances the seductive power of the model and its sense of possible control. The more extreme the weather becomes, the more we turn to the models for assurances that climate change can be managed or even re-engineered, although control of nature is what brought us to this crisis. It is

4   Felicity D. Scott, "When Systems Fail: Arthur Drexler and the Postmodern Turn," in *Perspecta 35* (Cambridge: MIT Press, 2004), 134–53.

5   Sylvia Kolbowski and Kenneth Frampton, eds., *Idea as Model: 22 Architects, 1976-1980* (New York: The Institute for Architecture and Urban Studies and Rizzoli, 1981), 1.

6   Paul N. Edwards, *A Vast Machine: Computer Models, Climate Data, and the Politics of Global Warming* (Cambridge: MIT Press, 2010), 115.

7   David Gelernter, *Mirror Worlds: or the Day Software Puts the Universe in a Shoebox... How It Will Happen and What It Will Mean* (New York: Oxford University Press, 1993). The reference to mirrors recalls the unease Freud characterized in his essay "The 'Uncanny'": "This invention of doubling as a preservation against extinction has its counterpart in the language of dreams, [...] the same desire spurred on the ancient Egyptians to the art of making images of the dead in some lasting material. Such ideas, however, have sprung from the soil of unbounded self-love, from the primary narcissism which holds sway in the mind of the child as in that of primitive man; and when this stage has been left behind the double takes on a different aspect. From having been an assurance of immortality, he becomes the ghastly harbinger of death." Sigmund Freud, *Collected Papers Vol. 4* (New York: Basic Books, 1959).

8   William Gibson, "Burning Chrome," in *Burning Chrome* (New York: Arbor House, 1986).

not surprising, I think, that the first intimations of this climate crisis in the 1970s seeped into the architecture culture and stirred the reactionary turn to anti-functionalism and abstract formalism that are still with us today.

In 1994 Henry A. Millon and Vittorio Magnago Lampugnani staged a magnificent exhibition of Renaissance models at the Palazzo Grassi in Venice[9] which then travelled widely. The models were very large-scale, indeed, to the modern eye, too large. In *On Longing*, Susan Stewart[10] writes of dollhouses, that "the miniature, linked to nostalgic versions of childhood and history, presents a diminutive, and thereby manipulatable, version of experience, a version which is domesticated and protected from contamination." The Renaissance models were not dollhouses but more like mirror worlds, wooden "building information models" made large enough for study, representation, and especially to instruct builders. It is easy to get drawn into the details of the great model commissioned by Filippo Brunelleschi for the cathedral of Florence. Millon quotes Antonio Manetti: "it seemed that [Brunelleschi] was concerned that whoever would make the model should not discover his every secret." Another wooden model, built by Antonio Labacco for Antonio da Sangallo the Younger's project for St Peter's Basilica in Rome, is about 80 centimeters wide and 1.5 meters tall, roughly 1:30 scale. These models were made for the workers to use and for the architect to refer to and modify, *in situ*.

The Renaissance models were made of plain wood, mostly without coloring or inlays, and the grain of the wood is quite present. The simplicity of Michelangelo's model for the façade of San Lorenzo church is enhanced by the surface grain, cracks and pin holes that pull the surface out, pushing back the form. The fact that the use of wood is ubiquitous in all these models lends them an appealing abstractness. This is not the illusionism of perspective, since the objects are three-dimensional, but it does have that "behind the mirror" feeling of both remove and presence that heightens the impact of these representations. Their large scale also enhances the immediacy of details and the uncanny quality of the not-quite-miniaturization.

In the early modern era of engineering, we can find, I feel, a similar 'mirror world' complicity between model, information, and construction in the works of the engineers Robert Maillart, Félix Candela, and Heinz Isler. In lieu of scale models, Maillart refined his engineering and designs of his two bridge types—the hinged arch (e.g., Salginatobel) and deck-stiffened arch (e.g., Schwandbach)—by observing each realization in service. After each bridge was completed, Maillart would closely monitor the patterns of cracks in the bridges' concrete to check his calculations. Each project allowed for a step-by-step evolution of type. His mathematics were sufficient, never arcane. He designed the pared-down form and details of his structures to mirror the idealization of uncomplicated calculations.

The first era of thin-shell and spatial structures in the post-World War II years was inspired by the uncanny simplicity of forms that could be derived from the elegant mathematics of thin membrane structural behavior, often made possible by the stark asymmetry of materials versus the labor costs of developing economies. Félix

9   Henry A. Millon and Vittorio Magnago Lampugnani, eds., *The Renaissance from Brunelleschi to Michelangelo: The Representation of Architecture* (London and New York: Thames and Hudson and Rizzoli, 1994 and 1997).

10 Susan Stewart, *On Longing: Narratives of the Miniature, the Gigantic, the Souvenir, the Collection* (Durham: Duke University Press, 1992).

11 Félix Candela was invited by Mario Salvadori to join me in September 1983 to teach a class on structures at the New School Parsons School of Design in New York. We kept in touch over the next decade and in 1997, before Candela passed away, I produced a 1998-2005 lecture series named for him, jointly organized by MoMA, Princeton, and MIT with Terry Riley and Stan Anderson. These were published by MoMA in 2008 as *Seven Structural Engineers: The Felix Candela Lectures*.

12 Rowland J. Mainstone, "The Dome of St Peter's: Structural Aspects of its Design and Construction, and Inquiries into its Stability," in *AA Files*, no. 39 (Autumn 1999): 21–39.

13 Another good example of the many ways that drawings and models can be productively and unproductively misread both in design and execution is the collaboration between Le Corbusier, Iannis Xenakis, and Edgard Varèse on the 1958 Philips Pavilion in Brussels. See Marc Treib, *Space Calculated in Seconds: The Philips Pavilion, Le Corbusier, Edgard Varèse* (Princeton: Princeton University Press, 1996).

14 Angela N.H. Creager, Elizabeth Lunbeck and M. Norton Wise, eds., *Science Without Laws: Model Systems, Cases, Exemplary Narratives* (Durham NC: Duke University Press, 2007).

15 Carlo Ginzburg, "Latitude, Slaves, and the Bible: An Experiment in Microhistory," in *Science Without Laws: Model Systems, Cases, Exemplary Narratives*, eds. Angela N.H. Creager, Elizabeth Lunbeck and M. Norton Wise (Durham NC: Duke University Press, 2007), 255.

↓ On a design by Michelangelo Buonarroti, model of the façade of San Lorenzo, 1518 ca. Courtesy Fondazione Casa Buonarroti

Candela built hundreds of hyperbolic paraboloids in Mexico during the 1950s and '60s. Each served as a test model and prototype for the next. Félix Candela once told me[11] that he limited himself to one page of calculations for his "hypar" shells. The form had to be both compelling and simple enough to require few calculations.

The practice of the Swiss engineer Heinz Isler also entailed the mirroring of object and image-model. Isler developed his use of models in the tradition of Giovanni Poleni's eighteenth-century two-dimensional hanging chain studies for St Peter's Basilica in Rome[12], and Antonio Gaudi's late-nineteenth-century use of three-dimensional chain and weighted string models for the shaping of the Colònia Güell Crypt and the Basílica de la Sagrada Família in Barcelona. These analog models were based on the fact that the "funicular" (i.e., small cord) shape of the chains or string models mirrors the minimal shape of the arch or dome in pure compression. Isler investigated dome shapes with a number of novel techniques including molded earth, inflated rubber membranes, and draped fabrics. He would cut cheesecloth patterns, spray them with water and hang them in his garden to freeze. These free funicular forms could then be measured and scaled to full-size thin concrete shells. While Félix Candela worked with the many variations of his preferred hyperbolic paraboloid shells, Isler was able to build thin concrete shells of often free non-mathematical forms.

The cover of *Time* magazine in 1964 showed the head of Richard Buckminster Fuller in the form of a geodesic dome, surrounded by models of his works. Fuller conceived the geodesic dome as a diagram (or *connectome*): the constellation of thoughts that form ideas, linked by the shortest paths. Only later did he materially realize the many versions of geodesics large and small, including the iconic Montreal Biosphere. For Fuller, these networks in space mapped mind, model and universe.[13]

MODEL SYSTEMS

The editors of the 2007 essay collection *Science without Laws: Model Systems, Cases, Exemplary Narratives*[14] wrote: "like biological systems, analog and digital simulations are of immense value precisely because they mimic in part the complexity of natural systems, which typically involve multiple processes, nonlinear interactions, feedback loops, and emergent properties." Biological model systems include *E. coli* bacteria or the fruit fly *Drosophila melanogaster.* They are chosen for their ease of use and effectiveness as substitutes for larger, more complex organisms. This resembles the analogous use of "cases" in law, medicine, and the social sciences detailed in the collection. Model systems direct us from the particular to the general, the individual to the universal. In his essay, Carlo Ginzburg quotes Marcel Proust: "People foolishly imagine that the broad generalities of social phenomena afford an excellent opportunity to penetrate further into the human soul; they ought, on the contrary, to realize that it is by plumbing the depths of a single personality that they might have a chance of understanding these phenomena."[15]

The German architect Frei Otto also "plumbed the depths" in his research on tensile structures with soap bubbles, fabric and net models. Georg Vrachliotis' catalog of the comprehensive 2015 exhibition of

↓ A funicular study model of
the church of Colònia Güell
in Antoni Gaudí's studio,
with weights, form and
thrusts mirroring those of
the executed work, 1900 ca.

Otto's models in Karlsruhe is titled *Thinking by Modeling*.[16] As you leaf through the volume of original models carefully photographed against black backgrounds, you feel the tension between the laboratory and the photographic studio. The models come across as objects of art rather than engineering instruments, just as occurs with Ólafur Elíasson's models. Parallel to Fuller's influence, Otto's ideas and commitment to an ethic as well as an aesthetic of lightweight ephemeral structures reached beyond the limited number of his built works. His three principal projects (the 1967 West German Pavilion at Expo '67 Montréal, the 1972 Roof for Olympic Stadium in Munich, and the 1975 Multihalle in Mannheim) were key turning points in architecture, engineering, and computation. All three communicated a new lightness and "transparency" in the culture of postwar West Germany, an important goal for Otto.

The Munich stadium brought together the engineers Heinz Isler, Fritz Leonhardt, Jörg Schlaich, and Rudolf Bergermann in collaboration with the architects Günther Behnisch and Fritz Auer. While Otto (who joined after the competition had been won) at first insisted that the stadium roof be designed through analog physical models, the complexities of its scale and nonlinear geometric behavior required that Schlaich and Bergermann, together with John H Argyris, develop a novel finite element method for analysis and design. This became the German framework for modeling lightweight structures. In turn, the Mannheim dome, a compressive grid shell adaptation of the Munich tensile cable grid, assembled a team of British engineers Ove Arup, Edmund Happold, and Ian Liddell, and advanced Alistair Day's "dynamic relaxation" numerical form-finding method. All these engineers played key historical roles after the 1970s. The two projects, Munich and Mannheim, initiated the two main strands of analytical and computational methods used for large deformation cable and fabric as well as grid shell structures. The reverberations of these key projects continue to be felt today in any discussion of the complex relationship of analog and digital structural models.

Frank O. Gehry's practice and model making can also be read as a model system in the literal sense and in the biological and case study sense. Unlike Otto, Gehry was able to create a powerful professional office to implement large-scale complex work. From early on, Gehry used building materials that could be manipulated at both model and full scale and extrapolated, often directly, using digitizing arms. His interest in fluid fish forms (of all "scales") as well as the overt use of aerospace digital modeling tools also echoes the traditional methods of naval architecture.[17] The progression of his models and model practices and their relationship to the built work thoroughly mix up the roles the models play as both instrument and representation and sculptural artifact.

There are other examples where model making is an analog model system that "mimic[s] in part the complexity of natural systems." Chuck Hoberman, for example, has created large-scale geometric kinetic models and sculptures that teach us a more complex way of imagining large-scale-deployable structures. Similarly, the Japanese engineer Kawaguchi Mamoru developed an innovative system of deployable structures first as a model system.[18] The proliferation of paper and Styrofoam models in the studio of Kazuyo Sejima and Ryue Nishizawa produces an immersive milieu of forms that are both atmospheric and, it seems, sublimated into the final work's often equal abstraction. Most haunting for me is the "House in a Plum Grove, Tokyo, Japan (Scale model 1:5) 1999–2004" by Sejima, in the MoMA collection.[19] This is an oversized,

---

16 Georg Vrachliotis *et al.*, eds., *Frei Otto: Thinking by Modeling* (Leipzig: Spector Books, 2017).

17 Soraya de Chadarevian and Nick Hopwood, eds., *Models: The Third Dimension of Science* (Palo Alto CA: Stanford University Press, 2004). In the essay "Fish and Ships: Models in the Age of Reason," Simon Schaffer writes "[Mark] Beaufoy [FRS] saw that unless ships were changed into forms more manageable by rational analysis, models would never generate useful data" (95). This could be read as an illustration of Frank Gehry's progression from fish-shaped lamps to complex building modeling.

18 Mamoru Kawaguchi developed what he called the "pantadome" through several projects as a means of erecting large span stadia via unfolding. See his essay "The Design of Structures – From Hard to Soft," in *Seven Structural Engineers*, 102–21.

19 Work by Kazuyo Sejima, *House in a Plum Grove, Tokyo, Japan (Scale model 1:5)* 1999–2004 is quite large at 142×136×130.3 cm. The model was shown in the 2016 MoMA exhibition *A Japanese Constellation: Toyo Ito, SANAA, and Beyond* curated by Pedro Gadanho. I organized a parallel symposium on April 30, 2016 which was later published as *Structured Lineages: Learning from Japanese Structural Design* by the MoMA in 2019.

↓ Kazuyo Sejima & Associates,
House in a Plum Grove,
Tokyo, 1999–2004. Scale
model 1:5. The Museum
of Modern Art, New York.
Courtesy Scala Archive

nearly 1.50m cube model of a tiny (7.50 m) paper-thin steel plate house in Tokyo. The large furnished model of a very small house leaves one with the uncanny feeling that it is the house that "mimics" the model.

Following in the Swiss lineage of the bridge engineer Robert Maillart, both Christian Menn and the younger Jurg Conzett developed bridge typologies that are readily grasped through both simple calculation and models. Both use scale models as their principal medium of design and representation. I know that Menn collaborated with a model maker to make detailed scale models of his bridges to serve as the principle documentation of his preliminary design, which was then finalized by others. The elegant Streicker pedestrian bridge at Princeton University was executed by the American engineer Ted Zoli in this way. A study of Menn's careful evolution of the "extrados" bridge design in both the Ganter and Sunniberg bridges clearly shows the sculptural sophistication, and structural simplicity, that emerged from this model system approach. This has continued in the work of Jurg Conzett, who collaborates closely with his partner Lydia Conzett. As I understand it, she makes the models of their bridge designs from sketches and conversations, working out the specific joint details and key proportions. In addition, both Menn and Conzett's models fully integrate topography, bridge, and flora, echoing the biological basis of model systems.

MODEL INSTRUMENTS

If mirror worlds and model systems can serve as categories that claim a holistic purpose for models as creative media, their narrower use to measure or simulate site-specific physical phenomena or characterize key geometries is instrumental. There are large-scale river basin models used to estimate flows in the design of flood control structures, and wind tunnel models used to design of tall buildings. From the 1960s, the wind tunnel technology of aeronautic engineering was adapted to include urban terrain and recreate the specific turbulent flow at the boundary layer between the ground and the wind. And because the key constraint on tall building design is the human perception of wind-induced lateral vibrations, the boundary layer wind tunnel is the only reliable means of simulating the complex turbulence that results as wind passes over topography, water, and cityscapes. In the case of the original World Trade Center Twin Towers engineered by Leslie Robertson, the wind acting on the building varied considerably depending on direction, season and for each twin as they took turns being windward and leeward.[20] Robertson was able to model this well in the wind tunnel, working with the wind engineering pioneers Alan Davenport and Jack Cermak.

For another landmark of the 1960s, the Sydney Opera House, the turning point in the long design process is best represented by the elegant wooden model of the parts of the sphere from which each "shell" was extracted. This geometric breakthrough had many parents, including the architect Jørn Utzon and the lead engineers Michael Lewis, Duncan Michael, John Nutt, and Jack Zunz, all assisting Arup.[21] After years of trying to devise a funicular thin shell form that would match Utzon's first sketch, they realized that it would be better to find a clear geometry for prefabrication and erection than to continue the search for an elusive mathematical membrane solution. In the subsequent years, the use of both physical and computational models at Arup would drive many of the innovations conceived by Arup himself and his partners. With Renzo Piano, both the structural engineer Peter Rice and the mechanical engineer Tom Barker and their proteges John Thornton, Alistair Guthrie and Andy Sedgwick used instrumental models extensively. The structural engineers and Piano made models of various structural parts, from the Beaubourg *gerberettes* to the ductile iron and ferrocement trusses of the Menil. The mechanical engineers developed

20 See Robertson's essay "A Life in Structural Engineering" (66–85) in *Seven Structural Engineers: The Felix Candela Lectures*, ed. Guy Nordenson, and our drawing of the WTC structure on p. 20.

21 See Françoise Fromonot, *Jørn Utzon: The Sydney Opera House* (Corte Madera, CA: Gingko/Electa Press, 1998). Her account of the design and construction, including the engineering, is, along with Marc Treib's Philips Pavilion book, a unique example of close reading of architecture.

computational fluid dynamic (CFD) models[22] to estimate and design air flows, and computational ray tracing and physical models to design natural and artificial museum lighting. Arup has also worked with computational and physical analog acoustic models, progressing all the way to full small-scale electronic simulations of concert spaces with natural acoustic qualities. Some of the physical acoustic models, like the water-based acoustic model of the Glyndebourne Opera House in the UK, are exquisite.

These model instruments are parts, not wholes. While some are highly seductive as objects, they do not mirror the full spatial and rhetorical worlds of the architecture and designs they parallel, nor do they represent a holistic medium of system representation or experimentation.

OBJECTIVITY

Writing about models in the journal *Log*, vol. 50, the architect Kiel Moe asks, "How did our models of architecture come to sanction its climate change-inducing pedagogies and practices?".[23] His critique of models of practice points to the fossil fuel basis of modern architecture, and can also apply to the earlier role of post-Renaissance architecture and engineering in advancing the ideology of human control of nature and power. I believe a close study of current models in practice would serve to illuminate this history.

The American anthropologist Clifford Geertz, in his contribution to *Science without Laws,* writes about rituals as model systems: "Confidence in the depth and substantiality, the "reality" of one's world, and of one's way of living in it, and thus of one's self, is, for humans anyway, not a natural given, but a social, cultural, and psychological achievement, recurrently threatened, occasionally destroyed. It is that achievement and that threat, which, among us [...] ritual can be seen to model."[24]

Architects and engineers make models and drawings. They do not build. The activity and craft of making models

and drawings, even those that are in part or entirely virtual, imply both contact with the reality of practice "in the field" and the domain of abstract thinking. At times, this displaced realm of making becomes a more structured ritual to address "the 'reality' of one's world."

I was encouraged to become an engineer by the sculptor Isamu Noguchi, who became a friend in the last decade of his life. He brought me to work in his studio with Sadao and, for one summer, with Fuller. I helped build models of tensegrity structures of wood and thread for the 1976 exhibition *MAN transFORMS* by Hans Hollein and Lisa Taylor[25]. Noguchi also introduced me to my first job as an engineer, and I worked with him and Paul Weidlinger on the 1984 *Bolt of Lightning... A Memorial to Benjamin Franklin* in Philadelphia. Noguchi had originally proposed the project in 1933. The 1984 version was a fresh start and was developed in physical and virtual models. When I started at Weidlinger in 1983, I worked on a 3D computer model for the structural analysis, which we digitized by dropping plumb lines off Noguchi's physical model. Noguchi would look at the virtual model on the low-resolution computer screen and approve our reading. I don't recall if he made new models from the computer-based geometry, but he must have. This was laborious, but slowing down the process made everything more intelligible, and thus satisfying for each of us. At the time I thought that Weidlinger had introduced the large, prominent cables, but it turns out the 1933 WPA proposal drawing by Noguchi[26] anticipated

→ Wind tunnel test of the WTC twin towers at Colorado State University, Fort Collins, 1964. Front Row: Alan G. Davenport, Minoru Yamasaki (architect), John Skilling and Leslie E. Robertson (structural engineers). Back row: Malcom Levy (Port Authority) and Jack E. Cermak. Davenport and Cermak were the pioneers of boundary layer wind tunnel testing. Courtesy Colorado State University Libraries

---

22   The use of CFD to model and design air circulation in buildings was, I believe, first introduced in the 1980s by Tom Barker, Peter Rice's "building services" engineer and partner at Arup, for projects with Piano and Rogers. An under-reported quirk of CFD models is their chaotic (non-linear dynamic) behavior: "forms more manageable by rational analysis" are required for fully progressive designs.

---

23   Kiel Moe, "Architectural Agnotology & Broken World Models," *Log 50: Model Behavior* (New York: Anyone Corporation, 2020), 157–62.

---

24   Clifford Geertz "'To Exist Is to Have Confidence in One's Way of Being': Ritual as Model Systems," in Angela N.H. Creager, Elizabeth Lunbeck and M. Norton Wise, eds., *Science Without Laws: Model Systems, Cases, Exemplary Narratives* (Durham NC: Duke University Press, 2007), 220.

---

25   Hans Hollein and Lisa Taylor, *MAN transFORMS: An International Exhibition on Aspects of Design* (New York: Cooper Hewitt Museum, 1976). The title is noteworthy as this was around the time of the 1973 oil and 1979 energy crises, just before the first publications on global warming by the NASA Goddard Institute for Space Studies then led by James E. Hansen.

them, influenced perhaps by Noguchi's then-developing friendship with Fuller. All this, recollecting now, did prime me to pay close attention to the interrelationship between the physical, analog models and computer-based or digital models necessary for calculation and, most often, fabrication. The means of representation thus become those of presentation and, as Vrachliotis writes, of the shift from "product of meaning" to "production of meaning."

This ritual performed through models is just another way of questioning objectivity, as Lorraine Daston and Peter Galison do beautifully in their book entitled *Objectivity*. Quoting them, and taking the liberty of substituting 'models' for 'images': "In the era of truth-to-nature, [*models*] were inspired passages to an idealized world; later, they became very much of this world, their automaticity aiming to make them, in their vaunted objectivity, all nature and none of us. In the exercise of trained judgment, [*models*] stood as bridges, part us, part not-us. Now, as [*models*] become part toolkit and part art, what are they? Nano-facturers use them as aesthetic objects, as marketing tags, all the while reaching through them to create and manipulate a brave new world of atom-sized objects. The scientific [*model*] begins to shed its representational aspect altogether as it takes on the power to build. Once again, [*models*] are influx. Once again, so is the scientific self."[27]

← Michael Hopkins & Partners, and Arup, Saline Airflow Model Test, Glyndebourne Opera House, Lewes UK, 1994 © Arup

→ Aldo Rossi, *Teatro del Mondo*, Venice, 1979. The wood schema floating along the stones of Venice. Photo Antonio Martinelli

---

26   See, for example, "Original proposal of Monument to Ben Franklin (Bolt of Lightning… Memorial to Ben Franklin) 1933," available at https://archive.noguchi.org/Detail/archival/96700. Accessed June 23, 2022. According to the Noguchi Foundation archivist, this may have been drawn by Noguchi but is unsigned.

---

27   Lorraine Daston and Peter Galison, *Objectivity* (New York: Zone Books, 2010).

READING BETWEEN THE LINES: THE LANGUAGE OF STRUCTURAL ENGINEERS

Gina Morrow

Versions of the phrase "engineering drawing is a universal language of signs and symbols" have appeared in countless engineering drawing textbooks since the early twentieth century and continue to do so today. A particularly evocative iteration published in the 1960s states: "[Engineering drawing] is a universal language; for the reader may be an American and the draftsman French, but the Frenchman can make the drawing so that the American can read it."[1] Not only is this visual language universal, the textbook suggests, but also its standardization transcends cultural difference. The notion that drawing is a form of language is hardly new territory for discussion, but the distinct way in which engineering representation is often mythologized as being rational, highly codified, and culturally agnostic is a flawed premise.[2]

On the contrary, engineering representation is often loosely defined and has come to be shaped by a variety of technological, economic, environmental, and cultural forces. These influences are frequently embedded and legible in the drawings themselves, highlighting the importance of drawing as both a reflection and agent of engineering thinking and design. This essay explores some of these dynamics at a general level and examines the way they play out in drawings by three of the engineers featured in the exhibition: Mamoru Kawaguchi, August Komendant, and Mahendra Raj.

1 Lincoln Electric Company, *How to read shop drawings: with special reference to welding and welding symbols. Welding symbols as standardized by the American Welding Society*, 1st ed. (Cleveland: Lincoln Electric Company, 1961), 1.

2 Among others, see Robin Evans' renowned essay "Translations from Drawing to Building," *Casabella*, no. 530 (1986) for an important discussion of the linguistic operations of architectural drawings.

3 See Ken Baynes and Francis Pugh, *The Art of the Engineer* (New York: The Overlook Press, 1981), 11.

4 For a thorough account of such miscommunication between engineers from the United States and the United Kingdom involving the production of merchant freighters during World War II, see John K. Brown, "Design Plans, Working Drawings, National Styles: Engineering Practice in Great Britain and the United States, 1775-1945," *Technology and Culture* 41, no. 1 (April 2000).

5   In California, for example, the 1933 Field Act mandated that all unreinforced masonry school buildings be retrofitted or re-built to improve their seismic resistance. The significance of this ruling incentivized engineers in California to rethink the way they made drawings and specifications. Some of the engineers from this period, who were pioneers in seismic design practice, directly attribute the Field Act to the superiority and rigor of drawings produced by California offices as compared with other American practitioners. See John Meehan, interview by Stanley Scott, *Connections: EERI Oral History Series*, vol. 25 (Oakland: EERI, 2017).

6   For a useful discussion of the role of drawing in the professionalization of engineering see John K. Brown, "Design Plans, Working Drawings, National Styles: Engineering Practice in Great Britain and the United States, 1775-1945."

↓   "Alphabet of Lines" in Thomas French, *Engineering Drawing for Students and Draftsmen* (NEW YORK: Mc-Graw Hill Book Company, 1911), 39

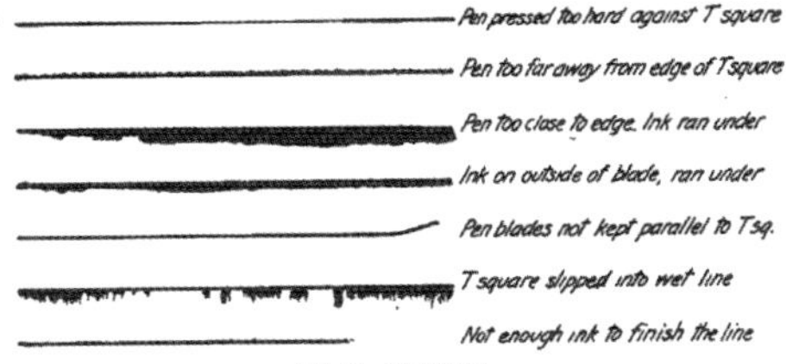

THE USE OF INSTRUMENTS   39

High-grade pens usually come from the makers well sharpened. Cheaper ones often need dressing before they can be used satisfactorily. If the pen is not working properly it must be sharpened as described in Chapter XIV, page 257.

FIG. 61.—Faulty lines.

The Alphabet of Lines.

As the basis of the drawing is the line, a set of conventional symbols covering all the lines needed for different purposes may properly be called an alphabet of lines. There is as yet no universally adopted standard, but the following set is adequate, and represents the practice of a majority of the larger concerns of this country.

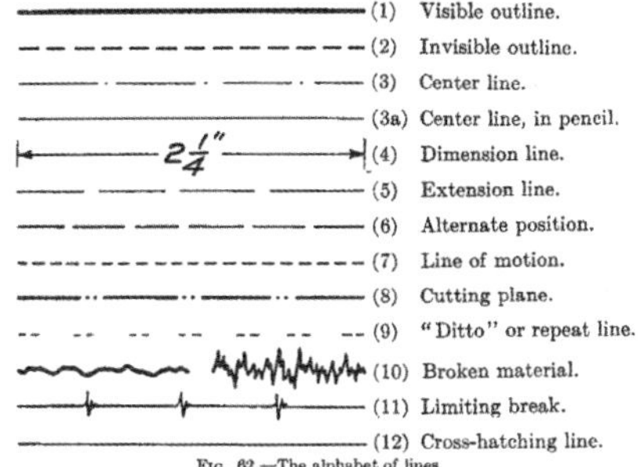

FIG. 62.—The alphabet of lines.

Structural drawings describe the primary supporting elements of a building and how they are designed to resist gravity and lateral loads through their connections and assemblies. While architectural drawings use poche and section to define the mass and the interrelationship of parts that allow people to move through a space, structural drawings divide buildings into points, lines, and planes to describe the flow of forces from the roof to the ground in a way that can be rationalized geometrically and mathematically. Concrete, steel, and timber have distinct drawing conventions that reflect their load path mechanics and the way they are put together in the field or the shop. These conventions, however, vary widely between structural engineers both domestically and abroad.

As far as languages go, engineering drawing is young. Historians Ken Baynes and Francis Pugh suggest that engineering drawing was born during the Industrial Revolution. They note, "Although it is possible to trace roots back to naval architectural draftsmanship and scientific and technical illustration at the time of the Renaissance, it was a distinctive form of production—the division of labor—that made engineering drawing essential."[3] While Baynes and Pugh write primarily about mechanical engineering (machines, locomotives, etc.), structural engineering followed a similar trajectory.

New technologies and manufacturing techniques necessitated advanced drawing methods for specifying rolled steel sections, standardized wood connection hardware, and steel reinforcing in concrete structures. Each material comes with specific labor and fabrication requirements, as well as analytical challenges. Differences in local fabrication practice as well as material availability caused technical drawing standards to diverge both domestically and internationally, and sometimes these differences could produce miscommunication between engineers, even those with a shared spoken language.[4] Within the United States alone, technical drawing practice differs according to factors like local environmental conditions (earthquakes, wind, flooding, etc.) and legal jurisdictions.[5] Even as drawing practice fluctuated, literacy in this developing graphic language was essential. Technical drawing became a key subject in every aspiring engineer's education and was the bedrock of an emerging professional class in the late nineteenth and early twentieh centuries.[6]

YOYOGI NATIONAL GYMNASIUM, MAMORU KAWAGUCHI

Kawaguchi designed the structure for the 1964 Olympic Yoyogi National Gymnasium, while working in the office of the prominent engineer Yoshikatsu Tsuboi. Kawaguchi has since been widely recognized for his innovative approach to construction sequencing and his development of hybrid structural systems, including unconventional uses of structural materials like pre-stressed stone, folded spatial structures, and mesh-reinforced air structures. The Yoyogi stadium is no exception; the structure is a distinct manifestation of Kawaguchi's interests and expertise.

Kawaguchi once wrote, "Some designers are enamored of the behavior of a structure only after it is completed, but I think the way

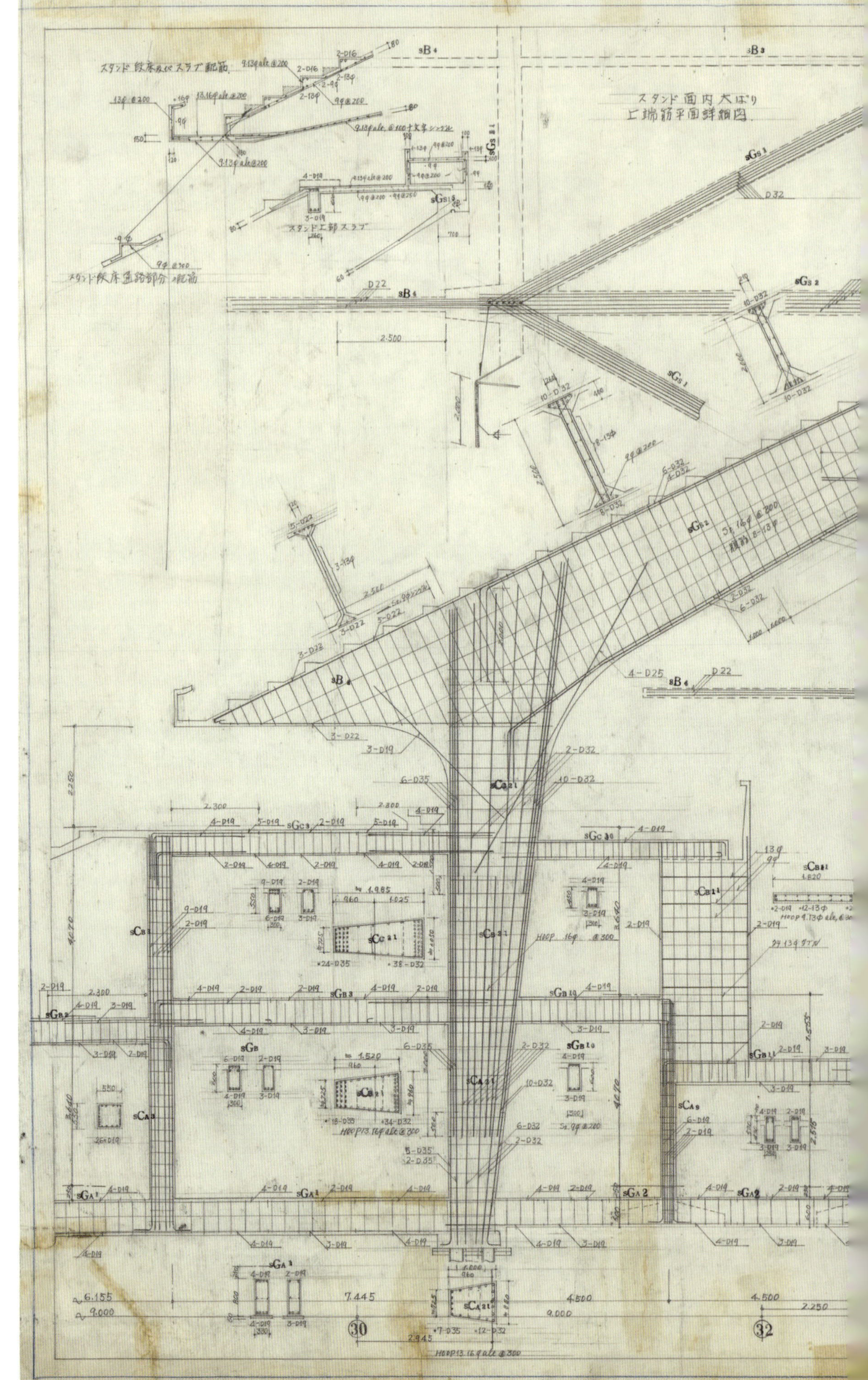

スタンド 段床及びスラブ配筋
スタンド上部スラブ
スタンド段床連絡部分 配筋
スタンド面内大ばり
上端筋平面詳細図

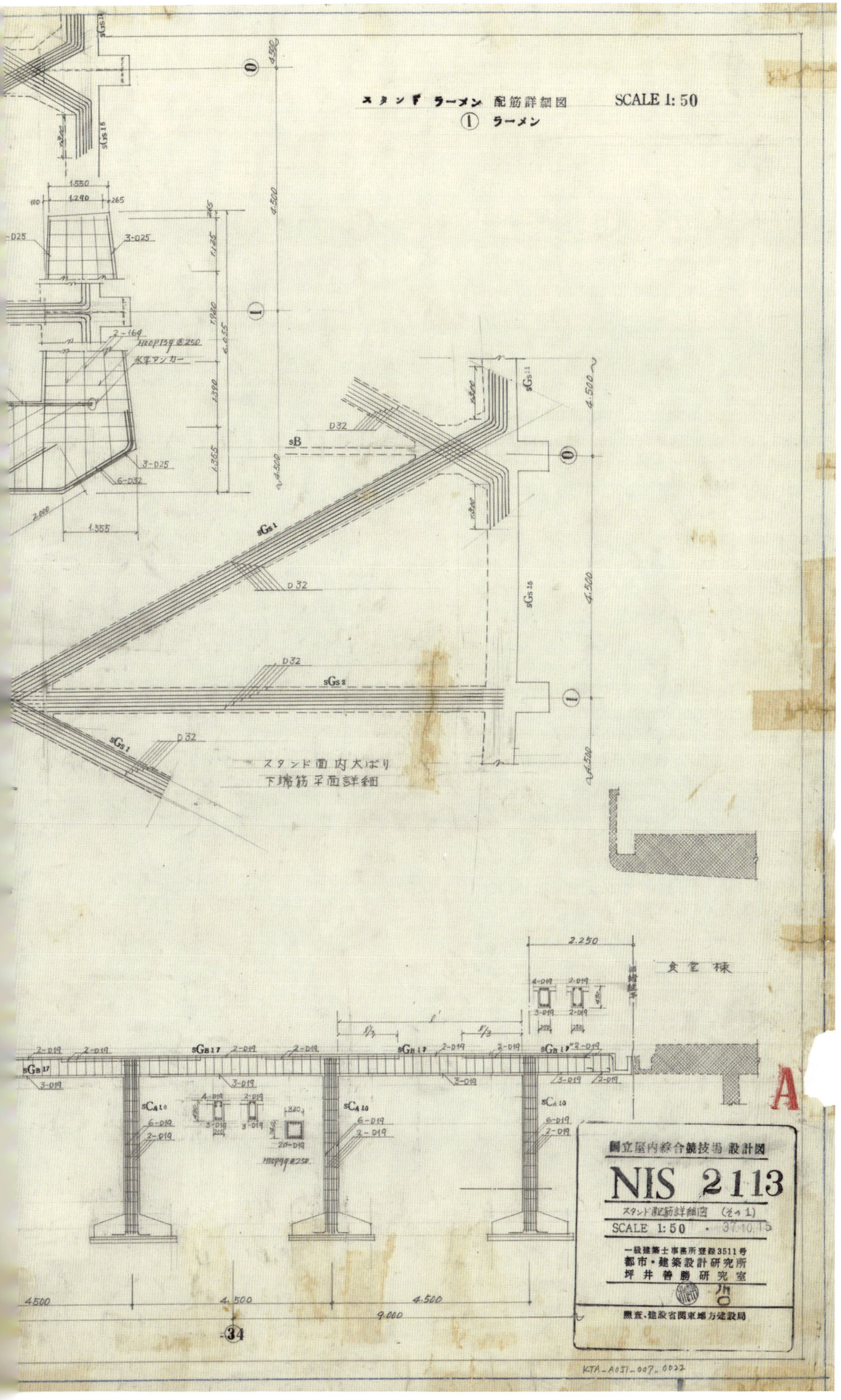

スタンド ラーメン 配筋詳細図   SCALE 1:50
① ラーメン
D25
3-D25
2-16φ
HOOP13φ@250
水平アンカー
3-D25
6-D32
sGs 1
D32
sB
sGs 11
sGs 16
sGs 3
sGs 1
D32
スタンド面内大ばり
下端筋平面詳細
2.250
貴賓棟
4-D19
2-D19
3-D19
2-D19
sGB 17
2-D19
2-D19
sGB 17
2-D19
3-D19
sGB 17
2-D19
sGB 17
3-D19
sCA 10
4-D19
2-D19
6-D19
2-D19
3-D19
3-D19
20-D19
HOOP9φ@250
sCA 10
6-D19
2-D19
sCA 10
6-D19
2-D19
3-D19
2-D19
4.500
4.500
4.500
9.000
34

國立區内綜合競技場 設計図
NIS 2113
スタンド配筋詳細図 (その1)
SCALE 1:50   37.10.15
一級建築士事務所登録3511号
都市・建築設計研究所
坪井善勝研究室
照査・建設省関東地方建設局

KTA-A051-007-0022

in which a structure is constructed is very important as well in terms of rationality and economy."[7] Starting in the 1980s, he developed a series of mechanical structures he coined "pantadomes." The pantadomes are folded into unique geometries so they can be lifted in place with a crane or hydraulic jacks. He called them "pantadomes" because their hinge mechanism is similar to that of the now obsolete drawing instrument, the pantograph—an early copying device used to duplicate the motion of a drawing utensil.[8] It is interesting to think about Kawaguchi's exposure to these instruments, which were long outdated by the time he designed the pantadomes, but might have been circulating during his studies at the University of Tokyo. Others have written about the unique pedagogy in Japan where engineers and architects are educated together, and one could imagine that this shared experience with the tools and craft of drawing could have influenced Kawaguchi's approach to structural design and representation.[9]

The drawing set for the Yoyogi stadium is immaculately detailed. It toggles impressively between scales and material, ranging from line diagrams of steel cable arrangements to color-coded concrete framing plans and intricate mechanical drawings of the cast steel joints. Many of the drawings are organized by a single component or a building zone cut in several directions: the skylight, the cable bundle, the auditorium stands, the cast connections, and so on. Unlike a "piece" drawing in the American sense, where a single element is drawn in isolation, the drawings for Yoyogi often combine and group structural systems on a page.[10]

While the roof usually gets all the attention, the reinforced concrete stadium structure is also noteworthy. Rather than schedule the reinforcing numerically in a table, it's almost all graphically represented. The building is full of unique geometry that requires sharp bends and hooks, and by drawing each configuration, there is less room for misinterpretation. A sheet like NIS2113 is particularly striking in the way plans and sections are distributed across the page to tell a story about the reinforcing system for the stadium. A representative section showing the vertical gravity system is indicated at the left of the page, with two partial framing plans above and to the right indicating the horizontal system. Beam sections are pulled off the primary drawing at a diagonal, parallel to their span direction, so that their reinforcement can be read distinctly from the overall section. Rather than spread the details across the set as one might expect, they are clustered on the same sheet, providing a concise indication of how the stadium is supported vertically and spans in and out of the page.

Kawaguchi designed steel castings to control the movement of the roof cables around the skylight, which were expected to experience large deflections during the construction. The castings were critical to the success of the project, and Kawaguchi developed physical models to test their rotation.[11] These connections are represented at a large scale and detailed like elaborate machine drawings. Lines of symmetry are drawn to represent the castings in section and elevation simultaneously, and this "halving" operation seems to reference the symmetry of the casting mold itself. The precise geometry and curvature of these components is so important to their operability that small geometry diagrams showing their underlying radii and curvature are also indicated on the sheet. The castings represent a significant engineering contribution in their tectonics and mechanical innovation, and their representation reveals their operability in a way that's difficult to comprehend in the completed building.

7   Mamoru Kawaguchi, "The Design of Structures – From Hard to Soft," in *Seven Structural Engineers: The Felix Candela Lectures*, ed. Guy Nordenson (New York: The Museum of Modern Art, 2008), 105.

8   *Ibid.*, 106.

9   For two excellent essays on this topic see John Ochsendorf, "Architecture and Engineering Education," in *Structured Lineages: Learning from Japanese Structural Design*, ed. Guy Nordenson (New York: The Museum of Modern Art, 2019) and Seng Kuan, "Introduction: Tange's Yoyogi, World's Yoyogi," *a+u*, no. 588 (2019).

10 For a useful discussion of piece drawings see John K. Brown, "When Machines Became Gray and Drawings Black and White: William Sellers and the Rationalization of Mechanical Engineering," *The Journal of the Society for Industrial Archeology* 25, no. 2 (1999) and Steven Lubar, "Representation and Power," *Technology and Culture* 36, no. 2 (1995).

11 For model images see Mamoru Kawaguchi, *Structure and Sensibility: Principles and Methods of Structural Design* (Tokyo: Kajima Institute Publishing, 2015).

←   Kenzo Tange, Yoyogi National Gymnasium, Tokyo, sheet NIS2113, stand details, 1962–1991. Courtesy The Kenzo Tange Archive, Gift of Takako Tange, Frances Loeb Library, Harvard University Graduate School of Design

12 This sequence of events is described
    in detail in August E. Komendant,
    "Kimbell Art Museum Fort Worth, Texas
    1967-72," in *18 Years with Architect
    Louis I. Kahn* (Englewood: Aloray,
    1975), 115-31.

13 See Guy Nordenson, "The Lineage of
    Structure and the Kimbell Art Museum,"
    Lotus International 98, 28-48.

14 Komendant, *18 Years with Architect
    Louis I. Kahn* (Englewood: Aloray,
    1975).

15 *Ibid.*, 122.

16 *Ibid.*

KIMBELL ART MUSEUM, AUGUST KOMENDANT

The drawings for the Kimbell Art Museum were produced in two parts by two engineers: Preston M. Geren and August Komendant. Preston M. Geren & Associates was the architectural and engineering firm selected by the client to be Louis Kahn's local partner. Komendant had worked with Kahn on the Richards Medical Research Laboratories and the Salk Institute for Biological Studies, and Kahn asked him to do some early consulting on the Kimbell. Geren was the professional contractually obligated to do the engineering, so Komendant eventually stepped aside. As the design work proceeded, Geren and Kahn's relationship became strained over numerous project delays, cost overruns, and the complexity of the design, all of which threatened the successful completion of the project. At a critical juncture toward the end of the design phase, Komendant was asked to engineer the upper level and roof structure in order to proceed with a structural system that better aligned with Kahn's architectural intent.[12]

Part of the magic of the Kimbell is that the structure is not what it seems. The famous cycloid shells that make up the roof look like a system of arches, but actually they behave somewhere between a beam and an arch, spanning the length of the structure as well as the transverse direction.[13] The beams that carry the mechanical ducts at the base of the cycloids appear to support the shells, but in reality the shells carry the beams and the beams just stiffen the cycloids.[14] There are also a number of deep "wall beams" which look like walls but in fact span longitudinally between columns. Regarding the wall beams, Komendant explains proudly that he eliminated several of the columns and walls supporting the upper floor level because they were not structurally necessary. He says simply of this decision: "The 104-footlong heavy walls could be designed as post-tensioned beams."[15] And so they were.

While there is clear pleasure in these games of structural performance, Komendant also values the legibility of the system. In his writings he qualifies the Kimbell in terms of its "honesty," moralizing the expression of the load path.[16] Important clues are distributed throughout the museum to convey the mechanisms of the structure. For instance, the arches at the end of the cycloid shells (which *do* behave as arches) are accentuated by the "lunette" window reveal between the arch and the end walls, so that it's evident the wall is not contributing to the arch action. There is another glass separation between the top of the "wall beams" and the bottom of the cycloid, lest anyone get confused and think the shell is supported by the longitudinal beams, which in turn are masquerading as walls.

The drawings toy with structural clarity and ambiguity on a number of levels. For one, there is a striking difference between Komendant's and Geren's approach to graphic notation. Geren's drawings are full of notes, dimension strings,

↓ August Komendant, Center Section Cycloids and Mezzanine Floor, sheet S15, 1970. Courtesy August Komendant Collection, The Architectural Archives, University of Pennsylvania

column numbers, and beam labels. The first few pages of the set describing the foundation and lower level (all within Geren's scope of work) are dense with information. Komendant entirely disregards the column numbering and dimensions put in place by Geren and establishes a numbered and lettered grid over the top of Geren's lower-level columns. Compared with Geren's five sheets for the foundation and lower level, Komendant has twenty drawings in total, eleven for the upper level and nine for the roof. Komendant establishes the structural system through repeated and sequential framing plans that are relatively free of annotation. Subsequent drawings focus on the structure in partial plans (North, Center, South) and sections to describe the concrete reinforcing in each direction. While Geren's drawings describe everything in a few compact pages, Komendant's set reproduces the same framing plan over and over, cutting serial plan and sections at different levels and orientations. The set gives the impression of a building being worked through and tested in the drawing itself.

Given the complex geometry of the post-tensioning strands in the wall beams and cycloids, most of these drawings *are* strictly necessary; however, it also seems Komendant utilizes the successive sections to articulate the load path of the whole building. By sequentially cutting through the cycloid shells with a dark pencil hatch, he has ample opportunity to demonstrate their dramatic spanning and support conditions which might not otherwise be legible. Sheet S15 is an example where many of the structural sleights of hand are examined on a single sheet. The drawing shows the condition of the end arches and the gap where they meet a wall, the gap at the wall beams, the thinness of the cycloid shells, a movement joint, and the double-skin floor.

Unlike Kawaguchi, however, Komendant resists representing the structure in small segments. The set almost never focuses on a single piece of the structure but rather uses sequence and section to explain which elements support each other and which elements span.

HALL OF NATIONS, HALLS OF INDUSTRIES, MAHENDRA RAJ

Mahendra Raj began his career as a civil engineer in India where he was thrown headfirst into structural engineering when he was assigned to work on the Chandigarh High Court and Secretariat, designed by Le Corbusier. Around 1960 he started his own practice and has since become known for his vast archive of unique and innovative structural designs, often in reinforced concrete, making effective and intelligent use of the material and methods of construction.[17]

The Hall of Nations and associated exhibition halls in New Delhi were commissioned to commemorate the twenty-fifth anniversary of India's independence from British colonial rule. A series of cast-in-place concrete space frames, the buildings represent the first such material adaptation of a space frame structure. Cast-in-place concrete, which can be imprecise and difficult to form *in situ*, was a daring choice for this project. Raj studied alternatives like steel, precast concrete, and combinations therein, but because of the scarcity of available materials and specialized labor,

17 See Mahendra Raj's essay "My
    Initiation into Structural
    Engineering," in *The Structure:
    Works of Mahendra Raj*, ed. Vandini
    Mehta, Rohit Mehndiratta, and Ariel
    Huber (Zurich: Park Books, 2016),
    22–35.

18 See Mahendra Raj, "Hall of Nations
    & Halls of Industries: Large
    Exhibition Hall Complex | A Case
    Study," in *The Structure*, 142–51.

19 For a description of the site work
    involved see Raj, "Hall of Nations
    & Halls of Industries," 142–49.

20 See note 4 on sheet 101.ITF.55C dated
    October 11, 1971 in *The Structure*,
    168–69.

cast-in-place concrete was the only viable choice to maintain the cost and schedule. Within these constraints Raj developed an effective way to design not only the structure, but also the construction sequencing. Raj had to analyze the structure several times over and under many loading conditions to account for the different ways it could behave during the course of construction.[18]

The drawings reflect the effort and planning that went into realizing a project with such an unorthodox material strategy. The drawings are not only rigorous and systematic, but also they make elegant use of the page, taking advantage of symmetries in the structure to demonstrate the economy of the building's form. The set includes a single drawing that names every straight member and every joint, setting out the geometry of the entire Hall of Nations with one overall plan and nine detail-plans along its lines of symmetry. The sheet includes a faint sketch of the basic pyramid that governs the form of the entire structural and architectural system—a subliminal message that this massive structure can be broken into something comprehensible. The patterning and nomenclature in this drawing are repeated throughout the set at greater levels of detail, a logic which instills confidence in the idea that the structure can be erected simply with reusable formwork.

Some of the most striking drawings are the details of the concrete joints where members intersect, an average of nine elements at once. The 25-centimeter rhomboid sections each have four reinforcing bars which must be woven together where they converge. The shape of the rhombus not only provides advantageous clear space for the bars but also resolves elegantly into a joint with crisp, sharp edges. The drawing of joint 111 shows several planar cuts of the same joint to describe the intricate threading of the reinforcing. The drawing operates as a design tool, a way to think through the spatial complexity of the reinforcement and to imagine the way it might be assembled on site. Traces of geometric guidelines are left visible beneath the drawing in a way that suggests its resolution. The isolation of the reinforcing in sections is a technique that gives graphic clarity to the drawing, but also establishes the continuity of elements across the joint. The large scale of the drawing enables Raj to show the possibility of creating laps between curved and straight sections of rebar where they meet to segment the concrete forming procedure and minimize the on-site bending of steel.[19]

Despite having scrupulously detailed the joint reinforcing geometry, a note on the drawings permits the contractor to make adjustments but also stipulates that a physical model must be produced. Note 4 on sheet 101.ITF.55C reads: "The contractor shall make prototype model of typical joints showing the arrangement of reinforcement through the joints for approval by the engineer in charge before execution."[20] Raj recognized that resolving these joints was crucial to the success of the project. While they appear to be fully resolved in his drawings, he knew it was important to implicate the contractor in the process of planning for their fit-up. The elegance of the completed cast-in-place joints is remarkable and contributes to the slenderness of the final structures, which were tragically demolished in 2017. The legacy of these buildings, for their ingenuity and clever adaptation of standard construction methods, lives on.

Raj, Komendant, and Kawaguchi, all roughly of the same generation, operating in different cultural contexts, exhibit shared interests and value systems in their drawings that are echoed in their personal writings and reflections on their work. Each drawing set underscores the importance of establishing underlying geometry, graphically describing complex forms, dividing structure into comprehensible parts, and articulating the load path, yet their execution of these ambitions is surprisingly diverse. While the Yoyogi set examines large sections of the structure at a time, the Kimbell drawings rarely narrow or focus on a specific element and instead examine the building in large, sequential sections, and the Hall of Nations proceeds methodically through a series of different scales from the entire building to a single joint detail. In each case the structure is fully articulated, but the approach is fundamentally different.

While it's not obvious to what extent these engineers directly contributed to the drawings or relied on experienced draftspersons, the drawings highlight the expertise and knowledge cultivated within their engineering practices. The variation of graphic dialects within these drawing sets illustrates their role as vehicles for invention and exploration. Each of these engineers wields this malleable language with great skill and deftness to reveal attributes of their structures that are not necessarily discernable in their built execution, but they evoke their design process and the way they work through everything from the resolution of the load path to the constructability of a certain detail. Their drawings reinforce the idea that this language is a nuanced form of creative and cultural expression that belies the rational purity with which it's often associated.

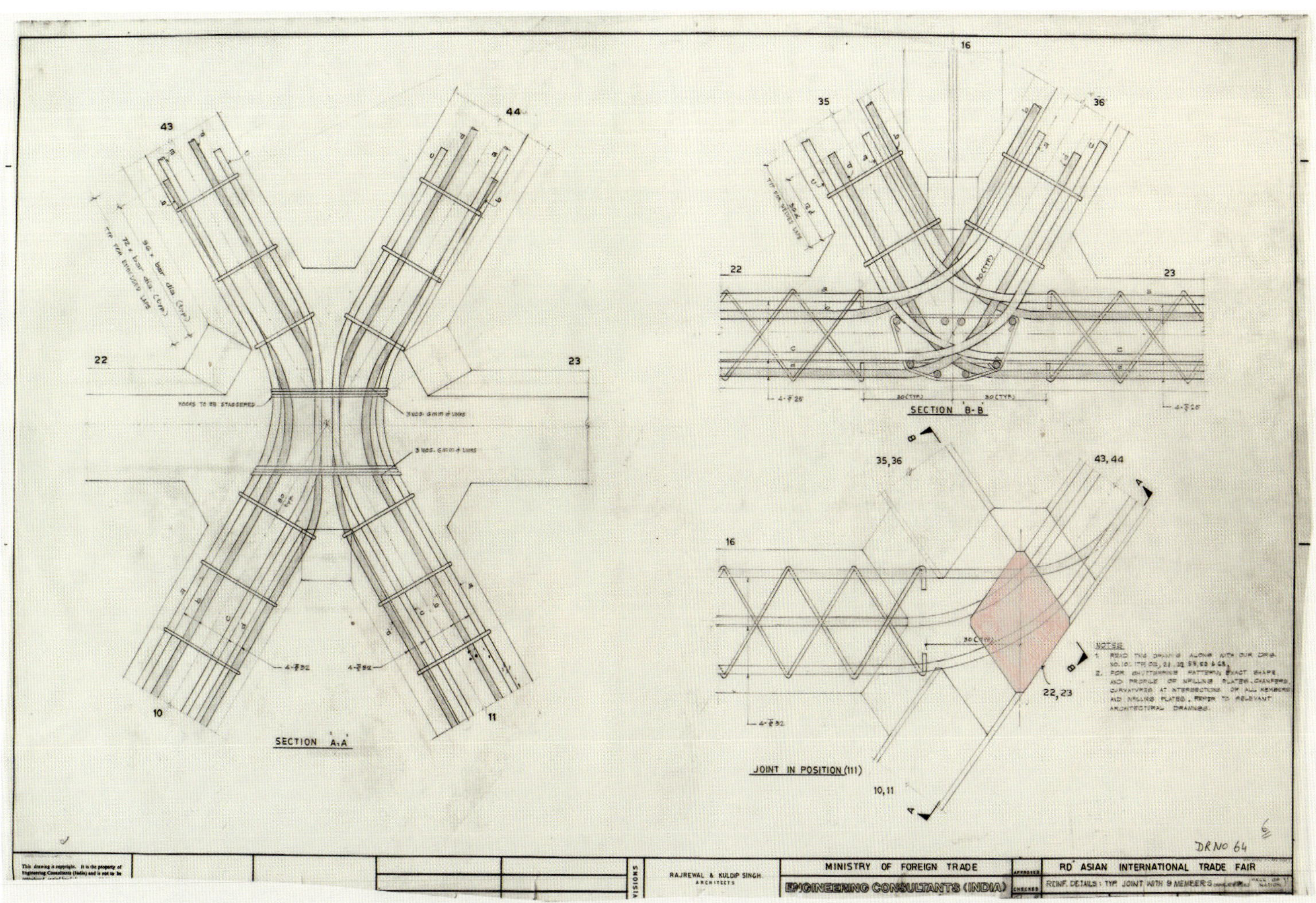

↑ Raj Mahendra, Hall of Nations, project,
Permanent exhibitions complex, New Delhi,
assembly details and types (joint 111), 1970.
Photo Georges Meguerditchian. Musée National
d'Art Moderne – Centre Pompidou, Paris.
Courtesy Scala Archives

SNOWDON AVIARY, ZSL LONDON ZOO

Already the home of a landmark of twentieth-century engineering—the penguin pool that had made Ove Arup's name famous in 1934—, in 1960, the London Zoo became the theater of an interesting design experiment, a collaboration between the architect Cedric Price, the engineer Frank Newby—who was heading up FJ Samuely and Partners following Felix Samuely's death the previous year—and the project's commissioner, Lord Snowdon. The three men created the first immersive, walkthough aviary in London, based on the principle of tensegrity, a structural solution Newby conceived that sprang from his direct experience in Samuely's 1951 Skylon project, and the close friendship he had had with Richard Buckminster Fuller since 1953. Two pairs of V-shaped tubular metal compression elements are held in equilibrium by a "ridge beam" made of two intersecting tension cables. This "organism" is the main support for a sub-system of intersecting tension cables anchored to the ground, which seem to make four tetrahedral tubular compression structures rise into the air. The entire structure is wrapped in aluminum mesh. The use of aluminum for the welded mesh and diecast tubular structure was highly innovative for the time.

→ Snowdon Aviary, ZSL London Zoo, London, 1964. Photo Sam Lambert. Courtesy Cedric Price fonds Canadian Centre for Architecture © Sam Lambert

1960–1964

ARCHITECT   CEDRIC PRICE

ENGINEER   FRANK NEWBY
                       FJ SAMUELY AND PARTNERS LTD

PHILIPS PAVILION, EXPO '58

	BRUSSELS, BELGIUM
	1958
ARCHITECT	LE CORBUSIER
ENGINEER	IANNIS XENAKIS

It is impossible to disengage the 480 seconds of Edgar Varèse's *Poème électronique*, Philippe Agostini's direction and Jean Petit and Le Corbusier's vision from the fluid sequence of organic space that was the Philips Pavilion, built in Brussels for the Expo '58. This total artwork played on the indoor/outdoor ambivalence between the architectural archetypes of the cave—a technological cavern of lights, colors, sounds and images—and the tent, and structural models of the shell structure that worked via compression and the tensile structure wrapped in post-tension cables. The pavilion's geometry was based on the intersection of 12 hyperbolic paraboloids, created from the ribbing of the main framework of 40-centimeter-diameter reinforced concrete. The resulting concavities were formed by prefabricated 5-centimeter-thick cement slabs embraced within a web of 7-millimeter steel cables positioned every 50 cm.

↓ Philips Pavilion, Expo '58,
Brussels, 1958. Courtesy
Royal Philips / Philips
Company Archives

YOYOGI NATIONAL GYMNASIUM

	TOKYO, JAPAN
	1961–1964
ARCHITECT	KENZO TANGE
ENGINEERS	YOSHIKATSU TSUBOI MAMORU KAWAGUCHI

For the 1964 Tokyo Olympic Games, Kenzo Tange envisioned two stadiums using avant-garde structural and construction technologies in a design that recalled the broad, sloping roofs typical of traditional Japanese architecture.

To cover a large surface area while leaving the space free of vertical supports, Tange was inspired by infrastructures; proposing a design that evoked suspension bridges, he created two structures with iconic, sleek-lined roofs.

The pool stadium has two tall reinforced concrete pylons supporting two steel cables, anchored to the ground, on which the roof structure is suspended. A series of pre-stressed cables descend in the form of a tent towards the edges of the seating structure.

The smaller basketball stadium follows the same principle, but with the use of a single pylon from which a curved steel cable is hung. Secondary cables are suspended from it, fanning out radially to shape and support the roof.

→ Yoyogi National Gymnasium, Basketball arena, Tokyo, Japan 1964, project. Courtesy of Frances Loeb Library, Harvard University Graduate School of Design

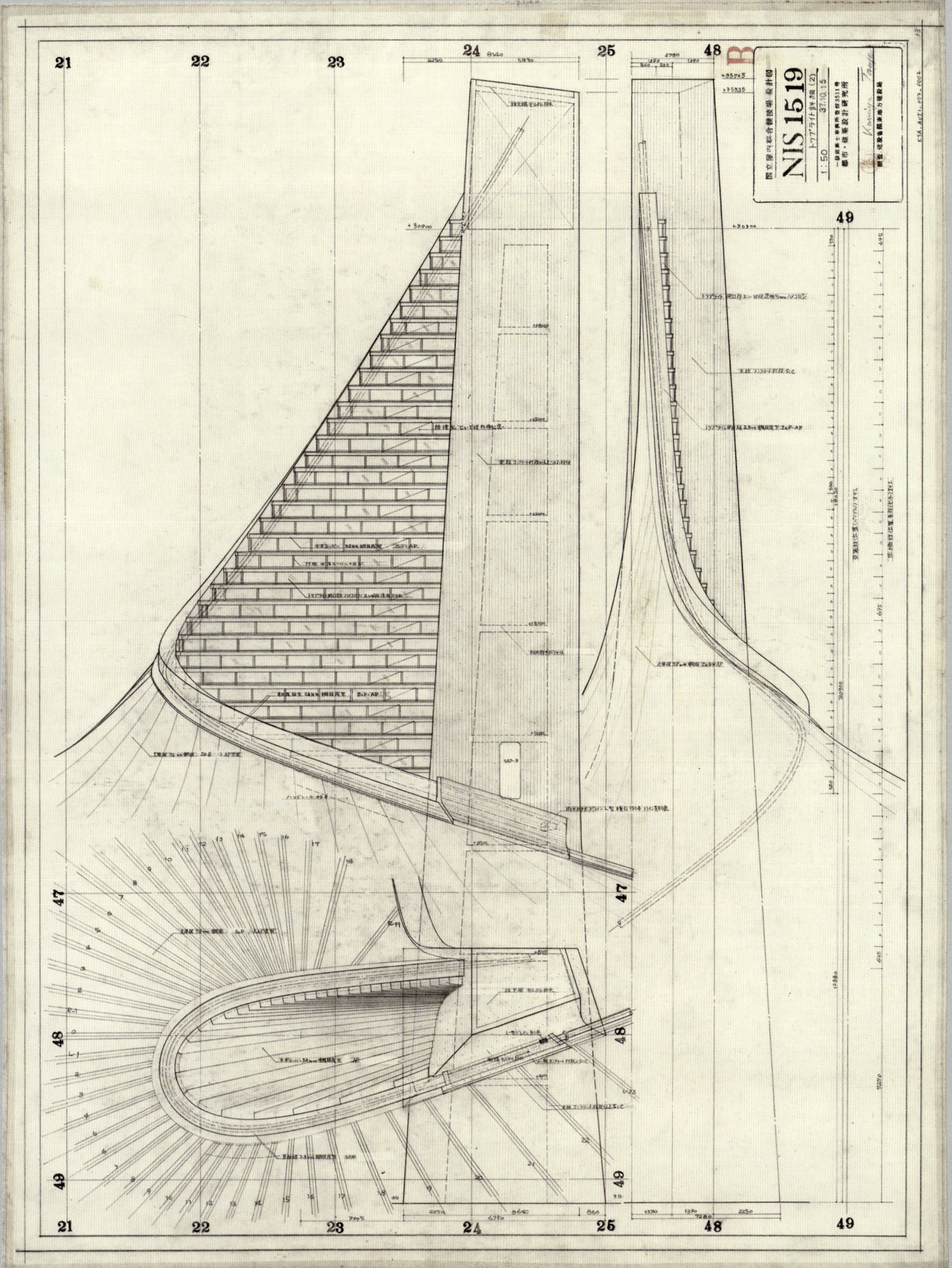

NIS 1519
トラフ及ヤグラ見上図 (2)
1:50
37.10.15
国立屋内総合競技場 設計図
都市・建築設計研究所
設計 坪井善勝海洋研究設計

SCHOOLS AND RESEARCH CENTERS

This section of the catalog and of the exhibition, set apart from the central focus on buildings and constructions of great structural value, is presented as an initial survey of the world of research and experimentation on the no longer strictly structural future of engineering.

Today, engineers are asked to augment their efforts with research on technologies, materials and techniques that can contribute to achieving the energy, environmental and social objectives of our day. All while being open to collaboration with digital culture, automation and information technology. This has led engineers who deal with buildings, spaces and landscapes to include in their work and research plans tools and aims that go well beyond structural studies, moving into broader and more technological areas, from new materials to the use of robots and electronic devices in construction and building management processes. There is experimentation with advanced technologies, and on the other hand, with "vegetal" environmental practices to combat natural or human-driven catastrophes. Urban design and management are considered from the point of view of the use of the most advanced digital technologies and artificial intelligence procedures.

This new and continuously expanding field of research has developed rapidly at the most responsive and organized schools and research centers, particularly those with a long-standing tradition of exchange and interaction between the spheres of engineering and architecture. So, to include a vision of the future of engineering applied to architectural and spatial matters in the exhibition, we decided to turn to some of the most important academic research centers, asking them to participate with projects representing the most advanced future prospects of their work.

As far as studies on new construction materials are concerned, we have the research groups from ETH in Zurich (The Block Research Group – BRG, at the Institute of Technology in Architecture) and the University of Stuttgart (Institute for Computational Design and Construction). Led respectively by Philippe Block and Achim Menges, both work on possible uses of synthetic and natural fibers, and on semi-artisanal processes in construction. Mike Schleich's team from the Technische Universität of Berlin (Institut für Bauingenieurwesen) presents the results of its research in the field of hyperlight concrete, introducing materials with great resistance properties, great ease of use and greatly-reduced ecological impact.

Remaining within the sphere of Europe and schools (in this case, schools of architecture), Greg Lynn and the Universität für angewandte Kunst in Wien show the results of their experimentation on robotics applied to the management of urban spaces within the Viennese Ring. Shifting to the North American sphere, the Space Exploration Initiative group from MIT led by Ariel Ekblaw presents parts of their research centering on materials and components designed initially for use in space exploration missions, and then to be integrated into everyday use. Guy Nordenson's team at Princeton and the Eucentre in Pavia work on dealing with natural disasters. The American team is focused on the effects of climate change in terms of rising sea levels, tsunamis and seaquakes. The Pavia group obviously works on contending with the effects of earthquakes, with particular attention to our national territory.

These research groups are present in the exhibition through site-specific installations they themselves designed and created for the interior and exterior spaces of the museum. The result is an interesting mix of prototypes, environmental installations, models, and graphic, photographic and video documentation that gives visitors an up-to-date idea of engineering applied to architecture in various ways.

KNITNERVI

UNIVERSITY

ETHZ

TUDelft

SWISS FEDERAL
INSTITUTE OF
TECHNOLOGY ZÜRICH

DELFT UNIVERSITY
OF TECHNOLOGY

TEAM   PHILIPPE BLOCK   MARIANA POPESCU
            SERBAN BODEA
            LOTTE SCHEDER-BIESCHIN
            KERSTIN SPIEKERMANN
            TOM VAN MELE

KnitNervi is an homage to the renowned Italian engineer and architect Pier Luigi Nervi. It draws inspiration from the striking reinforced concrete dome of the Palazzetto dello Sport to reimagine thin-shell, ribbed concrete construction. KnitNervi is a prototype of a flexible formwork system for concrete shells with highly articulated doubly curved geometry. The system consists of a bending-active gridshell, which serves as the primary structure of the formwork as well as the reinforcement for the final concrete structure, and a CNC-knitted textile falsework (KnitCrete).

KnitCrete allows for the realisation of an extended array of bespoke ribbed shell geometries. With this double-layered gridshell and fabric formwork system, expressive, compression-only concrete shells can now be constructed efficiently without the need for complex, wasteful moulds. CNC-Knitting offers the possibility of creating complex 3D geometries, which include functional features (e.g. channels, openings, grooves), in one streamlined production process. Active bending is a deliberate deformation method to elastically bend slender straight elements into curved geometries without falsework.

KnitNervi exemplifies interdisciplinary co-development in Architecture Engineering and Construction (AEC). To realise this goal, the Block Research Group (BRG) of ETH Zurich in collaboration with TUDelft developed the flexible formwork technology along with the architectural and structural design. The exchange between the various domain-specific software toolchains and data would have been impossible without COMPAS, an open-source computational framework for collaboration and research in the AEC industry.

Although it features innovative fabrication techniques, KnitNervi was materialised with conventional construction materials. To avoid concrete waste, the 65 mq installation embodies the moment, in a multi-stage construction process, just before the concrete is cast. Celebrating individualization and mass-customization, the installation breaks away from the prefabrication and standardisation paradigm of the twentieth century to re-define sustainable, structurally-efficient, thin-ribbed shell structures. KnitNervi aims to provide the exhibition visitor with an authentic spatial experience, a genuine "X-ray through the structure" and a glimpse on future construction which is smarter and more sustainable.as a critical component for a sustainable, future built environment.

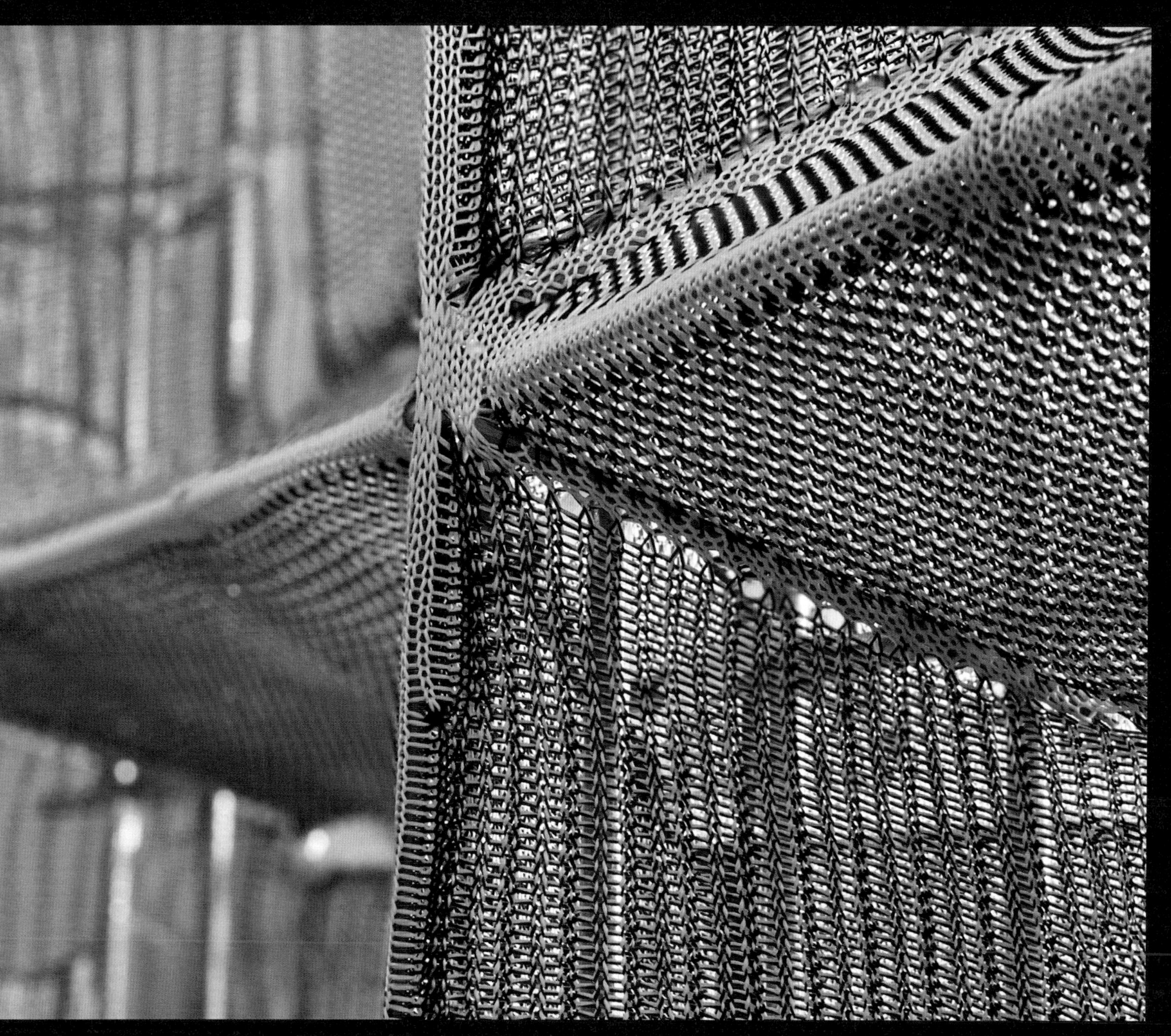

↑ The KnitNervi Pavilion
showcases advances in
flexible knitted formwork
systems for efficient
concrete structures.
© Block Research Group
Project by: ETH Zürich -
Block Research Group
and TUDelft

A WORLD OF RISKS OR A WORLD AT RISK?

UNIVERSITY

IUSS – EUCENTRE PAVIA

TEAM	ROBERTO NASCIMBENE	MARIO MARTINA
	GIULIA FAGÀ	FILIPPO DACARRO
	GABRIELE FERRO	RICARDO MONTEIRO
	RICCARDO PIETRABISSA	GERARD O'REILLY
	GIAN MICHELE CALVI	GUIDO ANDREOTTI

The IUSS as a whole and its PhD program in "Sustainable Development and Climate Change" aim to prepare future generations to redesign society and rethink development as no longer measured exclusively in terms of economic growth; instead, the central focus is the study of the complexity of interrelations between technological progress, availability of natural resources, migration, well-being and quality of life, climate change, the specific characteristics of territories, accessibility to water and food, etc. The numerous extreme events (earthquakes, tsunamis, explosions and many others) of the last few decades have underscored the great vulnerability of our urban areas worldwide, causing thousands of victims and enormous economic losses. The efforts of researchers have improved knowledge in the field of seismic engineering and risk in general, and have led to the drafting of useful documents geared towards the pursuit of a structural seismic response that will safeguard human lives. The achievement of a certain level of performance and a resilient urban system can only be possible if the entire societal system is able to respond appropriately to extreme events. Through experiments in laboratories—particularly Eucentre, represented in this exhibition and in close collaboration with IUSS—and the development of new knowledge, innovative technological solutions will be developed for a range of structural and non-structural elements typically found in home and work environments as well as the industrial and infrastructure sectors. Important technical experimentation will also be developed to serve society and simulate future scenarios.

→ ShakeLab, Eucentre, Pavia.
Photo Massimo Brega
© Fondazione EUCENTRE

UNIVERSITY

MIT

MASSACHUSETTS
INSTITUTE OF
TECHNOLOGY

SA+P
SCHOOL OF
ARCHITECTURE +
PLANNING

MIT MEDIA LAB –
SPACE EXPLORATION
INITIATIVE

SPACESUITS: SPACE ARCHITECTURE AT HUMAN SCALE

TEAM

VALENTINA SUMINI
XIN LIU
RAE (YUPING) HSU
PAT PATARANUTAPORN
MANUEL MUCCILLO

PARIDE STELLA
KATE MOLL
NICHOLAS DEMONCHAUX
DAVA NEWMAN
ARIEL EKBLAW

Humankind stands at the cusp of interplanetary civilization. In this decade, we are actively designing the technologies, tools, and human experiences of our *Sci-Fi Space Future*. Our community of researchers at MIT brings together design, architecture, engineering, and science to enable a transformative new future for space exploration and human spaceflight, while addressing the particular challenges posed by the extreme environment of space—from reduced gravity, to the absence of atmospheric pressure and radiation.

The MIT Space Exploration Initiative's exhibition for MAXXI presents a unique suite of interior and exterior environment spacesuits designed for day-to-day life in microgravity and planetary exploration—from a cyberbiome wearable, to seahorse and ocean-inspired prosthetic tails and gossamer garments, to a meditation on future inter-species living. These provocative design concepts highlight novel ideas for our future in-space habits, human behaviors, and activities—across both aesthetic form and scientific function. Creative re-envisioning of the spacesuit reminds us of the rich history of suit development, highlighted in the exhibit's inclusion of *SpaceSuit: Fashioning Apollo*,

while also pointing forward to the many suit concepts that will ensconce our spacefaring species as we design for and adapt to medium and long-duration human spaceflights to low Earth orbit, the Moon and Mars.

Designing and fabricating spacesuits offers us a compelling architecture and engineering challenge, in the spirit of MAXXI's *Technoscape*, as these objects function as the minimum housing units for space explorers on Intravehicular and Extravehicular Activities (IVA/EVA). We showcase the spacesuit as a unique space architecture concept at the most reduced, intimate scale: the human body. Through the MIT suit artifacts on display, we explore this possibility to transform the body in space by providing augmentation, enhanced performance, and functional fashion design that builds on our Earthly origins while leveraging the unique design affordances of the space environment.

The exhibit display reflects the unusual nature of our interdisciplinary design and engineering practice at MIT—we test these artifacts on parabolic "zero gravity" flights each year, where fleeting moments of true weightlessness provide the tantalizing opportunity to embody the future in microgravity.

→ Design by Xin Liu and Andrea Lauer. Photo Rob Chron

→ Design by Manuel Muccillo and Valentina Sumini. Photo Steve Boxall

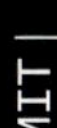

RESILIENT COASTS: FORESTS AND ADAPTATION

UNIVERSITY

PRINCETON UNIVERSITY

TEAM

PROJECT TEAM:
GUY NORDENSON
PAUL LEWIS
JOON MA
PATRICIA HAZLE
MAELIOSA BARSTOW
HELEN FIALKOWSKI
MITZY GONZALEZ
LISA RAMSBURG
TAKA TACHIBE
MICHELLE DENG

PROJECT COLLABORATORS:
CATHERINE SEAVITT NORDENSON
MICHAEL TANTALA
JIN SATO
SENG KUAN
BRENDA FRESHMAN
RANDALL KOCH
RENATA VALENTE
CARLO DONADIO

Resilient Coasts: Forests and Adaptation examines the cultural role and structural properties of forests and architecture as climate adaptation strategies in three regions around the globe—Rikuzentakata in Tohoku, Japan; Castel Volturno in Campania, Italy; and Neskowin, Oregon in the USA. Each region possesses distinct relationships to sea level rise, tsunamis, and to trees: as climate protectors, building materials, and entities that hold cultural capital.

Rikuzentakata, a small city in northern Japan, lost close to a tenth of its population in the March 11, 2011, by the Tohoku Earthquake and tsunami. The city's 10-year reconstruction plan—a massive infrastructural effort to raise the ground and build a concrete seawall—has transformed the coast. Rikuzentakata presents disaster response techniques deployed in one of the most tsunami-impacted and tsunami-prepared regions in the world. It exemplifies the impacts of post-disaster reconstruction and relocation on humans and ecosystems.

Castel Volturno, a city in which nearly half of the population is comprised of undocumented migrants, lies north of Naples along the Falerno-Domitio littoral coast on the Tyrrhenian Sea. A recreation route through the city provides walking and biking

access between previously non-accessible and abandoned natural features to mitigate coastal erosion and flooding, the region's primary climate challenges. Interweaving a complex socio-political environment controlled by the Camorra, the plan provides design interventions at the human scale: toilets, drinking fountains, solar-powered lighting, and shaded seating for civic accountability, safety, and solidarity.

Oregon faces a one-in-three chance of a high-magnitude earthquake in the next fifty years with little political, cultural, or infrastructural preparation in place. Responding to carbon-intensive engineering, the design for a tsunami evacuation tower in Neskowin, Oregon integrates earthworks, the forest, and architecture. Providing refuge in the immediate event of a tsunami, the steel and cross-laminated timber structure serves as an everyday sanctuary for wildlife and a gathering space for the public, while connecting adjacent natural landscapes over the course of long-term climate adaptation.

UNIVERSITY

TU BERLIN

TECHNISCHE
UNIVERSITÄT BERLIN

LIGHT AND LONG-SPANNING VS. INSULATING AND LOAD-BEARING

TEAM

PROF. DR. SC. TECHN.
MIKE SCHLAICH
DR. -ING.
ALEX HÜCKLER
MARIA SERRANO-MESA
ANNA MENDGEN
DIRK PEISSL

FALK MARTIN
FLORIAN ECKERT
ZEYNEP NAZ ÖZKAN
DETLEV KÖHLER
DANIIL SHTYRIKOV
FREDERICKE GLASSMAN

The Technische Universität Berlin is one of the 20 largest universities in Germany, with around 35,000 scholars studying in different campuses situated at different locations in Berlin. It is the heritage of the Königlich Technische Hochschule zu Berlin, founded in 1879. At Faculty VI "Planning, Building, Environment," architects and civil engineers, urban and regional planners, landscape architects and environmental planners, ecologists, sociologists as well as geodesists and applied geoscientists conduct research and teaching activities. The Department of Conceptual and Structural Design-Concrete Structure at the Institute of Civil Engineering is known for its research in the field of lightweight construction in civil engineering. After fifteen years of basic as well as application-oriented research and technical support of various construction projects, the Chair is one of the most important institutions in the field of infra-lightweight concrete and concrete reinforced with prestressed/passive carbon fibre reinforced polymer (CFRP) elements.

The potential of infra-lightweight concrete is not just demonstrated by numerous research activities, but also by various realized and currently pending real-life projects. The advantages of the heat insulating monolithic construction method in terms of robustness and durability, which when combined with the aesthetic potential of an exposed concrete façade, give rise to the hope that infra-lightweight concrete can contribute to building culture (*Baukultur*).

CFRP reinforced concrete can serve the construction industry, especially bridge industry, as an extremely material-efficient and economical building material for new buildings and repairs. This structural efficiency associated with CFRP can render the constructions realised with them extremely durable and, hence, sustainable as well.

Concrete, which has been infamous for being clunky and bulky, has thus begun to reinvent itself. The 'bad boy' is transforming itself—thanks to intensive research and development activities—into an efficient and innovative lightweight construction material. Accordingly, it can turn old views upside down and surprise people with completely new design solutions.

→ ILC Model. High-rise made of U-shaped elements. Anna Mendgen, Chair of Conceptual and Structural Design. TU Berlin

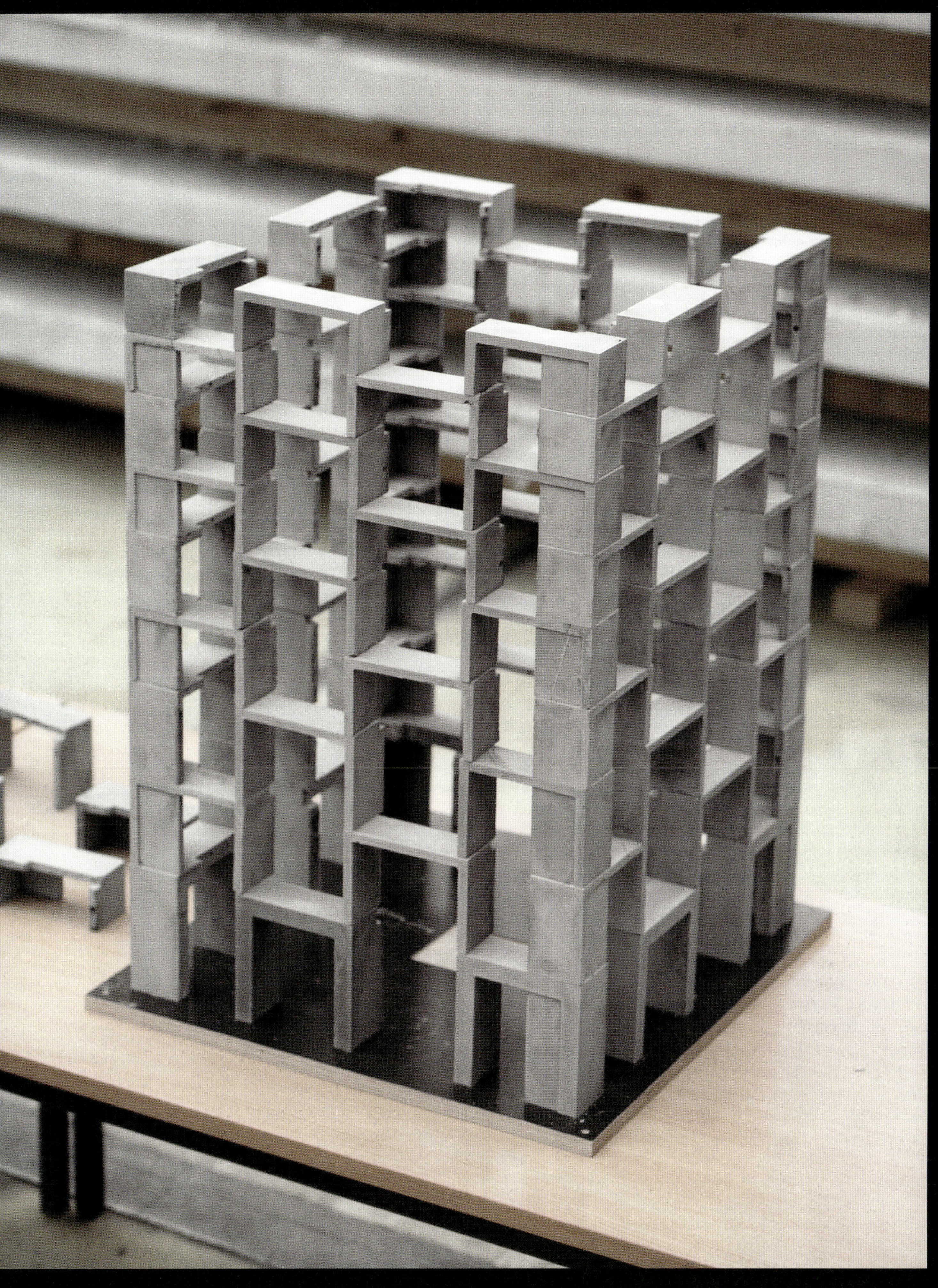

RECONFIGURABLE STREETS

UNIVERSITY

UNIVERSITÄT FÜR ANGEWANDTE KUNST WIEN

TEAM

STUDIO GREG LYNN
TEACHING TEAM:
GREG LYNN
MARTIN MURERO
VALERIA OSPITAL
BENCE PAP
KAIHO YU

STUDENTS:
TALA SAWMEH
PHILIPOVA OLGA
TOBIAS HAAS
ANASTASIA SEVCHENKO
LEON MACKOWSKI
JANNA EBERHARTER
NAOMI NEURURER
HELEN ANDRES
BENEDIKT SCHAMBECK

VIKTORIYA TUDHZAROWA
HAO WU
ANNA SALAKHOVA
LUCA ZANARINI
PHILIPP MA
TOMAZ ROBLEK
EBRAR EKE
ALINA LOGUNOVA
ANNA OVCHINNIKOVA
EYLÜL İÇGÖRE
NATALIA LASKOVAYA
ZUBIN TAN
JOYCE LEE
LALEH SADEGLOO
MARGIT APPLEGATE
ANAHITA DEHLAVI
JENNIFER FRANGIEH
ARKADII ZAVIALOV

ORGANISATION:
ASTRID TRINKBAUER
SABINE PETERNELL
AND BÄRBEL MÜLLER

FABRICATION:
PHILIPP HORNUNG

WITH THE
FRIENDLY
SUPPORT OF:
DIE ANGEWANDTE AND
THE INSTITUTE OF
ARCHITECTURE I OA

The mission of the year-long Reconfigurable Streets studio is to innovate the design of civic streets for a citizenry that has adapted to Covid-19 pandemic policies, transportation electrification, gig working, micro-mobility, and on-demand retail and dining delivery services, responding to contemporary culture, transportation, health policy, and urbanism with new ideas for use of streets. The studio's vision is to humanize technology and pedestrianize the built environment. The site for this reimagination of the street is the Ringstrasse in Vienna; a nineteenth-century urban scale experiment in land ownership, civic institution building, culture, politics, leisure and commerce. Six different teams designed the 4.2-kilometer-long street as a reconfigurable network of intelligent robotic infrastructure, street furniture, pavilions, equipment and energy infrastructure. Using electric mobility and autonomous navigation technology, the Ringstrasse is pedestrianized for festival, art, retail and gastronomy uses. The simulation of transport, configuration, assembly, and occupation is designed using game engine software. The scope of design encompasses building design, ergonomics, local manufacture, transport and construction logistics including assembly, demounting, transportation, storage, and re-use.

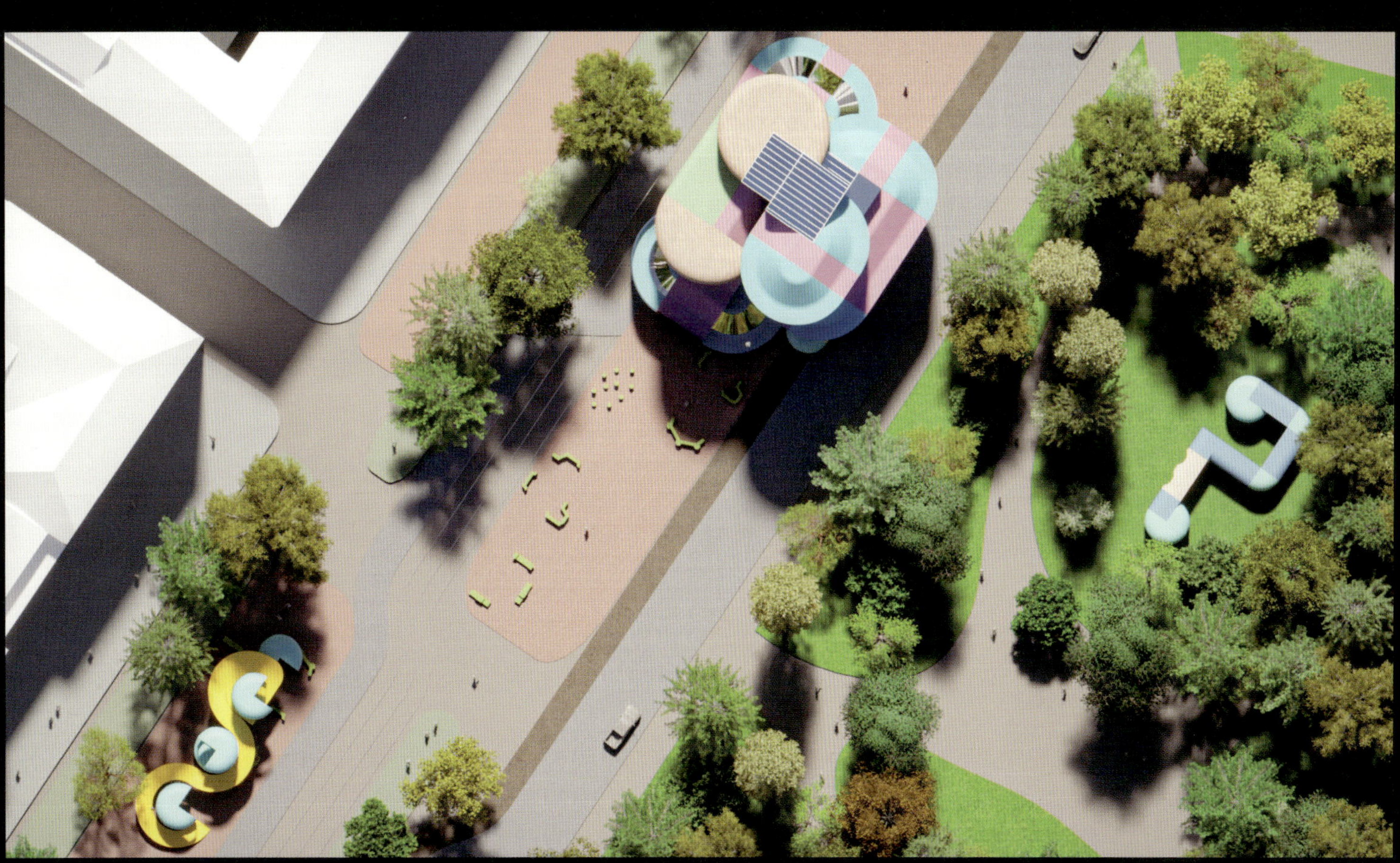

↑ Play & Connect. Team:
Ebrar Eke, Alina Logunova,
Anna Ovchinikova, Eylül
Icgören, Natalia Laskovaya

NATURAL FIBRE TECTONICS TOWARDS BIO-BASED AND BIO-INSPIRED ARCHITECTURE

UNIVERSITY

UNIVERSITÄT STUTTGART

TEAM

ICD (INSTITUTE FOR COMPUTATIONAL DESIGN):
PROF.
ACHIM MENGES
KATJA RINDERSPACHER
CHRISTOPH SCHLOPSCHNAT
CHRISTOPH ZECHMEISTER
NICCOLÒ DAMBROSIO
REBECA DUQUE ESTRADA
FABIAN KANNENBERG

ITKE (INSTITUTE OF BUILDING STRUCTURES AND STRUCTURAL DESIGN):
PROF.
JAN KNIPPERS
MARTA GIL PÉREZ
YANAN GUO

STUDENT ASSISTANCE:
CHRISTIAN STEIXNER
ALAN ESKILDSEN
XI WEIQI
XI PENG
IN COLLABORATION WITH:
FIBR GMBH, STUTTGART

PROJECT SUPPORT:
CLUSTER OF EXCELLENCE INTCDC INTEGRATIVE COMPUTATIONAL DESIGN AND CONSTRUCTION FOR ARCHITECTURE, UNIVERSITY OF STUTTGART

Living nature is characterized by ubiquitous and all-pervading diversity. Given the vast range of natural variation, it may come as a surprise that almost all load-bearing biological structures are fibrous composites. The Institute for Computational Design and Construction, and the Institute for Building Structures and Structural Design, both at the University of Stuttgart, have conducted numerous research projects exploring how the principles of biological fibre systems can be transferred to architecture. Based on advanced design computation, simulation and robotic fabrication, these explorations open-up a new approach to fibre-reinforced composite structures in architecture.

Our exhibit *Natural Fibre Tectonics* presents the next significant step in this research combining the effectiveness of bio-inspired fibrous structures with the advantages of bio-based fibre materials. It aims to bridge between the technical, as well as cultural dimension of fibrous systems in architecture and the rich repertoire of fibrous morphologies in nature. The full-scale display of a large fibrous slab explores novel, bio-inspired and bio-based tectonics, which are at the same time materially efficient, ecologically sound

↑ *Natural Fibre Tectonics.*
© ICD/ITKE/ IntCDC
University of Stuttgart

and architecturally expressive, and unfold deep interrelations between technology, biology and culture.

The exhibit is made of four slab modules, which are shown upright and thus expose the finely differentiated inner fibre structure. They are contextualized as a key structural component of our project Maison Fibre, a model for future fibrous habitat exhibited at the 2021 Biennale Architettura di Venezia. The exhibit shows how the research is further advanced through a load-bearing structure that is entirely made of robotically wound flax fibre, a material that is fully naturally renewable, biodegradable, and regionally available in Central Europe.

Natural Fibre Tectonics demonstrates how today's technologies enable a novel synthesis of bio-inspired design principles, advanced computational methods and robotic process, as well as bio-based materials. From this arises the opportunity to extend, or even rethink, our established canon of architectural tectonics as a critical component for a sustainable, future built environment.

FONDAZIONE MAXXI

PRESIDENT
Giovanna Melandri

ADMINISTRATIVE
BOARD
Caterina Cardona
Piero Lissoni
Nicola Lanzetta
Monique Veaute

SECRETARY OF
THE ADMINISTRATIVE
BOARD
Laura Gabellone

BOARD OF ADVISORS
Paolo Palombelli
Claudia Colaiacomo
Goffredo Hinna Danesi

DEPUTY MAGISTRATE
OF COURT OF AUDITORS
Enrico Torri

ARTISTIC DIRECTOR
Hou Hanru

EXECUTIVE DIRECTOR
Francesco Spano

DEPUTY EXECUTIVE
DIRECTOR
Rossana Samaritani

GRANDE MAXXI PROJECT
Margherita Guccione
    *Scientific Committee
    Manager*
Pietro Barrera
    Project Manager
Alessio Agresta

EXECUTIVE OFFICE
OF THE PRESIDENT AND
GENERAL SECRETARIAT
Laura Gabellone
    Head
Flavia Bagni
    Assistant to the President
Federica Cipullo
    Head of Registry Office
Deborah Compagnino
Cecilia Festa
Chiara Sbocchia
Raffaella Tebano
Donatella Saroli
    *Assistant to the Artistic
    Director*

LEGAL OFFICE,
TENDERS AND
CONTRACTS
Angela Cherubini
    Head
Valeria Quadrini

ADMINISTRATION,
FINANCIAL PLANNING
AND ACCOUNTING
OFFICE
Rossana Samaritani
    Head
Silvia Affinita
Francesca Civitenga
Eleonora Magri
Giuseppa Sparla
Federica Turchino

PRESS OFFICE
Beatrice Fabbretti
    Head of Press Office
Flaminia Persichetti
Elisa Cerasoli
    MAXXI L'Aquila

COMMUNICATION
OFFICE
Prisca Cupellini
    Head of Communication
Eleonora Colizzi
Cecilia Fiorenza
Giulia Chiapparelli
Olivia Salmistrari
Elisa Ingrosso
    MAXXI L'Aquila

PUBLIC SERVICE
QUALITY
Laura Neto
    Head
Stefania Calandriello
    MAXXI | MAXXI L'Aquila

TECHNICAL OFFICE
Elisabetta Virdia
    Head
Cristina Andreassi
Paola Mastracci
Claudio Tamburrini
Michele Sestini
Claudio Alagna
    MAXXI L'Aquila

HEAD OF PREVENTION
AND PROTECTION
SERVICE
Livio Della Seta

LOCATION PHYSICIAN
Cristiano De Arcangelis

WORKERS' HEALTH AND
SAFETY REPRESENTATIVE
Cristina Andreassi
Paola Mastracci
    *for MiC staff on temporary
    assignment*

MAXXI ARCHITECTURE
DEPARTMENT
NATIONAL MUSEUM
OF MODERN AND
CONTEMPORARY
ARCHITECTURE

Elena Tinacci
    Department Coordination

SENIOR CURATOR
Pippo Ciorra

DESIGN SENIOR
CURATOR
Domitilla Dardi

COLLECTION OFFICE
Laura Felci
    *Head of Architecture and
    Special Projects*
Simona Antonacci
    Head of Photography
Flavia Parisi
Alessandra Spagnoli
    International Projects
Chiara Castiglia
Eleonora d'Alessandro
Andrea Di Nezio

CONSERVATION AND
REGISTRARS' OFFICE
Viviana Vignoli
    Registrar
Serena Zuliani
    Conservation

ARCHITECTURE
ARCHIVES CENTRE
Carla Zhara Buda
    Head
Angela Parente
Claudia Torrini

MAXXI ART DEPARTMENT
NATIONAL MUSEUM OF
CONTEMPORARY ART

DIRECTOR
Bartolomeo Pietromarchi
Giulia Mastropietro
    Assistant to the Director
Eleonora Farina
    Curator

HERITAGE AND
CATALOG OFFICE
Ilenia D'Ascoli
    Head
Maura Favero

ART ARCHIVES CENTRE
Giulia Pedace
    Head
Giulia Cappelletti
    Cataloging
Valeria Dellino
    Image Licensing

CONSERVATION AND
RESTORATION OFFICE
Simona Brunetti
    Head
Maria Cristina Lanza
Stefania Montorsi
Marta Sorrentino

REGISTRARS' OFFICE
Roberta Magagnini
    Head
Marta Cesaretti
Francesca Commone

INTERDEPARTMENTAL
OFFICES

Monia Trombetta
    Head

CURATORIAL OFFICE
Monia Trombetta
    Curator – Head
Giulia Ferracci
    Curator
Luigia Lonardelli
    Curator
Elena Motisi
    Curator
Anne Palopoli
    Curator
Fanny Borel
    *Curator Assistant
    MAXXI L'Aquila*
Valeria Dellino
    Curator Assistant
Donatella Saroli
    Research

EXHIBITION
DESIGN OFFICE
Monia Trombetta
    Head
Silvia La Pergola
    *Senior Architect–
    Coordination with
    Technical Office*
Dolores Lettieri
    Senior Architect

Claudia Reale
Senior Architect

Benedetta Marinucci
Architect

Benedetto Turcano
Architect

EDUCATION, TRAINING AND CULTURAL ENTERTAINMENT DEPARTMENT

Irene de Vico Fallani
Head

EDUCATION OFFICE

Marta Morelli
Head

Giovanna Cozzi
MAXXI | MAXXI L'Aquila

Stefania Napolitano
Irene Corsetti

TRAINING OFFICE

Sofia Bilotta
Head

Marzia Ortolani

PUBLIC ENGAGEMENT OFFICE

Sofia Bilotta
Head

Silvia Garzilli

WORK EXPERIENCE AND CAREER EXPLORATION PROGRAM

Federico Borzelli
Head
MAXXI A[r]t Work project

Susanna Correrella

PUBLIC PROGRAMS OFFICE

Irene de Vico Fallani
Head

Stefano Gobbi
MAXXI | MAXXI L'Aquila

Giulia Lopalco
Carolina Latour

PUBLISHING OFFICE

Flavia De Sanctis Mangelli
Head

Chiara Braidotti
Chiara Cottone
Maria Pia Verzillo

LIBRARY OFFICE

Francesco Longo
Head

Jacopo De Blasio

DEVELOPMENT DEPARTMENT

Lucia Urciuoli
Head

EVENTS OFFICE

Paolo Le Grazie
Head

Leandro Banchetti
Ludovica Persichetti
Viola Porfirio

MARKETING, DEVELOPMENT AND MEMBERSHIP OFFICE

Maria Carolina Profilo
Head

Cristiana Guillot
Beatrice Iori
Giulia Zappone

SPECIAL PROJECTS OFFICE

Alessio Rosati
Head

Chiara Calabresi

MAXXI L'AQUILA

INTERIM DIRECTOR

Bartolomeo Pietromarchi

GENERAL COORDINATOR

Paolo Le Grazie

DONORS FRIENDS OF MAXXI

PRESIDENT

Alessia Antinori

PLATINUM

Adriana and Lodovico Rocca

GOLD

Alessia Antinori
Roberta Armani
Enzo Benigni
Founder Donor
Annibale Berlingieri
Founder Donor
Renata Boccanelli
Beatrice Bordone Bulgari
Flaminia Cerasi
Alessandra Cerasi Barillari
Founder Donor
Pilar Crespi Robert
Founder Donor
Anna d'Amelio Carbone
Founder Donor
Fabrizio and Elisabetta Di Amato

Erminia Di Biase
Founder Donor
Chicca Donnamaria
Yohan Benjamin Fadlun
Pepi Marchetti Franchi
Daniela Memmo d'Amelio
Francesco Micheli
Noemia Osorio d'Amico
Founder Donor
Ugo Ossani and Manuela Morgano Ossani
Marina Palma
Mirella Petteni Haggiag
Stefano Russo
Giuseppe and Benedetta Scassellati Sforzolini
Isabella Seràgnoli
Massimo Sterpi
Founder Donor

SILVER

Ludovica Amati
Francesca Antonacci
Mariolina Bassetti
Cristina Bastianello Ottieri
Lavinia Borea Carnacini
Massimo and Lorenza Caputi
Claudia Cornetto Bourlot
Emanuela Da Rin
Iolanda de Blasio
Luigi de Vecchi
Paola De Vincenti
Raffaella Docimo
Sabrina Florio
Marion Franchetti
Benedetta Geronzi
Anna Maria Giallombardo Gianni
Annette Gilka
GUCCI
Valentina Impallomeni
Roberto Lombardi
Paola Lucisano
Barbara Napolitano
Maria Fabiana Marenghi Vaselli
Matteo Marenghi Vaselli
Patrizia Memmo
Francesco Modesti
Vincenzo Morichini
Founder Donor
Gianluca Perrella
Chiara Pozzilli
Salvatore Puglisi Cosentino
Antonella Romiti
Federico Scrocco
Federica Tittarelli Cerasi
Founder Donor
Luisa Todini
Ludovica Tosti di Valminuta
Hendrik and Giacinta van Riel
International Friend

YOUNG

Giovanna dell'Erba

HONORARY MEMBERS

Gabriella Buontempo
Grazia Gian Ferrari
Paola Gian Ferrari Braghiroli
Piero Sartogo

AMERICAN FRIENDS OF MAXXI

PRESIDENT

Ginevra Caltagirone

CO-PRESIDENT

Alessandra Rampogna

BOARD OF DIRECTORS

Enrica Arengi Bentivoglio
Peter B. Brandt
Ginevra Caltagirone
Pilar Crespi Robert
Giorgio Gallenzi
Alessandra Rampogna
Massimo Sterpi

HONORARY MEMBER

Giorgio Spanu

GOLD

Francesca Bodini
Nancy Cain Marcus
Beatrice Del Favero
Kathy and Steven Guttman
Lisa Hedley
Andrew Lauren
Julie Minskoff
Claudine Nussdorf
Maribel Reyes
Nina Runsdorf
Carol Saper
Zach Sherman
Brian S. Snyder
Alice and Tommy Tisch
Leah Weiseberg

Thanks to all the donors who have chosen to remain anonymous

FOUNDING MEMBERS

ROME, MAXXI –
NATIONAL MUSEUM OF
21ST CENTURY ARTS

TECHNOSCAPE.
THE ARCHITECTURE
OF ENGINEERS

OCTOBER 1, 2022 –
APRIL 10, 2023

CURATED BY

Maristella Casciato

Pippo Ciorra

GENERAL COORDINATION

Alessandra Spagnoli with
Chiara Castiglia and Andrea
Di Nezio

**ASSISTANT CURATOR AND
RESEARCH COORDINATOR**

Luca Di Lorenzo Latini

**CURATORIAL AND
RESEARCH ASSISTANCE**

Chiara Castiglia

Andrea Di Nezio

**EXHIBITION DESIGN
AND TECHNICAL
COORDINATION**

Silvia La Pergola with
Stefano Campagna Pascale

REGISTRAR

Viviana Vignoli with
Monica Pignatti Morano

CONSERVATION

Serena Zuliani with Adele
Panizza and Flavia Sorace

IMAGE LICENSING

Giulia Pedace

Valeria Dellino

**EDITING OF AUDIO
GUIDE TEXTS**

Elisa Scapicchio

**AUDIOGUIDE PROJECT
COORDINATION**

Stefania Napolitano

**LIGHTINGS
COORDINATION**

Paola Mastracci

**ACCESSIBILITY
AND SAFETY**

Elisabetta Virdia

**SECURITY
COORDINATION**

Livio Della Seta

**EDUCATIONAL
ACTIVITIES**

Marta Morelli

Giovanna Cozzi

Stefania Napolitano

**PUBLIC PROGRAMS
AND VIDEO GALLERY**

Irene de Vico Fallani

Carolina Latour

Giulia Lopalco

**DEVELOPMENT
ACTIVITIES
COORDINATION**

Lucia Urciuoli

COMMUNICATION

Prisca Cupellini

Giulia Chiapparelli

Eleonora Colizzi

Cecilia Fiorenza

Olivia Salmistrari

PRESS OFFICE

Beatrice Fabbretti

Flaminia Persichetti

MARKETING

Carolina Profilo

Beatrice Iori

Giulia Zappone

**PUBLIC SERVICE
QUALITY**

Laura Neto

Stefania Calandriello

**COORDINATION
OF OPENING
EVENTS**

Paolo Le Grazie

Ludovica Persichetti

Viola Porfirio

GRAPHIC DESIGN

FIONDA, Torino

TRANSLATIONS

64 Biz

Matteo Bugiolacchi

Eugénie Antoinette
Goedheer

Valentina Moriconi

**VIDEO EDITING
AND SUBTITLES**

Emiliano Martina

TRANSPORTS

Apice Roma Transport srl

Expotrans SpA

Montenovi srl

INSURANCE

Willis Towers Watson

EXHIBITION SET-UP

Tagi 2000 srl

MULTIMEDIA SUPPLY

MangaCoop

**LIGHTBOX SET-UP
AND SUPPLY**

Tensocielo

**ELECTRICAL WIRING
AND LIGHTNING**

Sater4Show

GRAPHIC PRODUCTION

SP System

AUDIOGUIDE SERVICE

Orpheo group

IN COLLABORATION WITH

IUSS - Eucentre Pavia

Massachusetts Institute
of Technology-School of
Architecture + Planning-MIT
Media Lab Space Exploration
Initiative

Princeton University

Swiss Federal Institute
of Technology Zürich
(ETHZ) e Delft University of
Technology (TUDelft)

Technische Universität Berlin

Universität Stuttgart-ICD
Institute for Computational
Design-ITKE Institute of
Building Structures and
Structural Design

University of Applied
Arts Vienna-Institute of
Architecture

THANKS TO

Akademie Der Künste, Berlin

Architekturmuseum der TUM

Archivio Editoriale Domus

Archivo Torroja, CEHOPU-CEDEX

ARUP

Avery Collection Columbia University

Benedikt Redmann Photographie

CCA - Canadian Centre for Architecture

Christian Kerez Zürich AG

Erica Stoller - Ezra Stoller Archive (Esto)

Estate of Yuzo Mikami

ETH Zürich - gta Archiv. Institut für Geschichte und Theorie der Architektur

Fondazione Renzo Piano

Foster + Partners

Frei Otto Film - Simon K. Chiu

Fundación Arquitectura COAM

Grimshaw Architects

Harvard University Graduate School of Design

Hauke Dressler

Hoberman Associates

IHA - Institut pour l'histoire de l'aluminium

Instituto Lina Bo e P.M. Bardi / Casa de Vidro

Instituto Moreira Salles

Irish Architectural Archive

Iwan Baan

Karlsruher Institut Für Technologie (KIT) - saai | Archiv für Architektur und Ingenieurbau

Kawaguchi & Engineers

Kazuyo Sejima + Ryue Nishizawa / SANAA

Kengo Kuma & Associates

Kimbell Art Museum

Leonardo Finotti

Lisa Ricciotti - Photographe

Mahendra Raj Archives

Marc Mimram Architecture et Ingénierie

Museu de Arte Moderna do Rio de Janeiro

Niall Hobhouse - The Drawing Matter Collection

Norman Foster Foundation

Núcleo De Pesquisa e Documentação

OMA - Office for Metropolitan Architecture

Pace Gallery

Paul Warchol

Pei Cobb Freed & Partners Architects LLP

Peter Chermayeff

Ray Wachsmann

RIBA - Royal Institute of British Architects

Roger Viollet - Agence photo depuis 1938

Royal Philips / Philips Company Archives

RPBW - Renzo Piano Building Workshop

Seng Kuan - Harvard University, Graduate School of Design

Shukhov Tower Foundation

SOM - Skidmore, Owings & Merrill

State Archives of North Carolina

The Estate of Harry Callahan

The Estate of R. Buckminster Fuller

TIAA - Toyo Ito & Associates, Architects

Università IUAV di Venezia - Sistema Bibliotecario e documentale

Università IUAV di Venezia - Archivio Progetti

University of Pennsylvania, Stuart Weitzman School of Design | Architectural Archives

UNSW Arts, Design and Architecture

Utzon Center

Werner Huthmacher Photography

Wim de Wit

Yossi Milo Gallery

Zaha Hadid Architects

ZEISS Archive

SUPPORTED BY

MAIN PARTNER

CATALOG

EDITED BY

Maristella Casciato

Pippo Ciorra

HEAD OF PUBLISHING

Flavia De Sanctis Mangelli

RESEARCH

Luca Di Lorenzo Latini

EDITORIAL ASSISTANCE

Maria Pia Verzillo

EDITING

Chiara Braidotti

GRAPHIC DESIGN

FIONDA, Torino

IMAGE RESEARCH

Chiara Castiglia

Chiara Cottone

Andrea Di Nezio

LICENSING

Valeria Dellino

PROJECTS TEXTS

Luca Di Lorenzo Latini

Andrea Di Nezio

THANKS TO

Alessio Rosati

EDITORIAL PROJECT

FORMA

FORMA EDIZIONI SRL

Florence, Italy
redazione@formaedizioni.it
www.formaedizioni.it

EDITORIAL DIRECTOR

Laura Andreini

SPECIAL PROJECTS

Anna Mainoli

EDITORIAL STAFF

Maria Giulia Caliri

Raffaele Moretti

Elena Varani

LAYOUT

Isabella Peruzzi

TRANSLATIONS

Theresa Davis

Sonia Hill

PHOTOLITHOGRAPHY

Forma Edizioni